The Showstopper Lifestyle
☆ ☆ ☆

Valentino, Shawn
   The Showstopper Lifestyle: The Man's Guide to Ultra-Hot Women,
Unlimited Power, and Ultimate Freedom

ISBN: 978-0-615-33276-5

Design by Joy Sillesen
Cover Models: Cailin Mendes and Emm Jaye
Model Makeup: Jessica Winstead
Front Cover Designer: Timothy Whitfield, Timberwolf Photography
Cover Photograph: Payam Emrani
About the Author Photograph: Corrin Hodgson

www.showstopperlifestyle.com

This book is dedicated to Hugh Hefner, Nina Hartley, and Vince McMahon, for your valor and your vision, and for the education and the inspiration... Thank you for help setting the dream in motion.

THE SHOWSTOPPER LIFESTYLE

✩ ✩ ✩

THE MAN'S GUIDE TO ULTRA-HOT WOMEN, UNLIMITED POWER, AND ULTIMATE FREEDOM

By Shawn Valentino

☆ Table of Contents ☆

FOREWORD
☆ ☆ ☆

In 2002, I was feature dancing in an eighteen-and-over club in Ypsilanti, Michigan. I always preferred "juice" bars (no alcohol served) because the college crowd was permitted to attend shows, and there were fewer drunks in the audience to annoy me. I was very friendly with the crowds at all of my shows and spent a lot of time between sets mingling and talking. Most of the young men were pretty much interchangeable: enthusiastic, high-energy man-boys on the cusp of adulthood, excited to be so close to the Promised Land. I always liked these young men and took extra time to explain the Ways of Women to them, hoping they'd make fewer of the stupid mistakes so common to people just starting out on their sexual journeys. Some listened, most didn't, but I always gave the information regardless, wishing it would land on fertile soil.

Among the seventy-five thousand people I met this way, few stood out to the degree of meriting my contact information. That night in Ypsilanti I met the young man who grew up to be the author of this book.

Even though he's over twenty years my junior, there was something compelling about the young Shawn Valentino. He had braces and he wasn't the studliest guy in his group of friends, but he had personality, drive, and original ideas about life and love. When he told me of his plans to attend law school in Los Angeles, I suggested he look me up when he got to town. I've been his part-time mentor ever since, offering advice as he's worked to develop the ideas about life, sex, and relationships contained in the book you now hold in your hands. He appreciated my openness (non-monogamous, swinger, adult entertainer, sex educator), my educational background (BS in nursing, magna cum laude) and my career-long commitment to helping people integrate their sexualities into their everyday lives in a healthful manner.

Shawn has tremendous drive. Over the next few years he transformed his body into a compelling example of masculine beauty, picked up his law degree, and passed the bar, all while developing and refining his philosophy by testing it in the real world. Like me, Shawn wants to help people live happier, more fully realized lives, lives that they consciously choose for themselves.

I got emails and photos from him as he traveled all over the world having the time of his life. He always had questions about women and how to best communicate with them about his own nature. I always gave the same answers. Speak honestly and kindly. Be neither apologetic nor antagonistic.

Simply state the facts and let the women make their own decisions. Only our authentic selves can be happy, and Shawn has nurtured his authentic self. In his book, he shares what he's learned.

It takes self-awareness to overcome the conventional expectations of single men. The stereotypical "player," who promises undying love and total fidelity, even the prospect of matrimony, with no intention of fulfilling these promises will ultimately prove a source of misery to both his partners and himself. The self-effacing doormat, unworthy of a woman's affections, is likely to engender only unwelcome agreement in potential mates.

Shawn chooses to reject these toxic stereotypes. He tells the truth about himself and deals with the consequences, urging other men to do likewise. Those consequences can be hard to endure: scoffing from men, rejection by women, and an adversarial relationship with the expectations of contemporary culture. If his experience resembles mine, he's been called a jerk, a phony, afraid of commitment, shallow, indecisive, mean, withholding, weird, immature…and worse.

Far from being disrespectful of women, the Showstopper Lifestyle recognizes them as individuals with unique wants, needs, goals, sexualities, and desires. Its principles are predicated on honesty and acceptance of oneself and one's partner. The Lifestyle allows both men and women to break free of society's preconceptions. If a man doesn't have to lie about his intentions, a woman doesn't have to manipulate in order to keep a man. A woman of experience does not threaten a confident man. A woman with limited knowledge of sex offers such a man the opportunity to share his understanding.

With all the unhappy marriages out there (fifty percent still end in divorce or separation), isn't it time to look at different ways of building satisfying relationships based on respect, awareness, and acceptance of our potential partners and ourselves? Monogamy is fine for those who are monogamous, deadly for those who aren't. Open relationships are fulfilling for those who are non-monogamous, disastrous for those who aren't. Those who want to break free of society's constraints surrounding sexual and romantic behavior would be well advised to pick up this book.

—Nina Hartley
Los Angeles, 2009

☆ SECTION 1 ☆
Discover Your Inner Superhero

CHAPTER 1
Meet Joe Average
☆ ☆ ☆

"The average person does not know what to do with his life, yet wants another one that will last forever."—Anatole France

Ladies and gentlemen, my name is Joe Average, and I am here to tell you about my life. I am a forty-year-old American man. I have a beautiful wife and two kids, and I have been a loyal employee for my company for almost twenty years. I lived with my parents, and I went to school until I was 18. My parents cared for me greatly growing up, and they could not wait until I started a family of my own so they could play with their grandchildren. My childhood was fun, but mainly, I couldn't wait until I left home so I could be on my own, get a sports car, travel, date more women, and have my freedom.

At the time, I thought I would never get married. I dreamed of growing up and having a carefree existence where all my options were open. I went away to college after graduating high school, and was elated that I could finally live life without my parents' rules and constrictions. I drank, partied, enjoyed some wild sexual escapades, and had a blast with my friends during my freshman year. College was everything I ever imagined and more. Being independent was not only liberating but also empowering, and nothing in the world could beat the feeling of being free.

It was in my sophomore year of college that I met the love of my life, Betty. I knew she was the one when I first laid my eyes on her. I realized soon after we started dating that I would spend the rest of my life with her. She moved in with me my junior year of college. I didn't party very much anymore and saw much less of my friends, but it was so nice to have somebody to come back to every day after class. Betty was so special that I didn't mind giving up some summer school opportunities in Europe and spring breaks with my friends to spend more time with her. I knew vacation opportunities would always be there, but the chance at true love only comes once.

After I graduated, I got a solid job at a stable company. I did have an inner desire to travel a bit and get a little wild like some of my friends, but I knew that I had to think about the future because Betty started pressuring me to get married soon. There was a part of me that wanted to continue to explore the dating scene, but I felt as if I would never meet another girl like Betty and did not want to lose her. I'll admit that part of the reason was also that I lacked the confidence to really get out and date a variety of women.

We got married when I was twenty-five. We had our honeymoon in Niagara Falls, which was my first trip out of the country. She got pregnant soon afterward, and now we have two lovely children who bring incredible joy to our lives. I wake up every morning and go to my steady job from nine in the morning until five in the evening. I have two weeks of vacation a year and a beautiful young secretary who helps keep me organized.

There is nothing more fulfilling than having a reliable job to go to everyday and the same loving woman to come home to every night. Next month I am scheduled to receive a raise that will really help because our oldest child is going to be in college soon. I was hoping we could finally go on a European vacation, but Betty feels that it is not economically feasible now, and she is right. She is already upset that I finally bought that sports car that I have wanted for so long. Having a family sure is expensive. Many of my friends are now divorced, so I guess I am lucky that at least our family is still together.

So what does the future hold? If I save up enough money, I can put my children through college. Then if I plan everything perfectly and I'm lucky enough for my investments to pay off, I can retire from my steady job by the time I'm only sixty-five and then I can really enjoy my freedom. Yes, life is good.

The only thing is…I really would love that overseas vacation I have wanted to go on for so long. When I was in my twenties, I felt I had all of the time in the world, but now it doesn't seem like it will ever happen. Maybe I should have gone on some of those summer opportunities overseas or spring breaks with my friends. Speaking of my friends, I hardly see them anymore. Between my job and my wife and kids, my responsibilities have really taken a toll on having the time to hang out with my buddies. It doesn't help that many of them are miserable and/or broke from their divorces, while others are busy with their own families. I kind of miss the days before I was married when we were all young and could do whatever we wanted.

As far as being married goes, my wife is a great person and all, but perhaps we should have waited a bit longer before we decided to walk down the aisle. That way I could have experienced life a bit more and enjoyed my independence before settling down. Maybe this wish to travel and get out more is not only a desire for things I want to do now, but also regret from decisions I made in the past that now prevent me from doing those things. These days, I find that happiness is more of an emotion that I have to convince myself I have than a genuine feeling that is always there.

And I'm not the only one who feels this way. Unfortunately, my wife doesn't seem that happy either. Rarely a week goes by that she doesn't complain that she feels like she is getting old and her best days are behind her. I know that she has yearned for a vacation as well, but she doesn't think it's a smart move, given our financial situation. I have a sense that she stays with me more out of an obligation to our kids than for her own enjoyment. Speaking of my kids, as much as I love them, sometimes I feel the expenses, responsibilities, and constrictions that come with raising kids are overwhelming.

After all, how much do I really like that steady job that feeds us? I don't like my boss, and on most days, when I get there, I can't wait to leave. The highlight of my day at the office is talking to that sweet secretary…that beautiful, young, sweet secretary. She certainly isn't complaining about getting old or my financial decisions. In fact, if I didn't get married or have kids at such a young age, I probably wouldn't even have to worry about having to keep my stable job or have so many economic concerns. By the way, did I tell you how beautiful my secretary is?

I want to make it clear that I care about my family, but I also feel trapped in an endless routine that has sucked all of the excitement out of my life. These days, it is almost as if I'm that teenager again waiting to go to college and be free. Only this time, the decisions I have made have brought so many responsibilities that the type of freedom I seek is extremely difficult to attain without hurting my family. I have already seen the impact my friends' bad decisions have had on themselves and, even worse, their kids.

Oh, well, that is them, not me. I am happy after all. I am happy, I say. I am happy, I think.

Who am I kidding? I wish I had the power to make my own decisions and the freedom to enjoy life without worrying about the impact all of my choices have on others. Growing up, we are told to get a job and get married and have a family, and it is implied that we are selfish if we choose not to. Perhaps it is more selfish to merely do what is expected of us, instead of what we want to do and regret it later, and then have the people we care about pay the price of that regret. When I was young, I had so many dreams of seeing the world and exploring some of my wildest fantasies. Unfortunately, I lacked the confidence to make many of these things happen, and I was too close-minded to see beyond the typical social path that most people follow. Right now, I feel as if I'm a prisoner of my own decisions and would do anything to unlock these chains and be free again to live the lifestyle I really want.

CHAPTER 2
Introducing the Showstopper Lifestyle
☆ ☆ ☆

"This I believe. That the free, exploring mind of the individual human is the most valuable thing in the world."—John Steinbeck

Does the story of Joe Average sound familiar? It should, because these days, countless people face a similar plight and are perplexed by how to approach it. I hope this book will help those people to avoid becoming prisoners of their own decisions and to discover a different approach to life. I want all of you to open yourselves up to the idea that the dreams and fantasies all of us imagined as a child can be realized with the right mentality. For those of you who already feel trapped by your choices, I hope this book can help make the best of your situation and explore ideas that may lead to your happiness without hurting yourself or those close to you. There are too many glorious things in the world not to spend each moment being ecstatic about the miracle of being alive. The ultimate goal of the Showstopper Lifestyle is happily living life to the fullest and spreading that euphoria to the people who surround you.

By the way, I realize that many of you readers may be women. While this book is constructed as a guide for men, many of the principles it teaches will not only help you understand men more, but may also help you to get more out of your own life. After all, everybody wants to have the confidence to live life to the fullest.

When I was researching and telling people about my book, I talked about it being a self-help book for men, but, interestingly, it was women who had the most enthusiastic response. They would tell me that a book like this could help them meet better-quality men who would be more honest and understanding of their needs. I hope this book helps female readers gain a more open-minded view on life and relationships. Not only that, I anticipate that as a result of men reading it, you will encounter guys more in touch with your needs. The ideals of the Showstopper Lifestyle are universal.

So what is the Showstopper Lifestyle? It is the basic idea that people should spend their lives focusing on maximizing life experiences that bring them happiness without hurting others. It sounds pretty simple and in theory it is, but there is a reason that millions of people are unsatisfied with their daily lives. General lack of confidence and courage in pursuing their dreams, as well as societal pressures and expectations, often prevent them from living the lives they really want. Instead of focusing on what makes them happy, millions of people are struggling to deal with "safe" decisions that conform with society's ideals, but have lead them to boredom and misery.

While Mr. Joe Average, whom you met in the first chapter, is a fictional character, his dilemma is all too real. There are thousands, perhaps millions, of examples of good people with noble intentions who are trapped within the same unfulfilled existence. Statistics show that there is a solid chance you might even be one of them. People often become unable to do the things they really want because the decisions they make constrict their individuality to the point where their freedom is compromised. The reason is that most people are afraid to approach life thinking outside of the boundaries of the social constructs that have been practiced for hundreds of years, but are not necessarily the only option in our modern society. Joe Average is not an average guy because he was born "average," but because he has been unable to develop the inner strength to pursue the lifestyle he desires.

I want to stress from the outset that an essential element of the Showstopper Lifestyle is to approach life with an open mind. Before you read on, I want you all to do something. Free your mind! Free your mind of everything you were taught growing up. Free your mind of all of the social institutions that have been ingrained in you since birth. Free your mind and open yourself up to a way of thinking outside of the traditional social boundaries that restrict the way you may really want to live.

One of the main reasons so many people fall into frustration, boredom, and depression in their lives is that they do not approach life with confidence and an open mind. People all over are trapped in jobs they do not enjoy, relationships they want to end, and lifestyles they do not desire. Divorce rates have skyrocketed and the majority of marriages are unhappy because most people still refuse to approach life outside of the traditional way of thinking.

When we are young, most boys have dreams of fantastic success doing something they love, dating beautiful women, and exploring the world. Adults fill us with optimistic notions that all things are possible in this world if you work hard and believe in yourself. Ironically, at the same time, from the time we are children most of us are told that the measure of a happy existence is a stable job, marriage, and kids to carry on our legacies.

As we grow up, many of the fantastical hopes and aspirations we envisioned as children are marginalized, and we are convinced that we are selfish if we pursue them. All too often, the grandiose dreams and the wide-eyed excitement with which we view the world when we are young gradually fade away and are replaced by "reality checks" of conformist ideals and structures of how we should be living. The principles of the Showstopper Lifestyle allow you to sustain that sense of adventurous joy most of us have in our youth and utilize it to live your dreams as an adult.

The main goal for this book is to help you discover what makes you happy in life and to focus on spending every possible moment doing these things that bring you joy. I will explain how to develop confidence in yourself as an individual and not to rely on others. This inner power is paramount to living the Showstopper Lifestyle. This lifestyle will help you create your own world where you are the master.

Please do not get me wrong. There is nothing wrong with getting married, raising children and working a steady job, and it is true that many people are perfectly content in that lifestyle. For millions of people, maximizing life experiences means coming home to a loving wife and playing with their children, but these numbers are decreasing every day. Statistics prove, however, that people should be exploring other options. You should not feel afraid to go against social expectations of what a traditional life is. Instead, you should approach each day knowing what makes you happy, and focusing each moment on doing these things, whether they fit social expectations or not. That is the ultimate freedom and the essence of the Showstopper Lifestyle.

That is why I want all of you to approach this book with an open mind. I do not want to tell you how to live nor do I want you to think of the contents of this writing as a condemnation of a traditional lifestyle. Instead, think of it as a different mode of thinking that leaves your heart and mind open to all of the wondrous possibilities this world offers. If you decide not to get married, have kids, or work a stable job, you are not a failure because there are many other paths to fulfillment. This book will help you explore these paths.

You will learn that the main key to living out your passions is developing confidence in yourself and taking the initiative to broaden your mind and go for your dreams. Like Joe Average, everybody has a superhero inside of them who can make all of their ambitions possible, but most have not harnessed that inner power. I will take you through steps on how to find that heroic side by building your self-esteem and belief in your abilities. We will discuss how to avoid giving in to outside pressures and judgments and focus on what you like to do, not what you are supposed to do. You will discover that when you have the inner confidence to be happy with yourself without the need of others' company or assurance, your power will be unlimited, and your friendships and relationships will also flourish.

Many of you are reading this book because you want to expand your dating options and want to be able to meet beautiful women. This work is not meant to merely be a guide to picking up women, but mainly an exploration of principles that make you a more open-minded, confident and well-rounded person. If you utilize some of the ideas explored in the book, you will find that you will be more desirable and attractive to the opposite sex. Over the years, I have developed the ability to attract many gorgeous women, despite not being rich or having a traditional look. As many of you know, my skills with women even attracted national attention when Tyra Banks interviewed me on her show.

I will show you how to meet and date more women without being afraid of rejection or heartbreak. The main reason I've been able to get girls is because I am comfortable with myself and my lifestyle and I am able to convey that confidence in an honest, entertaining manner that gets women excited. We will look at the psychological principles that operate behind the dynamic between men and women. Then I will explain the skills and strategies of how to get what you really want out of a woman while analyzing the mystery of what women are really looking for.

For those of you ready to settle down into something serious, I have outlined an approach to your potential relationship. The most important thing to remember is that settling down does not mean settling. You should make sure the person you are looking for is somebody who complements your life, and not someone you are with merely because you are lonely and they fill a void. Many people get into relationships to build their sense of security or self-esteem, but you will find that when you are already confident and secure with yourself, you will have much better connections with your partner. Everybody should have a sense of standards of what they are looking for in a mate when deciding to commit, and you should choose the best person according to those standards. Hopefully upon reading this book, you will get into relationships not just because you need to be with someone, but because you really want to be with that someone.

For those of you already married or in a relationship, I will offer tips on how to minimize the drama and make that relationship more exciting. If you are with someone you are unhappy with or unsure of, I hope this book can help you make a decision on how to move forward with or without that person. There are too many couples out there going through the motions and remaining together just for the sake of having somebody in their life. A bad relationship is not only unproductive, but also unhealthy for all parties involved. I will teach you to how to look at the quality of your relationship and decide if being in it is allowing you to maximize your life experiences. One thing I have learned over the years is that the secret behind a successful bond between partners is not too different from that of what makes a happy single person. It is the mentality that life should be spent exploring new thrills and adventures, instead of settling into a monotonous existence and creating unnecessary drama.

This book is not only a result of studying my own life experiences, but also a compilation of years of research on thousands of subjects. There are certain points in this book that I will stress repeatedly because I want all of you to ingrain these messages in your head. Before anything else, remember to free your mind. If you do so, I think you will find that you will not only be living the lifestyle you only dreamed of before, you may also find the inner strength and happiness that everybody seeks but many never find. If you read this book with an open mind, I hope you will discover your own ability to attract ultra-hot women, attain unlimited power and experience ultimate freedom. You will discover that if you are spending each moment doing what makes you happy, then you are living the Showstopper Lifestyle.

CHAPTER 3
The Making of Shawn Valentino
☆ ☆ ☆

"All fantasy should have a solid base in reality."—*Max Beerbohm*

Shawn Valentino. Sounds too Hollywood to be real, you may say. Well, in a way, you would be right. Shawn Valentino may not be my real name, but it is more of an identity I have created that fits certain parts of my character. My philosophy has always been that life should be a blend of reality and fantasy, and my personality blends the two to create a life of escapist excitement without losing track of my goals and the people I love.

When I was researching my book, people were curious as to what the central theme would be. Although the contents of this work are difficult to summarize in a few sentences, my response would always be that it is a self-help book based on my own life to teach people how to build confidence and maximize life experiences. I wanted to share the belief that an "ordinary" person can live a fantasy life if his dreams are extraordinary. The topics I cover in this book would lack gravitas if you did not know more about me and how my experiences have shaped my ideas.

Some of you may have seen me on television, read about my views, or seen my pictures, and many who have may have some type of preconceived idea of who I am and where I come from. Most of you likely know nothing about me but a vague notion of my views and my lifestyle. That is why I wanted to share with all of you a bit of my life story. Instead of giving you a straight biography, in the process of introducing myself I wanted to present some of the concepts that I will elaborate on over the course of this book. In the mean time, let me give you some background on what led to the birth of Shawn Valentino and the Showstopper Lifestyle.

When I discuss my philosophies on life and share my open-minded view on various social topics that are usually approached with a close mindset, people often get the misconceptions that I was a spoiled rich kid, suffered a traumatic experience as a youth, was severely hurt by some woman, or am rebelling against my family or society. Maybe people come to these conclusions because they are just unaccustomed to someone who lives so far off the social norm, but nothing could be further from the truth. Millions of people who viewed me on *The Tyra Banks Show* saw my lifestyle criticized as "overcompensation" for some type of bad experience. The fact that many people do not take the time to understand the ideals behind those who have a different way of life shows that they cannot think outside the box. I want to explain what led to the formation of my views and show you that being different does not mean something is wrong with you, but simply that you have a unique set of values that diverge from "the norm."

First of all, I was lucky enough to have a fantastic childhood. The culture my parents came from taught them that once you have a child, your whole life should be dedicated to taking care of them. While the selfless dedication required for parenting is one of the reasons I do not want to have a child myself, I was a fortunate beneficiary of their undying love and care throughout my youth. They not only showered me with their affection and pointed me in the right direction, they also surrounded me with a tremendous circle of friends that I have kept to this day.

The combination of loving friends and family throughout my life has been instrumental for me in maintaining balance and stability. Whether I am living out an exciting adventure or suffering a profound tragedy, they keep me grounded. I know not everybody is fortunate to be born with a perfect family, but everybody has the choice to make friends with quality people who make a positive impact on their lives. I have learned that no matter what lifestyle you choose, it is absolutely vital to have caring people who are there for you in good times and bad. That is one thing I always stress to anybody who asks me for advice. In the quest to live out your fantasies, do not lose focus on the real people in your life who care for you. If you do, you will find that the dreams you seek can transform into a hollow nightmare.

When people hear about my adventures and travels around the globe, many come to the conclusion that I must come from a wealthy family. I was lucky enough to grow up in the beautiful suburbs of Michigan, but it was hardly Beverly Hills. In actuality, we were very middle-class, and my parents had to work extremely hard for every dollar they earned to raise me and put me through school. While I cannot say it would not have been nice to be able to afford anything I wanted as a child, I feel that my humble upbringing has given me a greater appreciation for the exciting things I have done as an adult. It has made me work extra hard to make sure my lack of finances does not inhibit me from enjoying the beautiful people, places, and things life has to offer. I wanted to stress this fact because I do not want any of you to feel that you need to be rich to travel, date gorgeous women, or live out whatever dreams you may have. The very premise of this book is that a "regular" guy from any income bracket can live out his fantasies if he has an open mind, focus, and balance.

As I said before, people often draw the wrong conclusion that my own desire to remain single and not have children stems from some type of awful childhood event or being a product of a broken marriage. Actually, my parents had a very stable marriage, and I rarely saw them get into as much as an argument. My mother and father had an arranged marriage in a third-world country and barely knew each other at their wedding, but they grew to love each other over time and through shared experiences. It may have not been a classic story of "love at first sight," but their caring arose from coming to America together and building a new life in a completely different culture. Perhaps that is why my view on relationships is so open. I feel that when two people have a family, it does not necessarily have to be some type of fairy tale romance, but that the only true type of love comes from friendship based on respect, trust, and communication built up over years.

Right now, I wanted to point out that my parents were married for thirty-five years, and only my father's passing due to cancer ended the relationship. Again, I did not arrive at my philosophies because I witnessed a crumbling marriage as a youth. On the contrary, I grew up in a very stable household with loving parents who provided me with everything I could want.

The reason I think the way I do is because the strong upbringing my parents provided me allowed me to develop an independent, confident mindset based on strong core principles. While I appreciate the traditional family dynamic I grew up in, I never found the life my parents had very appealing for myself. While I believe they were genuinely happy, their life together seemed to lack the passion and spontaneity that I feel are the very core of what makes our world so exciting.

From a young age, I felt that people should be more open to the idea that getting married and having kids is not the only way to achieve happiness. Most young kids at some point say they will never get married, but the majority of them end up going down the aisle at some point. (Unfortunately, these days, most of them also end up in a courtroom going through divorce proceedings.) Even as an adult, I have been consistent in the belief that marriage is not for everybody, and I feel you should not be pressured by anybody into a wedding if you feel that it is not for you. I am not against the idea of getting married or having kids, only against the misconception that your life is incomplete if you do not.

While respecting the love my parents had for each other as well as myself, I always sought a more independent, exciting lifestyle. Much of this free streak may have been due to the fact I was an only child with two working parents. Living alone much of the time from a very young age, I was forced to develop my own set of hobbies and interests to keep myself entertained. During that magical time, I gained the ability to have a great time without having to rely on the company of others. From those early days, I also learned the beautiful idea that being alone does not equate to being lonely. I will repeat that concept over and over and want you all to grasp the idea that most people fail to understand. Being alone does not mean being lonely! If you train yourself to not be reliant on others for enjoyment in your life, you will discover that true happiness comes from within yourself. Once you achieve this inner joy, you will not only be happy on your own, but the relationships you have with others will thrive.

Although many of the principles of my lifestyle stem from developing a strong sense of independence as a youth, my parents played a vital role in shaping core elements of my life. My father was a strict disciplinarian who always stressed the importance of education with his unconventional tactics. When I would bring home report cards, a "B" might as well have stood for bomb because my dad would blow up that I had not received an "A." One time I tried to convince him that a "B" was as good as an "A" and he promptly informed me that I was as dumb as a duckbilled platypus if I actually believed that. Thankfully, I was blessed with the innate ability to do really well in school without working very hard, and usually brought home really high marks. This early emphasis on education was an integral part of my adolescence and adult years because I learned that with intelligence came immense respect.

That is another important point I want to stress. With intelligence comes immense respect. If I were to do some of the wild things I have done and did not have real life smarts as well as a law school education as a base, then I may not have had the maturity and discipline to balance my lifestyle with my goals. At the very least, I might not have honed the writing skills to properly convey the concepts that I have learned from my experiences. I may have been lucky enough to be a naturally gifted student, but without my father's drive to see me succeed, I may not have passed two bar exams and I would likely not be writing this book right now.

I am not trying to convince you that attaining a graduate degree is the only signifier of being smart, but only that maximizing the educational opportunities you are given will open up many more options in all walks of life. Even if you are not a person who excels in the classroom, if you make smart decisions in your personal life, then you will not only be ahead of many people who are more educated, but people will respect you.

Even though he was skilled at intense motivational speeches, the main things I learned from my father were by example. That just goes to show all of you parents who are reading this that your children will learn more from your actions than they will from your words. I witnessed how he took care of our family, while simultaneously helping out his brothers and other relatives back in his home country. He was also excellent at maintaining relationships with all of the people he cared about over the years and they all held him in high regard because of it. One thing that disturbs me about people who get into relationships is that they often neglect the friends and family members who have been there for them throughout their lives. Although he never talked about these things, I learned from watching him that I would need to stay close to all of my relatives and the friends I have made over the years. All of these wonderful people were by his side when he passed away and have supported our family since our loss.

Witnessing the importance of maintaining close ties with family and friends from a young age made me understand that these people will always be there for you through good times and bad. As I said before, being single does not mean being lonely. I am able to fully enjoy my single life because I make steady efforts to stay in touch with the individuals who mean the most to me. I may not be in a monogamous relationship, but I have many different ent people with whom I share emotional bonds. That is why I never feel the need to be in a romantic relationship for love and companionship. Again, be sure to make an effort to appreciate those who care about you. Relationships come and go, but friends and family last forever.

One of the main judgments I have come across from people who do not know me well and are perplexed about why I do not desire to be in a relationship is that I had a bad relationship with my mother as a child. That could not be further from the truth. The reason I enjoy dating a multitude of women is that my lifestyle does not lend itself to a committed relationship. I am constantly traveling and I feel there are too many beautiful women in the world for me to settle down with just one. It is not because I had some absent or irresponsible mother figure. My mother is just about the sweetest person in the world, and we are very close friends. Although she could not even begin to imagine some of the wilder aspects of my lifestyle, she raised me well and allowed me from a young age to spend time alone and create my own world.

There is something magical about the mind of a child and the infinite possibilities the world presents to them. Most people lose that wondrous vision as they grow up and become overwhelmed by the self-imposed worries and stresses of daily life. Many people ask me what my secret is to being so happy all the time. I tell them the sense of wonder and excitement from my youth is something that never left me. It is this vision that allows me to explore the world and enjoy the beautiful things it brings. When people ask my mother if I have gotten a job at a law office yet, she merely tells them that I am in my own world doing what makes me happy. As I said, she may not know about the specifics of my lifestyle, but nobody understands more about the mentality that makes me who I am.

The combination of my father stressing the importance of education and my mother granting me my personal freedom resulted in me both doing well in school and developing interests that kept my world fascinating. Unlike so many parents who are overly protective of their children, they gave me the freedom to essentially do whatever I wanted as long as I did well in school and did not hurt myself or anybody else. I never really had a curfew or any types of restrictions. Although I could have exploited that freedom and gotten into unhealthy habits, I never tried alcohol, smoked, or did any drugs when I was young.

For all of you grade-school teens reading this book, I wanted to stress that there is nothing cooler than being strong enough to resist the temptations of these substances. You will be more productive in life and be more attractive to the opposite sex if you have a clear mind. Although I see nothing wrong with having a drink here and there as an adult, the enjoyment in your life should come from the joy within your soul and not be a result of the manufactured effect of chemicals. When I talk to young people, I tell them to stay away from the temptations they are not mature enough to handle and to instead spend time enjoying quality moments with friends and family minus drugs and alcohol. Sure, there may be peer pressure to do these things to be cool, but when you stay true to your principles, then you will be the one setting the standards for what cool is. I never even tasted a sip of alcohol in high school, and I was one of the most popular people in my school.

Although I was not much of a partier as a youth, other interests helped shape who I am. One of my favorite hobbies when I was a young child in the late 1980s and early 1990s was watching movies. Much of my current fascination with seeing the beautiful people and places in the world came from my obsession with the magical world of the movies as a youth. While many people view films and fantasize about the spectacular sights and the sexy women on celluloid, I knew from a young age that I had to make those fantasies a reality. When I first laid eyes on Marilyn Monroe in The Seven Year Itch, the idea of the surreal blonde bombshell was something I felt I had to have when I grew up. When I watched Tom Cruise put on his aviators and flash his megawatt-smile in Top Gun, I knew I had to exude that same type of charm and coolness. When I saw Superman fly to some of the world's most famous attractions, I felt I had to see these landmarks of our world. The sensational motion picture images I viewed as a youth remained embedded in my mind, and I internalized the idea that my life should be no less a fantasy than those shown on the silver screen.

As much I have always loved movies, nothing in pop culture has aroused my passion more than the wild and wacky world of professional wrestling. Laugh if you may, but it was watching the characters of the ring as a young child that influenced some of my characteristics I developed as I grew older. The sense of theatrics that the WWE/F brought to the screen was electric, and I was enamored by the phenomenal spectacle. The charismatic performers embodied a confidence that I emulated from a very young age. While so many people look up to superheroes in comics and on screen, wrestlers are proof that real people can possess larger-than-life comic-book character attributes. My early years of watching countless movies and hours of pro wrestling greatly influenced the ideals of The Showstopper Lifestyle.

When you decide what type of lifestyle you want to live, it is important to examine your strengths and weaknesses. I feel that my strongest qualities are confidence and charisma. My confidence gives me the inner strength to live a unique life and do many of the things others desire but are afraid to do. My charisma allows me to display this confidence in a likeable fashion and in a manner where that sense of excitement can radiate to others. Those qualities came together when I became class president in high school. I learned during the election process that there is nothing wrong with promoting yourself and your abilities. Most people go through their lives afraid to display their strengths because they may be accused of showing off. There is nothing wrong with exhibiting the qualities and skills that make you unique as an individual. If you can do so in a nice, charming manner and don't take yourself too seriously, you will not come across as being arrogant.

When I won the class presidency, my already powerful sense of confidence grew exponentially because I had convinced a wide majority of students in the school that I had the skills to be a leader. Although I had always believed in my abilities, I really learned that it is possible for a regular guy such as myself to achieve success.

Let me elaborate on what I mean when I use the description, "regular guy." None of us should ever view ourselves as ordinary because we all bring something unique and beautiful to the world. We should always have it ingrained in our mind that we have the ability to do extraordinary things. When I say "regular" I mean that I did not fit the profile of somebody one would imagine is a popular, charismatic leader. I was not tall and did not have a traditional look. I was a minority in a nearly all-white school. In my pre-braces days, I had a mouth full of teeth more crooked than a broken down railway. I did not drink or date a different girl every month like so many of the "cool guys" do in high school. In a time of my life where brand names were everything, I chose to wear unusual flashy fashions instead of what was trendy. My mother sometimes tells me that if I hung my shirts on a street corner, people might mistake them for traffic lights.

Despite all this, I became leader of the free world. Well, maybe not, but at the time, a Class A high school of more than two thousand students was its own world anyway. Of course, we all know now after the 2008 election that being "different" is not an obstacle to any goal. I would like to say that I am proud to have opened the doors for Barack Obama during my historic high school presidential victory.

Seriously speaking, my point is that there is no specific profile for what makes somebody popular or successful. The idea is that you should take your own unique qualities and confidently display what makes you special. Confidence does not come from conforming to what people think is cool. You will find that being comfortable with who you are and displaying it with passion and poise will make others think that you are the measure of coolness. Emphasize the strengths you have and present them to others, while attempting to improve your weaknesses without dwelling on them.

Not everybody can be the best, but everybody can be the best they can be. That is one of the core principles of the Showstopper Lifestyle and something I will continuously stress through the course of this book. In high school, I had not reached the point where I was completely comfortable with who I was, and I certainly was not ready to live completely carefree or approach beautiful women without any type of fear. What I was able to do, however, was discover the characteristics and form the principles that would enable me to follow my dreams in the future.

By the way, if you are reading this and you are in high school, make sure you live these years to your fullest and utilize every moment to discover what makes you unique as a person. High school is often a good microcosm of the world, and if you can develop a level of confidence during these young years, you will have a good base to live your dreams in the future. Of course, you should always try to maximize each moment in life no matter what age you are, but this is a time where most of you usually have healthy parents and minimal financial and personal responsibilities and concerns. Take advantage of this freedom and security.

In addition to giving me immense confidence, as fate would have it, winning the presidency would allow me to be in class to hear a speech that influences me to this day. My high school principal and I always had a great relationship. I still recall barging into his office and asking him for the keys to his car. Yes, we had that type of relationship. For all of you *Saved by the Bell* fans, just think of Zack Morris and Mr. Belding. He always admired my confidence and unique personality, and I just thought he was a cool guy who understood what was important. Sadly, he had decided to retire during my senior year. Thankfully, he was to give a retirement speech in my leadership class, the final lines of which will echo in my mind forever. Although he delivered it to a class of at least fifty people, he looked directly at me when he said, "I want you all to remember this. If there is one thing in life I have learned, it is this. Don't do what you have to do. Do what you want to do. Nobody ever put a grade-point average or salary on their tombstone."

That speech influences me to this day. The ideal of living life doing what makes me happy instead of worrying about doing the things that I "should be doing" now encompasses my very existence. After all, I probably should be writing a legal brief right now, but here I am sitting by a computer with a huge smile on my face, writing about an inspiring speech I heard over a decade ago.

I took the words of my principal's retirement speech to heart at the University of Michigan, where I completed my undergraduate studies. While most people advised me to get a degree in something practical like business or economics, I decided to major in American Culture. I knew I was going to law school, and I was told by counselors to focus on classes I would do well in. I spent my college years taking classes I absolutely loved, such as film studies and social science courses. I developed a keen awareness of social issues, and enhanced my writing skills to the point where my professors would use my papers as examples on how to properly construct essays. While those skills do not appear to be marketable in the real world, they played to my strengths and my passion for writing. If it was not for those classes and my terrific teachers, I probably would not have the skills to be writing this book right now.

When I show people my pictures and explain to them the principles of the Showstopper Lifestyle, they often expect to hear wild college stories of drunkenness and orgies in sorority houses. In actuality, I was not a party animal at all at U of M, and could probably count on one hand how many parties I attended. When I had finished my studies there, I had yet to touch an alcoholic beverage in my life. My most fun moments in college were watching classic movies for my film classes and watching wrestling every Monday night with my friends while chomping on some type of greasy cheesy food. For you Wolverines reading this book, no keg-fest can compare to the intense pleasure of some Ultimate Cheese Bread from Mr. Pizza. Though I did not live the typical beer-drenched party life many students experience in college, I had a blast doing the things I loved. Stay true to yourself and do what you enjoy instead of what is expected. Remember the words of my principal's speech. Don't do what you have to do. Do what you want to do.

While most students stressed out about getting a high-paying summer job, I spent my summers in college traveling the world with my parents and seeing famous landmarks across the globe. More importantly, I was able to become closer to my family and enjoy priceless memories that I can never recreate. A good summer job can look good on your resume and I am not discouraging anybody from trying to obtain one, but also take some time during your extended time off to see the world and enjoy vacations with your family. Trust me when I tell you that I do not regret foregoing summer employment for magical moments with my mother and father.

I mentioned earlier that as a child I was heavily influenced by watching movies and wrestling. One of the main problems people have in today's media age is that too many people try to live their own fantasies through watching celebrities. Instead of living vicariously through the media, people should incorporate some of the better qualities they witness in their favorite stars into their own personalities.

During college, I learned how to exude star quality and coolness from watching the icons of classic movies, when Hollywood really was a "dream factory" that produced timeless stars. I studied the movements, gestures, and mannerisms of actors such as James Dean, Montgomery Clift, and especially Rudolph Valentino. I saw *The Sheik* in one of my film studies classes and admired how Valentino exuded sultry sex appeal and became an icon of "the Latin Lover." Possessing exotic features myself, I saw that I could use my "different" look to my advantage and become physically appealing toward women. More importantly, I also started to realize that it is not so much of a look, but more the confidence and magnetism you exude that makes you attractive to women. The image of Valentino is one I feel all men should study if they want to attract large quantities of women, and watching him in college was a great learning experience.

My college years also happened to be the time when professional wrestling reached the apex of its popularity. Monday Night Raw and Monday Nitro were the most highly watched shows on cable television. While "Stone Cold" Steve Austin, the Rock, and "Hollywood" Hulk Hogan were the biggest superstars, my favorite character was a cocky young rebel named "the Heartbreak Kid" Shawn Michaels. For those of you who do not follow wrestling, Michaels is the epitome of the flashy, charismatic star with an electric presence that makes wrestling so exciting to watch. He had a swagger in his movements and a confidence that often bordered on arrogance, but it was all done with a wink and a smile. The mixture of the flashy persona, the self-assured aura, and his reputation as a bad boy who got all the women was the very personification of what I felt I could exhibit if I honed some of my attributes. He even called himself "the Showstopper," and the excitement his presence generated made that name the perfect title for the lifestyle that is the namesake of this book.

Despite my open-minded attitude, one thing you may have noticed is that, unlike many college graduates, I had not been partial to alcohol and I hadn't dated a string of different women or gotten in an early long-term relationship. At age twenty-two, I had never even tasted an alcoholic beverage. Some may feel that I missed out on some great experiences, but I think sometimes it is what you don't do that defines who you are. While I began drinking occasionally after college, I never developed a need for it to have a good time the way so many people who start drinking at a young age seem to do. Since I never had a desire to consume alcohol while growing up, I could still enjoy my hobbies and my time with friends without the bottle. As I said before, control your substances; otherwise, the substances will control you.

Anybody who didn't know me growing up but has seen my pictures or has heard about my reputation as someone who is highly skilled with women may be shocked to hear that I was still a virgin when I graduated from college. The fact that I did not feel the need to have sex or date during my school years, but later appeared on national television as a "womanizer" and am now writing a book in which one of the main focuses is how to get beautiful women proves there is no timeline to do so. I could have been sexually active younger but chose not to because I enjoyed doing other things and did not wish to complicate my life at the time. I feel the fact that I was single throughout my youth has made me much more comfortable with being independent as an adult.

I am not necessarily advocating waiting that long to have sex or be in a relationship, but I do advise that you wait until you are ready instead of giving into peer pressure or your own curiosity or desire to be cool. You may find that you enjoy such activity much more when you are more mature and developed in other facets of your life. The ideals behind why I decided to wait are consistent with why I get so many women today. I stayed true to myself and did what made me happy instead of what was expected of college-age adults.

As you can tell, up through college, I lived a terrific life and was very comfortable with myself as a person as well as with my accomplishments. At the same time, while I was very happy, I did not live a life that would be considered adventurous by most standards. My plan after graduation was to go straight to law school in Los Angeles to study entertainment law, but my parents convinced me to go to school closer to home in the Midwest at the University of Illinois by offering to give me a car. I agreed to their request and this set in motion a chain of events that would change my life forever. When the time came for me to move to school, my parents reneged on their promise to give me their car. Suddenly the prospect of spending three years at Illinois did not seem so appealing. I knew I had to make a tough decision

This is no disrespect to the University of Illinois, but I knew in my heart that I belonged in Los Angeles. Hollywood is the city of dreamers and I felt I had to be there to make my dreams come true. I attended my first class at U of I and then proceeded straight to the counselor's office and withdrew from school. My parents were obviously livid with me for quitting school, and even I was a bit uneasy at having to delay my law school education by a year. Instead of being down about having my law career postponed, I looked at the bright side of having a free year to do as I wished.

You know how there are those seemingly inconsequential moments in your life when you make a little decision that will have a huge impact on the course of your life? On an ordinary Friday evening a few days after I returned home from Illinois, a friend of mine picked me up to go to lunch at Chinagate, one of our favorite restaurants in college. If any of you reading this live in or near Ann Arbor, you must go there and get the almond chicken! Anyway, as we began our drive, he had the sudden urge to make a detour to a gentleman's club, or strip bar as most of us like to call it. At the same time, we were craving that delicious Chinese food. We had to make a quick choice before hitting the highway whether we wanted chicken breasts or women's breasts in our face. At the flip of a coin, our car turned around to head to the strip club.

Although I enjoy going to these institutions, I am not a fan of wasting money on lap dances. The idea of spending my money just to get teased does not appeal to me. What I do enjoy is the camaraderie with guy friends when lounging at the club. Even more exciting is hanging out with sexy, open-minded women in a fun environment. I will discuss the pros and cons of the strip club experience later in this book, but right now I'll just talk about this unforgettable night. Not too long after entering the club, I had a gorgeous Turkish woman named Leila fawning over me. Not once did she try to hustle me for money, but spent more time trying to get to know my interests, not to mention my phone number. She told me that she was married to an older guy who was abusive to her and that she would like nothing more than to spend a night out with a "sexy younger guy." At this time, I was only twenty-two years old, and the idea of hooking up with a twenty-eight-year-old belly dancer was quite a fantasy. We exchanged numbers (and kisses) before I left, and my friend had the look of a proud father as he congratulated me on my potential flame.

It was one seemingly minor decision on a seemingly ordinary day but the events which took place that day triggered a side of me that wanted to explore more of the fantasies I had developed as a wide-eyed youth with big dreams. That day we were confronted with a choice between doing what was safe and familiar, and going someplace that may not have been as comfortable but which presented adventurous possibilities. This symbolic decision resulted in an encounter that boosted my confidence and motivated me to take more chances in life, including being more outgoing with women. Inspired by my enjoyment of this moment, I would spend my year off exploring my courageous side, not only pursuing increasingly gorgeous women, but also traveling the world and learning about different cultures.

Soon after meeting this sexy beauty, I read something that I feel should be required reading for all young men, Hugh Hefner's *Playboy Philosophy*. Published in the early years of the Playboy Empire, when various aspects of Hefner's lifestyle were considered taboo, this is a brilliant guide for men on how to be more open-minded and live life to the fullest. I learned that the underlying concept of Playboy was not so much the sex, but the idea that a man can live his life carefree with a passion that rekindles and realizes his dreams and fantasies as a youth. These are some of the very same ideals that underline the Showstopper Lifestyle which I developed in the years that followed. The similarity in philosophies between myself and Hefner later earned me an invitation to the Playboy Mansion on my birthday, which was obviously a dream come true.

In the preceding pages, you have read about some of my background, from my childhood through my college years, and I have introduced to you some of the concepts that will be elaborated further in this book. Up until this point, my life may not seem all that spectacular on the surface. It is really in the years after college that the "Shawn Valentino" character was born and the Showstopper Lifestyle was created. From the moment I had made the choice to drop out of the University of Illinois, not to mention the symbolic decision I just described, nothing would ever be the same.

Over the last few years I have dated more women than the majority of men in the world do in their whole lifetime. I have traveled to more than forty countries, met glamorous celebrities, and have experienced countless incredible adventures. I did all of this while completing law school and passing multiple bar exams. Through these experiences, I have developed such an extreme self-assurance and sense of passion about every moment life brings that rarely a day goes by that something special and unique does not take place. I have created an aura of excitement that often radiates to others who surround me. It is because of my desire to share with people how to develop this confidence that I have written this book.

The ideals and skills I have learned from my numerous experiences will be discussed over the course of this writing. You must remember, however, that the more "thrilling" and "sexy" aspects of my lifestyle would not be possible without the core principles I developed in my early years. From a young age, I had parents who taught me about hard work, discipline, and most importantly, caring about the people close to me. I had forged friendships with quality people with high goals who have supported me and kept me grounded. My confidence made me very comfortable with doing things that made me happy instead of worrying about what other people thought. Spending plenty of time alone as a youth allowed me to have fun without being needy for companionship. Growing up watching larger-than-life characters helped influence my own sense of flash and charisma, not to mention my alter ego name.

If you did not figure it out by now, the name Shawn Valentino combines the names of my favorite wrestler, Shawn Michaels, and one of my favorite actors, Rudolph Valentino. The Shawn Valentino persona I crafted is part flashy and flamboyantly charismatic wrestler and part exotic sex symbol, and it represents me when I am at my most confident and adventurous. When I am in this mode, no obstacle seems too difficult and no woman seems too beautiful to be unobtainable. One of the things you will learn in this book is that everyone has their own unique superhero inside them, and if you cultivate this inner magic, you will feel that all things are possible.

My point in writing this biographical section is that in order to find the fantasy hero that all of us can become, you must first forge the real relationships and form the strong principles that will be the core of who you are. Whether you are having an intimate dinner with your family, or at the top of a Himalayan mountain with a supermodel on each arm, these principles will be the foundation of your happiness. If it were not for the special people and the strong beliefs that have made me who I am, then the making of Shawn Valentino and the fantasy of the Showstopper Lifestyle would not be possible.

CHAPTER 4
Becoming a Showstopper
☆ ☆ ☆

"Thoughts become words. Words become actions. Actions become habits. Habits become character. And character becomes your destiny."—Unknown

Everybody has the ability to live the Showstopper Lifestyle. All of you have the potential to maximize your life experiences and focus on doing what makes you happy. I know it sounds easy in theory, but first there are steps you should take to become the "showstopper" of your dreams.

From the introduction, I have repeated that in order to live an enjoyable life, you have to be happy with yourself. I realize that confidence and inner strength do not develop overnight, but by taking measures that improve yourself, you will discover that your self-esteem will grow. Some of these steps may seem like simple common sense but let's face facts. The idea of being excited about your life should be the norm, but too many people choose to unnecessarily complicate their lives and end up unhappy. Remember, don't complicate common sense! Many of you may have already followed some of the guidelines I am about to present, but there are too many people who neglect the basic principles that allow a person to enjoy their days here on earth.

☆ *Step 1: Maintain a close relationship with your family.*

One of the most important aspects of maximizing life experiences is to develop strong lasting relationships with quality people who enrich and enhance your life. Most importantly, you should forge a strong bond with your parents and other family members and maintain that closeness throughout your life. There is something comforting about having people who care about you without any conditions attached, and nobody really offers you that love like your parents. Generally, parents do not judge you based on things such as what you look like or how much money you make, but mainly want you to be good people living happy lives. As I explained in the previous chapter, I was fortunate to have wonderful parents who have cared for me and supported me throughout my youth. Their unconditional love still fills me with comfort, and even in my toughest times, I am assured that there is somebody who is always there for me.

Hopefully, you are similarly blessed with loving parents who will be there for you through good times and bad. Take time to show your appreciation for what your parents have done for you, and as you grow older, make sure you treasure every moment you have with them. Sitting and having meals with them at home and sharing conversations will make you closer. Of course, enjoying your time together at home is essential, but often it takes a break from the comfort zone to bring people closer together. Try to schedule at least one vacation a year with your parents. You will find that traveling together will strengthen your family bond and give you memories that you can cherish and remember forever. It does not have to be to an exotic destination, but just go somewhere together where you will have a shared experience.

Taking frequent vacations with my parents not only brought us closer together, but gave me an international perspective on life that helped me as I grew older. It may not sound "cool" to travel with your mom and dad, but the wonderful memories you enjoy with your family not only make all of you happy, they will make you a stronger person. (As a bonus, they will likely pay for everything.)

If you are living with your parents right now, do not take them for granted. Enjoy and appreciate every moment you are lucky enough to spend with them. If you are not living with your parents right now, try to spend a few moments each day to call them, because that little gesture goes a long way in showing you care. No matter where I am, I make an effort to call home every day. Not only does the repeated contact make them feel good, but you will find that just hearing their loving, reassuring voice will make you content as well. Sometimes, absence makes the heart grow fonder, and you may find that when you do not live with your parents, you may want to see them more. No matter how busy you are, take time to be with your family whenever possible. Maintaining strong ties with them will provide you with a foundation of strength and support that will last the rest of your life.

Your mother and father will not always be around, but if you enjoy each moment you share with them when they are alive, you will discover that your memories of them will fill you with joy even after they are gone. My father has passed away, but his presence lingers on in my heart and mind and all of the immeasurable love and support he gave me in his life strengthens my spirit.

In addition to keeping a strong relationship with your parents, make sure that if you have brothers and sisters or cousins, they are your best friends. I am an only child, so I don't know what it is like growing up with siblings, but I have cousins in my age range, and we love each other and have a blast every time we get together. Strong relationships with these relatives are extremely important because you are tied together by blood, but the power dynamic is not one-sided, as it is with your parents. You should consider these family members a blessing because you generally have common experiences and you share a lineage that brings you together. Too often I see siblings who spend so much time arguing and fighting instead of developing a special friendship that will last forever. Life is too short to have petty disagreements, and if you have enough of them, it can ruin a relationship. If you establish a close relationship with these loved ones, you will keep the family bonds that can add depth to your soul, and you will have a sense of security that somebody is always there for you.

Constructing an excellent relationship with your family is one of the most significant factors in obtaining the well-balanced attitude that will make you successful in all of your endeavors. The closeness with your relatives will provide you with a sense of inner peace that is necessary for you to attain the self-confidence in order to achieve a blissful existence. If you do not have that peace with yourself, none of your accomplishments will make you content. For me, having a great connection with my family provides me with a powerful foundation that keeps my heart and mind happy even when I am in my lowest moments. Without that strong base of special people, it doesn't matter if you are dating the most gorgeous women or visiting the most beautiful destinations in the world. I have been fortunate enough to do both, but I must say that without my loved ones, my life would be much emptier.

☆ *Step 2: Surround yourself with friends who have a positive impact on your life.*

I understand that not everyone is lucky enough to come from a stable family. There are many people who come from broken homes or have parents who are not there for them. There is also a saying that you cannot choose your family, but you can choose your friends. You should always make smart choices in selecting a strong, supportive circle of friends who have a positive attitude and genuinely care about you. I have friends who came from abusive parents and shattered families, but who look to their circle of friends to provide the stability that a family typically creates. There are too many talented people who can do wonderful things with their lives, but who are brought down by negative "friends" surrounding them. Having a solid set of friends can help keep you on the right path as well as steer you away from the negative forces of the world.

As I said before, maintaining high-quality relationships with family and friends is one of the greatest sources of strength you can have in life. Hopefully, you have already established some of these connections, but if you haven't, there is no time like the present to search for quality individuals who enhance the enjoyment of your life. The key to this is to find what types of activities you are interested in and become involved in those hobbies. When you participate in interests you enjoy, you will inevitably find interesting people with whom you have something in common. Take time to get to know those you connect with and you may find a friend for life.

With the advent of the internet, you can easily search for avenues in which you can pursue those interests and meet people who have similar likes and dislikes. There are also community programs, classes and organized sports to meet people who share your lifestyles and hobbies. Of course, if you are in school, there are countless groups and sports activities for just about anything you can imagine. Developing closeness with people while doing something constructive will provide you with emotional fulfillment, and you can slowly eliminate the more destructive "friendships" that only serve to impair the quality of your life. Use common sense in finding those with a positive attitude towards their own lives, and you will see that they can positively impact yours. As I mentioned before, I have been lucky enough to have incredible friends from a young age. The support circle of caring people who have high goals and are fun to spend time with keep me focused on the right path and fulfill my need for companionship.

One of the central themes of this book is that a person should not need somebody in their life to be happy. The necessity of having a stable set of friends and family may seem to contradict this notion, but it really does not. Having good relationships with friends and family ensures that you will always have good people around, but they also will not demand to be a constant and permanent part of your everyday life. Their companionship gives you the freedom to be more comfortable being single because their love and support will minimize your need to be in a romantic relationship. The nature of a relationship with your friends and family generally does not have the unstable nature of a romance, and it is more likely to last.

This stability without the drama will not only help you become more secure with yourself, but having these bonds will also aid you if you do decide to settle down and enter a serious relationship. Many studies, including my own, have shown evidence that a person who does not have a strong connection with family and friends will have trouble later in maintaining strong romantic relationships and families of their own. If you enter a relationship already having a strong base of people around you, you will be less likely to be entering it because of loneliness and less inclined to unnecessarily continue it if it goes bad.

No matter what age you are, learn to develop these strong ties. This will provide an immense comfort throughout your life, whether you decide to stay single or enter a relationship. Remember, romance can come and go, but friends and family will last forever. When you have this love and support, living the Showstopper Lifestyle becomes much easier.

☆ Step 3: Construct your lifestyle around things that make you happy.

In addition to developing a circle of quality people in your life, you should also discover a set of activities that make you most happy. Too many people are discontented with their lives and create unnecessary drama because they are not focused on doing what they love. Everyone has something they enjoy doing. You should write down your interests and identify a path in life that correlates with your enjoyment of living. After you find the hobbies that bring joy to your life, you should attempt to live a lifestyle that allows you to maximize the time doing what you love.

I learned early in life that I love to help people and that I am passionate about writing. Being a lawyer allows me to assist others while exploiting my writing skills in writing legal briefs and memoranda. Additionally, writing books gives me the creative freedom to use my literary skills to convey my views and beliefs in a manner that advises others on how to get the most that they want out of life. As you can see, I have parlayed my interests into my career path so what I do for a living will not feel like work.

Of course, your hobbies may not always correlate with your strengths or be marketable in the workforce, but being aware of your interests and spending as much time as you possibly can engaging in them will at least bring you happiness in your personal life. In addition to writing and helping people, I really enjoy being surrounded by beautiful women as well as traveling the world, ideally both at the same time. These are interests that make me happy during my personal time. That is why I choose to remain single and not get involved in long-term jobs. Avoiding these commitments gives me the ability to date various women without worrying about drama and jealousy, and it allows me the freedom to circle the globe without neglecting my responsibilities or being asked questions from a significant other. Again, I analyzed my interests and constructed my lifestyle in a manner where I could maximize my life experiences. As a result, I am happy nearly every moment of my life and the few moments I am not are exceptions and not the norm. If you develop activities you enjoy and build your lifestyle around them, then you will make the most of your precious time on earth.

☆ Step 4: Maximize your educational opportunities.

In order to have a lifestyle where you do the things you love, you must possess the tools that will allow you to succeed. That is why you want to make the most out of every moment you are in school and get an education that prepares you to live out your dreams. Remember, with intelligence comes immense respect. I went to law school, but I am not saying that you have to obtain a graduate degree to be smart. In fact, I know many grad school alumni who are not very bright about life. What an education does when used properly is broaden your horizons and build a bridge that can lead you to your goals. If you make the most out of school, then your power will exponentially grow, as will your confidence.

My law school degree not only allows me to explore various career paths that can lead to financial success, but it also fills me with a feeling of accomplishment that I have achieved a level of learning that very few people have. While doing well in school may seem nerdy when you are young, as you get older, you will find nothing is cooler than being smart. When I say I have passed multiple bar exams, I am instantly more attractive to women and, despite the usual lawyer jokes, I gain respect from men and women alike. Even though I have spent much of the last few years traveling and working odd jobs instead of practicing law, the fact that I have a strong education has given me a backbone to allow me to be creative and explore various avenues. An education expands your options, both professionally and personally, and the more opportunities that are available to you in life, the stronger you will become, both in your career and at home.

★ Step 5: Health comes before all else.

Good friends and family and a solid education are meaningless if you do not have your health. It is amazing to me how people are willing to put so much time and struggle into things such as making money, going to school, or having a serious relationship, but so many of them refuse to put in the effort to improve their body and their health.

Simply working out about four hours a week can make a world of difference in your appearance and your physical well-being. Most people comment that I have a pretty good physique and ask how I attained it. The answer is that I am disciplined enough to make sure that I always spend a few hours a week to focus on my body, no matter how busy I am. I have a gym membership and make sure I work out at least four times weekly there, doing a mix of yoga, cardiovascular, and strength training. I do not even eat all that healthy, but when I see myself getting out of shape, I know it is time to eat a more balanced diet before things get out of hand. If you have trouble seeing your shoes, it should be a sign that you are neglecting your well-being.

Even if you have never worked out before, it is never too late to start. The two most common excuses people present are that they do not have time or that they cannot afford a gym membership. First of all, everybody has time. Most people spend forty hours a week working a job to support themselves and often their families. Ask yourself how good that financial stability you work so hard for is if you are not healthy enough to do what you want to do. Everybody has at least four hours a week, and that is all it takes to make a significant difference in your look and overall fitness. The cosmetic gains that show from working out will improve your confidence and self-esteem.

Additionally, the physical benefits that come with the improved appearance will give you more energy and likely a longer, healthier life.

If cost is your concern, most cities have some type of gym giving special deals, and if you search hard enough, you will likely also find community centers where you can exercise for a cheap price. Let us assume that you find a gym membership for twenty dollars a month. Even if you are getting paid minimum wage, that is only about three hours of work a month. I understand that the economic times are tough, but just remember how vital your overall health is not only to your quality of life, but to any problems you face along the way. If you do not want to spend the money, or simply do not want to work out at a gym, that should not mean that you cannot keep fit. Anyone can do some running or jogging outside, or various types of exercises in the comfort of their own home. There is, quite simply, no excuse for not paying attention to taking care of your body.

The reason most people do not put in the time for strength and cardio-vascular training is because they are either too lazy, or they have a misplaced set of priorities that cause them to neglect their body's well-being. Again, you can have the most brilliant mind or the largest bank account, but you may find it is all useless when your physical condition deteriorates. If you have not done so already, schedule at least one hour a day for four days a week to work out, eat reasonably healthy, and you will find that both your physical and mental health will improve.

☆ Step 6: Feel your confidence and self-esteem grow.

As I mentioned earlier, confidence and self-esteem are not items that you can purchase bottled up in your corner grocery store. If they were, they would be the biggest-selling items of all time. Unfortunately, if you lack these attributes, they most likely will not magically develop overnight. Just realize that if you find life brings you to an unhappy state of mind, it should not be permanent, and you can always turn things around. We are lucky to be on this earth, and everybody deserves to be as happy as they can be. If you take the steps outlined in this chapter, you should find your confidence growing and, along with it, your passion for life.

Many of the steps I outlined in this chapter may seem like pure common sense. That is a good thing, because the more these essential steps to achieving happiness in life are obvious to you, the closer you are to living the Showstopper Lifestyle.

CHAPTER 5
The Lucid Dream
☆ ☆ ☆

"What is happiness to you?"—Julie Gianni (Vanilla Sky)

What is happiness to you? In theory, this should be the easiest question in the world. Nobody knows about your likes and dislikes more than yourself, yet so many people in the world are unhappy and spending much of their lives doing things they don't enjoy. From working jobs they cannot stand to being in relationships with people they are not compatible with to wasting time needlessly worrying about nonsensical matters, there are too many people out there not taking advantage of their precious time on earth. There is a good chance you may be one of them. No matter how content you are, I want you to stop now and take about ten minutes to think about the people you care the most about, the places where you love being or desire to be, and the things you love doing, then write those things down. Take your time if you cannot think of these things right away, and then come back to reading this book.

Do you have your passions written down? Chances are, you did not write them down or even think about them, and that may be your first sign of a problem that plagues too many people in the world. Human beings simply do not focus enough on their happiness or even take the time to understand themselves enough to discover the things that bring them joy and allow them to maximize life experiences. In the movie *Vanilla Sky*, which I will reference many times in this book and which I recommend all of you to see, Cameron Diaz's character, Julie Gianni, asks Tom Cruise's character, David Aames, "What is happiness to you?" It is the simplest and most profound of questions, and it is one we should always ask ourselves because the answers may change over time. We should discover the things we love the most in this world and attempt to revolve our lifestyle around doing them to the best of our ability. In the film, David is awakened to the possibility of creating his own universe, like a work of art, where he is the painter illustrating his idea of the perfect world and then living his ideal existence. They introduce this concept as "the lucid dream."

In technical terms, the lucid dream is one in which a person is aware that they are dreaming while the dream is in progress. When the dreamer is in a lucid state, he or she is able to actively participate in and often manipulate the imaginary experiences to take control of the environment. I am not going to give you a scientific explanation of the subject, but I want you to take that very concept and apply it to your life. With a clear mind, discover the people, places and things that make you the most happy, and take control of your life so as to live every moment in this universe as if you are living your own lucid dream.

The first step is obviously to determine what your idea of happiness is. If it sounds simple, then write these things down so you have documentation of where your passions lie. Don't forget to not complicate common sense. These interests do not even have to be realistic, as you will find that even your wildest fantasies can come true you if you concentrate on making them happen. The key is to understand what your definition of an ideal existence is, and then build your life around achieving this personal utopia. You may feel that the decisions in your life have made it impossible to strive toward the fulfillment you seek. Then you may want to reexamine those choices and see what you can rationally and voluntarily change so you can take steps to enjoying your life to the fullest without those around you suffering. Even given your best efforts, you may not be able to live the life you are passionate about, but you owe it to yourself to think positively and do the best you can.

Let me use my own life as an example. My basic idea of a perfect life is to maximize the amount of quality time I can spend with my friends and family, travel the world, and be surrounded by beautiful women, without having to be committed to a steady job or a significant other. Unfortunately, I was not born rich nor am I financially well-off at the time of this writing, but I realized I do have something perhaps more valuable. I have the freedom to live my life according to my own standards and to make decisions spontaneously without doing substantial harm to myself or those around me.

It did not happen overnight, but I concentrated hard on finding work where I could get paid without being committed to a consistent schedule Also, as much as I love women, I have been smart enough not to be involved in a long-term relationship. As a result, I have been free from weekly office responsibility or any obligation to a girlfriend or wife. I may not make large sums of money, but I am my own man and I make enough to fund my lifestyle. Additionally, since I book my schedule week to week, I am always available to spend time with my friends or relatives. Since I have a clear understanding of the lifestyle I want to live and made my decisions around those goals, I have been able to become master of my own universe and live out my lucid dream.

I see myself as living proof that every person can carve out his own utopian world because I have been able to do so coming from very humble upbringings and having very limited financial resources. Despite this, I have been able to travel to more than forty countries, hook up with countless beautiful women, and most importantly, spend lots of quality time with those I love. Do not accept your limitations. Just understand what makes you happy, then exercise control of your mind and free it to the possibility that everything you desire can come true. When you have achieved peace in your mind and body, and are able to clearly concentrate on doing the things you love to the best of your ability, then you are living the lucid dream.

CHAPTER 6
The Best Exercise Not of This Earth
☆ ☆ ☆

"Yoga is invigoration in relaxation. Freedom in routine. Confidence through self control. Energy within and energy without"—*Ymber Delecto*

One particular activity can bring your mind and body peace. I have already stressed the benefits of working out and getting a gym membership to improve not only your physical and mental well-being, but also your confidence and self-esteem. In my opinion, the best exercise you can possibly do does not require you to join a health club and that is yoga. Practicing the art a few times a week is a fantastic way not only to improve your body's strength and flexibility, but also to revitalize your nervous system and achieve relaxation. I am new to yoga myself, so I am not going to give you an in-depth explanation of the principles or the benefits of the exercise, but I can tell you, based on the few months I have done it, that I have never felt better.

Getting started is easy. All you need to do is find a book or a DVD that illustrates the various postures and stretches. I would suggest also buying a yoga mat and CD of relaxing music. Once you do so, you are ready to practice at home at a cost of less than fifty dollars. It is one of the best investments you can possibly make because the benefits for your physical and spiritual well-being are immeasurable.

For those who are more serious about it or the ones who cannot motivate themselves to exercise at home, try finding a local yoga instruction class. If you are a member of a gym, they generally have a schedule of free classes going on both during the day and evening. In fact, it took me nearly six years of being a member at Bally Total Fitness before I realized that I was able to attend these classes free of charge. If you already work out at Bally or one of the other bigger clubs, you should look into what courses are offered. If you are not, I stress repeatedly that a gym membership is an excellent, economical way to motivate you to stay in shape. This will not only be terrific for fitness reasons but will also be a social experience where you can meet others with similar interests. As a bonus, if you are a guy in the class, you will likely be surrounded by women, many of them single. It may be a great venue to showcase the skills you are learning in this book. Many men are apprehensive about yoga because they think it is mainly for women. Well, use that misconception to your advantage and go meet these ladies who are taking the initiative to do something positive. Not only do you have the opportunity to meet girls, but the bodily benefits and discipline you will receive from the exercise will vastly improve your sexual flexibility and prowess.

In fact, the principles of yoga are not all that different from those of the Showstopper Lifestyle. The ideals of staying positive, maximizing your potential, and not worrying about the judgment of others are paramount. The underlying theme is to summon the strength in your mind and body to do the best you can. There is no better mantra—not only for yoga but for life in general. Not everybody can be the best, but everybody can be the best they can be.

The exercise is all about maximizing your body's potential, while achieving inner peace at the same time. It truly is the union of mind, body, and soul. Nearly anybody of any age can do yoga because it is not strenuous enough to cause severe pain or injury. The stretches will strengthen and tone your physique, enhance your flexibility, and regulate the physical and physiological functions of your body. Most importantly, the emphasis on proper breathing and relaxation will put your whole body and mind at ease.

I feel the mental part of the practice is most important. In life, the mind has so much control over the body, not only when it comes to exercising but also in motivating you to do the things you want to do. The Showstopper

Lifestyle is all about forming the mentality to focus on doing the things you love no matter what people may think of you. When you are in a yoga class, you are essentially in your own universe, even if you are in a room full of people. The soothing music in the background will put you in a trancelike state, and you will ease your body into positions you could never imagine. The beauty of it is that you are in a place where nobody is judging you. It is all about summoning your mental and physical energy to the best of your ability. Frankly, no matter how flexible or strong you are, everyone in a yoga class is usually in some type of ridiculous pose, so there really is no place for anybody to be critical. Even if you are practicing in your own home, you will feel as if you are somewhere else, a location where it is always peaceful. Just relax and enjoy the journey on which your mind and body take you.

Through this book, I encourage you to get out and travel the world. Even if you decide not to, at least take my advice to enter the magnificent world of yoga, and you will feel as if you have been transported to another dimension. That is why I call it the best exercise not of this earth.

CHAPTER 7
Being Alone Does Not Mean Being Lonely
☆ ☆ ☆

"You cannot be lonely if you like the person you are alone with."—
Wayne Dyer

So far, I have outlined the principles of the Showstopper Lifestyle and have explained the essential steps to living out your dreams. There is nothing more vital in this pursuit than your strength as an individual. One of the major reasons so many people are unhappy in their lives, get into bad relationships, and make poor decisions, is that many never develop the ability to enjoy their lives as single, free-thinking individuals. Most people are too scared to do things by themselves, and many are wary that people will think of them as selfish or strange. You need to realize that in order to be content with yourself as well as with those you care about, you need to be able to have a good time without relying on others.

The concept of needing to be secure in being alone in order to have fulfilling relationships with others may sound contradictory but it is not. I am not saying that you need to isolate yourself from society and do everything alone, but you should train yourself to create your own excitement so your personal happiness does not rest on the actions and emotions of others. You will find that when you have the ability to construct your own universe where you are in control of your fate and are able to do the things that bring you pleasure while not reliant on others, you will feel immense power. Just keep the idea in your mind that being alone does not mean being lonely.

This was a concept I discovered when I was a young child. As I explained earlier, being an only child with two working parents, I learned early in life how to immerse myself in my own hobbies and be completely happy. I had many friends I had fun playing with, but I was just as satisfied being on my own. That ability has stayed with me and has given me tremendous strength as I've gotten older. While it is something I learned as a youth, age should not be a factor in developing your individuality. No matter how old you are, you need to surround yourself with quality people who make a positive impact in your life. At the same time, make sure you spend some time by yourself, not only doing the things you love, but also examining your priorities and goals.

That is why I recommend to everyone that they spend at least a year of their lives living alone. It is truly the best way to become completely comfortable with yourself as an individual because, at the end of the day, there is nobody influencing your thoughts or your actions. When you live alone, you have the ability to spend every night doing what you want, and you can examine each day and formulate your own thoughts on how it went. That type of self-analysis is much more difficult if someone else is always around when you are home. Additionally, the inner strength you will develop having to take care of yourself will assist you in all of your endeavors. Hopefully, sooner or later you will discover that you are secure with doing the things you love on your own and will feel deeply empowered by that ability.

Just get the idea out of your head that you are lonely because there is nobody there with you. One of the biggest fears humans harbor is the fear of being alone. That is because they associate the idea with isolation and depression instead of strength and independence. When you are on your own and in charge of your own decisions and their consequences, it is an incredible learning experience. You will find the power that comes with it will make you more secure and confident as an individual and more outgoing and intelligent in how you approach others.

If you develop the strength to be happy with yourself, eventually you will discover that you will become closer to the ones you love. Focus on the fact that you are able to choose when you want to see the people you care about, and that you are with them because you *want* to be with them, not because you have to. Having that choice to spend time with your friends and family and significant others only when you truly desire to, instead of out of necessity, will help your relationship with these people thrive. I have seen countless relationships go sour because of poor decisions in living with someone that you are not compatible with. Be careful before you decide to give a person that much access to your personal space. Again, when you can live alone and be happy, you will make smarter choices about who you decide to live with if you eventually choose to do so.

Even if you do not decide to live on your own, make sure you schedule some time alone every week, preferably every day, not only to think about things, but also to do what you love. It gives you the opportunity to get some perspective on life as well as cultivate your hobbies. For example, I love movies, as most people do. When I have a free day, I will go to a theater and spend all day watching films by myself. Most people might think that is strange or dorky. On the contrary, I am doing what I love and am completely content to go there on my own without relying on another person's schedule. I get to form my own ideas about the films I watch without the opinions and influence of others. I know that I am enjoying myself and have plenty of friends to go out with if I want, but sometimes I just choose to be alone. The key is to not worry about how others perceive you and be secure with your own actions. When you are doing what you love, the judgments of others will be irrelevant.

You may be thinking that all of the activities you are passionate about require another person. When you focus on spending time alone, you may not only discover new passions in your life, you may also find that the things you feel you can only enjoy with others you can do on your own and have just as much pleasure.

The individual strength you will develop when you are happy on your own will open up a whole world of options. For me, I am able to go out anywhere from seminars and events to bars and clubs and easily meet people because spending so much time alone has built my confidence in approaching others. When you are by yourself, you are sometimes forced to talk to people you may be afraid to or unmotivated to when you have the comfort of people you know already there. Breaking out of your comfort zone is often a good thing because you may be introduced to a whole world of people you may not make contact with otherwise. Additionally, the confidence you will radiate will draw others to you. There is nothing more attractive than a person who is secure with themselves and genuinely excited about their lives.

Perhaps most importantly, when you are satisfied with yourself as an individual pursuing your passions, you will be less likely to get into a bad relationship. If you have noticed, at no point in this chapter have I said that you cannot have a significant other in order to do the things you love yourself. This is not so much about being single as it is being strong. That strength is what will guide you both as an individual as well as with loved ones surrounding you.

There are so many people who get into relationships simply to have somebody in their life and not because they truly want to be with that person. That is an incredibly unhealthy way to begin dating someone and almost inevitably will end in disaster and heartbreak for both parties. When you are confident with yourself, you will be smarter and more choosy about who you allow in your life.

As much as I love the movie *Jerry Maguire*, one of the most frightening lines in the movie is one of the most famous, and that is when Jerry tells Dorothy, "You complete me." The very idea of needing somebody else to feel complete is something I am sternly against and it is one of the primary causes of bad relationships. A good relationship is based on two people who complement each other, not complete each other. There is a major difference between the two. One signifies that you are content as an individual and you feel that becoming closer with this other person will add to that happiness and help you grow as a person. The other means that you are entering a relationship because there is some type of empty void in your life and you are relying on this other person to fill it.

Unfortunately, you often come to realize that when you do not have personal satisfaction in your life, relying on another's emotions to fulfill your own existence may bring you temporary joy, but it will not fix the underlying problem. Getting into a relationship based on loneliness or unhappiness with your individuality is one of the primary reasons divorce rates are so high. It is also why so many people remain with a partner even after things go bad. You will find that when you are a strong individual who can do things alone, you will be less likely to be a prisoner to an unhealthy bond with another person.

Of course, it is perfectly natural for human beings to seek companionship as we are social creatures by nature, but that does not have to come from a committed relationship. Too many people have the misconception that if you remain single, you will eventually become some lonely old person with nobody to take care of you. Remember, the first steps to living the Showstopper Lifestyle include building quality relationships with friends and family without the drama of commitment. If you combine those relationships with the ability to enjoy activities on your own, you will never feel lonely, and you will always have people to care for you, no matter what your situation might be.

Having people there for you through tough times does not only come with commitment, but comes from love and caring as well. Who decided that you need to be married to have that type of compassion in your difficulties? When my father passed away, I did not have a significant other, but I was surrounded by loving friends who came to my aid and assisted me through that difficult time. If I choose to remain single throughout my life, I am assured that when other obstacles come my way, there will always be people who are there for me. Do not be overcome by the fear of loneliness.

As you can see, the effects of individual strength ripple out to all areas of your life and soon you will realize that by being happy alone, you will have more quality people in your life, not less. Additionally, you may pursue activities that you were afraid to before, or did not do because you were too reliant on other people's schedules. As you get older, you may find it more difficult to coordinate time with those you care about. If you are content in doing what you love alone, then you will not be so reliant on others.

One of the main things that amazes people about my lifestyle is how I am able to travel the world on my own. For most, the very idea of getting on a plane and going overseas is a bit of a scary thought. It is a manifestation of people's natural fear of the unknown. When you develop the ability to face the world alone, eventually seeing the world will not be such a foreign concept. I will discuss how I journey across the world and how you can too in a later chapter. Right now I want to focus on helping you build the mentality to do so.

Just ingrain in your mind the importance of asserting your own individuality. Whether you are looking to meet beautiful women, travel, or simply face each day with a positive attitude, it all revolves around the inner strength that forms the core of your personality and your pursuits. The Showstopper Lifestyle is about self-empowerment and freedom to make your own choices, and the concept of being happy with yourself is essential to live the way you want to live.

CHAPTER 8
Without Goals, Your Dreams Are Just That
☆ ☆ ☆

"There is fate, but it can only take you so far. Once you get there, it is up to you to make it happen."—Angel (Can't Hardly Wait)

One of the most memorable experiences in my life took place when I was in Orlando for Wrestlemania 24. Since I am an enormous wrestling fan, it is an extra-special time of year for me because I always stay at the same hotel where the wrestlers reside, and I get to meet my favorite superstars. One day, a friend and I were sitting in the lobby when we were approached by Tony Atlas, a legendary performer who was also a bodybuilding champion. He needed a ride to the gym and soon we were working out with a former Mr. Universe! After the exercise, he ran through his daily routine with us to optimize our results. As he did so, he explained why so many people work out every day but achieve minimal improvements. He pointed out people who were lazily lifting weights or talking on their cell phones during their workout. The average person at the gym is not focused or motivated by goals that will make the most of their time there, and that is why they never attain the body they want. I feel that this is a fitting metaphor for why most people do not maximize life experiences during their time on earth.

Just like that lifter at the health club who is not capitalizing on his potential, the average person often settles for going through the motions in life because they do not have the a sense of aims that will lead them to maximum fulfillment. If you do not have a set of goals and passions that drive you to success and happiness in your everyday existence, you will not make the most of your time on earth. These targets should not just be related to education and career, but also encompass enjoyment in your personal life. You should always be content with who you are and what you have, but you should also aspire to greater success in all avenues. I have always lived by the principle to always be happy, but never be satisfied.

No matter what stage you are in your life, make certain you always have a series of objectives to shoot for both in the short term and in the bigger picture. When I was growing up, I was always a dreamer and knew that I wanted to live a lifestyle that differed from the norm. While many young adults dream of getting a high-paying steady job, a loving wife and eventually kids to carry on their legacy, I was never excited by those things. When I was in high school, my dreams were to one day be a Hollywood entertainment lawyer, date a bevy of supermodel-caliber women, travel to more than a hundred countries, show up on *People* magazine's "50 Most Beautiful People" issue, and to do extensive charity to help the less fortunate, all while retaining strong ties with the people I love. Years later, I am living in Hollywood, have passed the California Bar Exam, have dated a plethora of gorgeous girls, have been to more than forty countries, and am still waiting for *People* to take notice! That last part was just a joke…I think. Most importantly, I feel I have remained close to the people I care about and have laid a foundation for success that will allow me to assist those who were not lucky enough to have the same opportunities that I did.

No matter how lofty your ambitions may be, it is vital that you strive to make the most of every minute you are alive. Each day, you should wake up with the purpose to pack as much pleasure in as possible before going to sleep. Even if you are pleased with your everyday life, ask yourself if you could be doing more. Life is not just about what you do, but also about what you do not do. Every day we have an infinite amount of choices, and you need to make sure the path you choose takes full advantage of the gifts you are blessed with. Sometimes people forget that we are on this planet for a limited amount of time and waste too much of it consumed by unnecessary worries and conflicts. There are also those who settle in a routine of activities they do not enjoy, accept that they cannot do better, or refuse to take measures to improve. If you are not thrilled with the very miracle of being alive, you need to take steps to grasp this passion. When you lose your zeal for life, you lose the ability to make the most of your existence.

After my father passed away, all types of philosophical questions arose in my mind and I had some deep discussions with my friends about them. One of the most intriguing thoughts that came to my head was wondering how people would change their lifestyles if they knew ahead of time the day they would die. Do you notice how we often only really recognize the value of things, whether they are our health, possessions, or the people we love when they are in jeopardy of being taken away? It often forces us to make extra efforts to appreciate and enjoy them in a way we never do when we assume they'll always be there.

Let me give you an example from my personal life. When my father was alive and well, he was often stressed out and overcome by worries. He brought needless conflicts and problems into his life, which added unnecessary complications. Although he was a great family man, he often took out his frustrations on my mother and me, either through angry outbursts or generally moody behavior. Since I am a relatively laid-back person, I was never as close to him as I could have been. When he found out he had cancer, he suddenly had a new awareness of how precious his time on earth was, and was much nicer and more grateful for those around him. Similarly, I took extra steps to become closer with him that I did not do when he was in good health. It should not take an imminent death to appreciate what is important to us.

Don't get me wrong. I'm not telling you to live each moment with the thought that you may be gone soon. On the contrary, I am urging you to live with the exuberance that showcases how thankful you are for being here and alive. Keep your eyes on the larger-scale vision of what you want to accomplish in life, but also concentrate on smaller everyday goals that build toward this grand portrait. You should construct your lifestyle around the pursuit of maximum pleasure and minimal anxiety. Since I have always been very aware of the core values that are important to me, I wake up every morning excited about the adventure that awaits me that day. Because of this focus, I have enjoyed experiences that most people only dream of.

My friend once told me that my life is like a movie. I write my own script and then I live it. You need to realize that you are a star of the greatest film of them all—your life. You have the entire world at your fingertips for your settings and you have millions of wonderful people to be in your cast. The amazing thing about it is that you are the scriptwriter and have control over adding as much action, adventure, dramatic thrills and romance as you desire. When you discover how to achieve the power to direct the screenplay of your dreams, you will indeed feel like a superstar.

Right now, I am asking you to stop reading and take some time to seriously think about ten goals you have in both your personal and professional life. These objectives will focus on the ideals of maximizing life experiences and minimizing worries. Write them down and place the list somewhere that it is readily available and will not disappear. Take your time to seriously think about the people, hobbies and career path that you are passionate about. Make sure your goals correlate with enjoying the ideals you value to their utmost extent. Do not commence reading again until you have outlined this core set of values and ambitions. This will be the Constitution for your own Showstopper Lifestyle, and you can make amendments as time progresses.

CHAPTER 9
Confidence Is the Key
to Living Your Dreams
☆ ☆ ☆

"Once we believe in ourselves, we can risk curiosity, wonder, spontaneous delight, or any experience that reveals the human spirit."—E.E. Cummings

There are numerous factors that combine to allow you to live the way you want to live in pursuit of your goals. The central attribute you must possess to get everything you desire out of each moment of your life is confidence. It encompasses you and feeds you with positive energy that strengthens your mind and gives you the power to seek out and accomplish all of your goals, both personally and professionally. Whether you want to meet quality people, rise up the corporate ladder, start a business, travel the world, or date a plethora of gorgeous goddesses, confidence is the key to living out your dreams. It is the most vital trait of one who wants to live the Showstopper Lifestyle.

Unfortunately, this is not a characteristic everybody is born with, and there is no magic potion that will suddenly make you a confident person if you do not believe in yourself. Too many people see the lifestyle of their dreams as just that, something unobtainable that only exists in a parallel universe. This book has already outlined various key components you can improve in your life over time that should build your self-esteem and inner strength to make this utopian universe a reality. Maintaining closeness with friends and family, getting a good education, taking the initiative to travel, weeding out the negativity in your life, and understanding your passions are but a few of those factors. In order to enhance your skills to do these things, however, you simply have to ingrain in your mind that every moment in life is a gift, and if you are not maximizing it doing what you love, you are wasting it.

I hope by the time you are finished reading this book, you will put into practice some of the ideals that I explain and develop the confidence to get all you want out of your life. Although I go into detail about the various factors that build your self-assurance, right now I want to make a simple plea to all of you who do not believe in your abilities and focus too much on what you perceive you are lacking. Everyone in the world is blessed with incredible talents, and all of us have flaws. The key is to harness the capacity to do good things and eliminate the negative energy from your body. Nobody can go into your mind and bolster your self-belief for you. The power lies in you to take full advantage of your strengths and use that power to do everything your heart desires.

Let me give you an illustration as to why so many people in the world are miserable and afraid to live the way they want to. Most people see their dreams as unattainable fantasies locked up in an airtight metal fortress. Inside this fortress reside the people they would love to date, the job that brings them joy and riches, the lovely landmarks they wish they could see, and the close family life that creates their fulfillment. This seemingly impenetrable blockade is made up of the deepest fears in their minds and hearts: their misguided need to conform, their worries about being judged, and worst of all, their feeling that they are not worthy or able to break this barrier. If you do not believe in yourself, you will forever be standing outside its mythical gates. With confidence, you will discover the magical key to this fortress, and soon you will be basking in the glory of your dreams.

CHAPTER 10
Live Every Day As If It Is Your First
☆ ☆ ☆

"Children find everything in nothing; men find nothing in everything."—
Giacomo Leopardi

No, this chapter title is not a typo. When people who really understand me try to describe my lifestyle to others who do not, they say that I am a guy who lives every day as if it's his last. I am not going to disagree with that description per se, but I feel it is both semantically and practically incorrect. Treating each day like it is your last has the connotation that you are living as if there is no tomorrow. On the contrary, my theory on life is that you should enjoy each day as if there were no yesterday. I advise people to live every day as if it is their first.

When we are children, everything is exciting. As we are experiencing things for the first time, there is a feeling of awe that overcomes us. This childlike wonder with which we view the world as a youth is something we should strive to maintain throughout our lives. The innocence that fills our hearts when we are kids makes every new adventure exhilarating. Can you recall the first time you went to the movies or your parents took you to a ballgame? Does any feeling compare to the excitement of seeing your friends when you are a child? Do you remember the first time you shared a kiss or went on vacation?

There is a certain thrill that accompanies the initial occasion we experience an event in our life. The idea behind this philosophy is to urge you to capture that pure emotion in a bottle and that you should treat each moment with the same enthusiasm as if you are experiencing it for the first time. If you can sustain that feeling, every day in your life will feel special.

People often ask me what my secret is for being so genuinely enthusiastic about life all the time. It is because I have been lucky enough to carry on the magical ability most lose as they get older, and that is to approach each day as one that has infinite possibilities. This vision prevails even if I am doing something I have done before. I may be looking at the same California shoreline every day, but each time I see something different that makes it more spectacular than the last. When I see the people I care about, no matter how often I see them, I try to appreciate just how fortunate I am to be sharing those moments with them, just as I did when I was a youth. If you can harness this ability, even the familiar will feel as magnificent as when you first laid your eyes on it. You will never get tired of seeing your loved ones, but cherish each instance you are blessed to be with them.

When life becomes a chore and things start to become old and boring, even the hobbies, the places, and the people you love, then you are losing the very charm of what makes our existence on this earth so meaningful. There are so many people going through the motions in life, alive but not truly living. They are doing things that have no emotional effect on them, and even lose appreciation for the people they care about after awhile. If you are one of those people, you need to alter your perspective on your experiences and harness your ability to recognize the value of your precious time on earth. Nothing should ever appear plain to you, even the seemingly mundane and ordinary, because every breath and every sight you enjoy is a gift. We are all on this planet for a limited duration, so why not be excited about every bit of it?

I urge you to be grateful for every second you are on this planet and approach each moment with the captivated heart of a child. Even though we all grow older, when you can capture the sensation that made everything so new and exciting as a youth, you will find you will remain forever young. You will not feel as if there is no tomorrow, but instead that there are an endless amount of days that will bring fascinating escapades that will fill you with bliss. Live every day as if it is your first, and you will be eternally bathing in the fountain of youth.

CHAPTER 11
The Railroad Tracks of Aging
☆ ☆ ☆

"Nobody grows old merely by living a number of years. We grow old by deserting our ideals. Years may wrinkle the skin, but to give up enthusiasm wrinkles the soul."—Samuel Ullman

Some of the most memorable commercials from my childhood were a series of ads run by Toys ' R' Us with the theme being "I don't wanna grow up." To this day, these remain some of my favorite advertisements of all time. Even after graduating from law school and traveling around the world, I still see myself as somewhat of a big kid. While most people lose their excitement for life and their childlike wonder for the world as they grow older, those are sentiments I have kept in my heart. As I said, I live every day as if it is my first. People often look at my lifestyle and comment that I need to "grow up." The idea of growing up in our culture is something I have never understood, and the criticism to me is ridiculous. Who defines the standards of being a grown-up, and why do we have to put a time limit on doing what we love because others tell us that "we need to grow up?"

Here is the timeline that our cultural standards try to put on our lives. We go to school and enjoy minimal responsibilities until we are eighteen. After that, we go to college and get our first taste of freedom, so we are allowed to drink and party while we get an education. Soon after finishing our schooling, we are supposed to get a steady job that will give us financial stability so we can eventually buy a home to raise a family. Since we need to meet somebody with whom we can plan that family with, it is not long after starting employment that most people get married. By your early thirties, you are supposed to have children of your own and raise them. That is the general expectation our society has of how a person should grow up, and when a person is way off that expected avenue, they are often deemed as being stuck in their childhood.

Unfortunately, because of these social constructs, many people make lifestyle choices that lead them to unhappiness. I look at this timeline like a set of railroad tracks and we are the trains. Joe Average was one of those people who remained on this railway. In fact, people expect us to stay on these tracks through the different phases in our lives and make the various stops that will lead us to being "grownups" with an education, a job, a spouse, and children. When people ask me why I do not have a job and have no plans on getting married or having kids anytime soon, I simply tell them that life is not a railroad. There isn't just one set of tracks that leads to a specific destination. The beauty of life is in the anticipation of the unexpected, and the idea that every day has endless possibilities. Unfortunately, people make decisions that limit these choices in fear of the unknown, and end up later regretting it.

Instead of ending up like Joe Average, a good man who once had big dreams but who chose to follow the expected road in life and got trapped by his choices, you should not succumb to social definitions of what it means to be an adult. In actuality, your only standards you should hold for yourself as you get older is that you take care of your own responsibilities and maintain ties to those who care about you, while not intentionally harming others. Of course, you should follow the law, be respectful to your fellow man, and be able to financially support yourself so as not to be a burden on your loved ones, but besides that, you do not need to be accountable to anybody. Your lifestyle should be measured by the things that bring you happiness and how you share that joy with others, not by how others think a person of your age should be acting.

Let me use my own life as an example. I did not party or drink like most people in college but chose to enjoy myself going to movies and watching wrestling and doing other things I was passionate about. I did not get into serous relationships, nor did I have wild sexual escapades in my school years, but it was simply because I had other priorities at the time, not because I couldn't do so. I am a law school graduate who has passed the bar in multiple states so others would say I should be working in a law firm. Instead, I have been working temporary gigs and traveling the world. Most people my age are either getting married or in a serious relationship. I am dating many women at the same time and am completely honest and unapologetic about it. Despite the fact that I am not living the life of a traditional "grownup," I am ecstatic every day I wake up and loving every moment of it.

Similarly, you should not feel that just because you are a certain age you have to behave a certain way. You should live every moment doing what you love, not what others would love you to do. Too many people are caught up in worrying about the long-term ramifications of their every activity, instead of appreciating the moment for the blessing that it is. John Lennon said, "Life is what happens to you as you are busy making other plans." Instead of judging every action as a track on a structured railway that will lead you to specific destinations, let things flow and allow yourself to enjoy the ride. If you do so, you will live out your dreams. If others are judging your lifestyle, it is generally because they have insecurities about their own. If life is a railroad, it is not one that follows only one set of tracks, but an open field where the train can go on many paths. Your main responsibility as the person who steers that train is that it leads you to one destination everyday: the place in your heart that makes you happy.

CHAPTER 12
Focus on Your Own Life
☆ ☆ ☆

"Life is too short to be living somebody else's dream."—Hugh Hefner

You might be wondering how long it took me to write this book and how much I prepared for it. In truth, I have been preparing for years, and the stories and philosophies that I have compiled are a result of a lifetime of learning from my experiences. For almost a decade, I have sent out emails of my adventures to a list of hundreds of my friends and acquaintances. It laid a tremendous groundwork for this book, as it made me formulate my views and convey them to people to not only entertain them, but hopefully to inspire them. The responses to these emails have been fascinating, and emotions have ranged from excitement and laughter to shock and disgust, but most of all, those who have replied have told me they are in awe of my lifestyle. Many have been spellbound by my ability to live by my own set of rules, and some commented on how they live vicariously through my escapades. Although I am flattered by the compliments, it also showcases a disturbing trait common to human nature. The inability of people to focus on their own lives and actually carry out their own dreams is one of the primary reasons so many people are unhappy in this world.

If you can spend more of your life focusing on your own goals and concentrating on spending each moment doing things that make you happy, you will be a much more successful and content individual. As with most of the concepts I explain in this book, it sounds simple in theory, but gets unnecessarily complicated. People spend too much time needlessly worrying about what others are doing or thinking, instead of taking responsibility for their own actions and aspirations. When you are discussing the events of someone else's life that have no bearing on your own, ask yourself if this time is better spent doing something productive that can improve your own life. Do not waste your valuable time being judgmental or agonizing about the life choices of those who do not affect your own. What this often really indicates is that something is hollow in your own existence, and this can be detrimental to your relationships with those around you as well as your own well-being.

Perhaps the most harmful and common type of distress occurs when people are too concerned about the opinions of others. If you worry endlessly about how people perceive you, this will take an awful toll on your psyche. The best way to combat this is to have confidence in your own abilities and realize that you cannot get into another person's mind and control what they are thinking. Too many people are constantly in fear of everything, from how their boss examines their work to how their friends feel about their worth to how the opposite sex views their attractiveness. This anxiety stems from a sense of insecurity. If you live your life on your own terms and are not overcome by the judgments of others, then you will find that people will respect you and that their opinions will be irrelevant.

Almost as fruitless as tormenting yourself over the decisions or opinions of others is attempting to live out your own dreams through them. When somebody tells me that they live vicariously through me, I respond by telling them that if they desire the lifestyle I enjoy, they should experience it for themselves. From the exotic travels to the beautiful women to my general enthusiasm about life, there is nothing I am doing that you cannot do yourself. It is all about the power of the mind and harnessing the positive energy to focus on your passions, whatever they may be. In fact, if the choices you have made inhibit you from doing what you want, it is time to reexamine your decisions and restructure your priorities so you may do so. Of course, try to do so in a way you do not hurt those you care for or the ones who depend on you. Just realize that you are not helping anybody if you are unhappy with yourself. It comes back to knowing what is important to you and constructing your daily life around those pleasures as best you can.

The lack of meaning that many people attach to their own way of life is a primary reason the media has become such an enormous influence on our culture. It has become commonplace for people to use celebrities or athletes as an outlet to project their own desires, dreams and frustrations. Is there a reason why so many become incensed about the trivial acts of famous people that they don't even know? How does the fact that Janet Jackson exposed a breast, Tom Cruise jumped on a couch, or Britney Spears shaved her head affect your own life? Entertainers and competitors are meant to entertain us, not serve as substitutes for pursuit of our own goals. Do not become obsessed with a star's actions or attach yourself to a sports team's fate because of a sense of boredom or lack of purpose in your own life. What you should really worry about is what this indicates about your own existence if you are so consumed by those who have no relation to you.

Additionally, do not become obsessed with the lifestyle, the possessions, or the accomplishments of others, whether it is a superstar or your friends. Hugh Hefner made this observation when describing his lifestyle, "The interesting thing is how one guy, through living out his own fantasies, is living out the fantasies of so many other people." Although it is good to have heroes you look up to, do not live through them. Use their lives as inspiration to carry out your own aspirations. There is nothing more pathetic than someone who lives vicariously through others because they are too scared to live the way they want to. The Showstopper Lifestyle is all about living out your own fantasies without worrying about the criticism of others. If you acquire the mental strength to fix all your efforts on doing positive activities and bringing happiness to yourself and those around you, you will soon find that it will be others who will be amazed by your life, and you will explain to them how they can live out their dreams.

CHAPTER 13
Rich Friend, Poor Friend
☆ ☆ ☆

"It is easy to feel rich any time. Just count all the things you have that money can't buy."—Kevin Eikenberry

One of the biggest trends in our culture in recent years has been the movement to escape the constraints of a traditional nine-to-five job to build your own business and enjoy your "freedom." Although I am in complete agreement about the toll a regular office job can potentially take on your soul as well as the benefits of pursuing self-entrepreneurship, much of the literature and lectures in association with this trend are fundamentally flawed. Some of our world's most brilliant minds provide advice on how to make decisions that maximize your power and freedom, but ignore some of the prime reasons why those are voluntarily taken away.

Robert Kiyosaki wrote arguably the most famous of these recent books, *Rich Dad, Poor Dad*. It compares the two father figures in his life: his actual biological dad and his friend's father, who taught him about managing money. The book is fascinating, and I highly recommend reading it, but keep certain caveats in mind. It does not examine the fact that one of the major reasons the autonomy of humans is limited is not only their inability to make sound financial decisions, but also choices they make in their personal life. When you decide to get married, be in a serious relationship, or have children, your options in life often become seriously limited. Now, I am not telling you to be single and childless your whole life, but to examine the constraints on your independence as well as your employment decisions that taking those steps creates.

To illustrate, I will present my own version of Kiyosaki's dichotomy. One of my closest friends while I was growing up opened up his own business a few years ago, and it has become an enormous financial success. We will call him Ron, for the sake of protecting his identity. When we were teenagers, Ron and I had very similar interests and enjoyed an awesome time whenever we hung out. He was a laid-back guy who was fun and carefree and always enthusiastic and excited about life. After we graduated from high school, we drifted apart a bit, and in a few years, I went to law school, while he started his own sports store.

In the ensuing years, Ron opened up a few stores that have thrived, and he has also gotten married and had two children. During this same time period, I have never even had a steady job nor opened up my own business. There have been stretches where my bank account was as likely to be in the negative as in the positive, while he was a millionaire who owned multiple homes. In terms of the standards that most people measure success by, I would be a failure compared to my rich friend.

Now let us look at things from another perspective. While Ron has money, real estate, and a wife and kids, he also lacks freedom to make his own decisions and spontaneously do as he pleases. He has told me about his desire to hook up with different women as well as to travel to various places. Unfortunately, he cannot sleep with other girls without lying or cheating on his spouse and attempting to hide it. Financially, he can afford to travel to wherever he wants, but with his responsibilities to his businesses and his children, it makes things difficult. Mentally, he is weighed down because of these responsibilities. Most of the time, he is living the same day over and over again, and his existence is monotonous and mundane.

At the same time, while I may not enjoy the monetary stability that Ron has, I have the luxury of having the freedom to do whatever I please, whenever I want to do it. I am able to date whatever women I want without having to be deceitful to anybody. I can travel and visit loved ones without restrictions. I may not be working a steady job, but my law degree offers me countless opportunities for high-paying jobs, and I am not limited as far as where

I can take a position. Since I do not have family responsibilities, I do not have the pressure to make so much money. I only need to be in charge of my own welfare; thus my decisions primarily affect only myself. Consequently, I am capitalizing on my freedom by casually dating a multitude of women and traveling the world while spending quality time with friends and family.

As you can see, there is more than one way to define success. It is not always measured by values of traditional society because often those standards restrict one's individuality rather than enhance it. Even if you are a flourishing entrepreneur, it does not necessarily mean you enjoy more freedom than one who is not. Often, you can become prisoner to the decisions you make, and your power is limited because you are bogged down by your responsibilities, even if it is not a steady job. People always complain about jobs they hate and the monotony of the workplace, but they need to remember that the very reason many of them have to sustain their employment is because of the choices they make.

Again, this is nothing against raising a family, but the fact is that there are millions of people who are miserably going to jobs they hate to support spouses they are not fond of either. Even if there is no ill will toward the significant other, I have met countless people who would trade in the benefits of this so-called stability for the ability to be a free spirit unfettered by any boundaries. The main reason you pursue employment is to have an enjoyable life anyway, and if your work is not resulting in happiness, then what purpose is it really serving? So for all of you people who are making the decisions that will shape your lifestyle, keep in mind that the true measure of wealth is not so much in your assets, but in the ability to utilize your skills to make the most of the enjoyment of your days on earth. Even if you are not financially well off, if you are maximizing life experiences and focusing your energy on doing activities you love, then you truly are rich.

CHAPTER 14
The Man, the Mansion, and the Motivation: The Playboy Influence
☆ ☆ ☆

"The individual remains the all important element in our society—the touchstone against which all else must be judged."—Hugh Hefner

One of the biggest influences on my lifestyle and my views has been *Playboy*. Of course, just about every living and breathing male has heard about *Playboy* magazine and its legendary founder, Hugh Hefner. The thoughts most people associate with *Playboy* are the gorgeous nude girls in the magazine and the decadent parties at the Mansion. Like most hormonal teenagers, for me getting hold of a magazine was akin to a prospector discovering gold, and the thought of going to the legendary home was the most surreal fantasy one could imagine. It was amazing to me how so many respected celebrities would shed their clothes to grace the pages of the publication, and for me, the bunny symbol represented the living dream.

As I got older, I recognized that *Playboy* was about more than naked girls and sex, as there are plenty of adult magazines and videos that are more titillating in that respect. What set it apart from the others are the beautifully artistic manner in which the photographs are presented, and the impeccable quality of the editorials and the content. Yes, folks, people do look at *Playboy* for the articles. The most famous and influential of these came in the early years of the magazine from the editor himself: *The Playboy Philosophy.*

If you have not read Hugh Hefner's timeless work, which explains the principles behind the Playboy Empire, you owe it to yourself to do so. Like anything good in life these days, you can find it on the internet. In fact, I feel it should be compulsory reading for all young adults because it is a fascinating exploration of the closed-mindedness and the hypocrisy that plagues our society, not only when it comes to sexuality, but free thinking in general.

When I first read it, I felt Mr. Hefner was reading my mind and transcribing my views on life. The lifestyle he describes is not just about the erotic adventures and the attractive ladies, but the idea that a person should spend every moment of his existence living life to the fullest. It is about having the courage to live your own unique life in a world that brainwashes the masses into conformity and mundanity. It is about not being bound by social restrictions and institutions, but creating your own universe where you are king and the world is your kingdom, like a lucid dream. The underlying theme behind the philosophy is that a person should be a free-thinking individual unafraid of pursuing self-pleasures. This does not just include sex, but living with a zest for everything that makes you happy. Hefner emphasizes that this enthusiasm for the joys of life should not inspire condemnation or sympathy, but should be celebrated as a pursuit of making the most of every moment you are alive.

As you can see, the ideals behind Hef's philosophy largely coincide with the principles of the Showstopper Lifestyle. While thanks to *Playboy* and other influences, plenty of progress has been made in the ensuing years in opening people's minds towards these ideas, the world still largely frowns upon those who stray away from social institutions and restrictions. Even nearly fifty years after its first publication, the hypocrisy and judgmental attitude of the masses toward those who are chasing a dream that does not fit the societal norm plagues individuality in our culture.

With the ideals of *The Playboy Philosophy* already ingrained in my mind and influencing my lifestyle, one of my main goals when I moved to Los Angeles for law school was to meet Mr. Hefner and to visit his famous home. I finally got the opportunity to meet the man himself at an annual convention called Glamourcon. I am not the type to be in awe of celebrities, but I will admit it was truly an unbelievable experience. I was arriving at the convention, and at the exact same moment, I saw a limousine pull up in front of the hotel where it was held. Curious about who was inside, I glanced back and saw three of the most magnificent blonde goddesses one can possibly imagine emerge from the vehicle. Then out came the legend himself, and he looked as young and glamorous as ever. I stood, astonished by his presence, as he walked by surrounded by his gorgeous entourage. When I followed him up the stairs to the event, it defined the phrase walking in the shadow of greatness.

Hefner has always been a hero to me, not only because I admire his success and everything he stands for, but also because I have always seen parallels between our upbringings. Like me, he was a regular guy from a conservative Midwestern family who loved his parents but felt their lives lacked the passion and excitement he desired in his own. He had an extraordinary imagination that allowed his fantasies to become a reality. Not only that, he had the courage and fortitude to stand up for his beliefs, and he built his empire and his livelihood as a celebration of his unique vision and lifestyle. I have not even begun to reach his level of success, but to me he is proof that people should not live vicariously through others, but to live out their dreams. Hefner said the "Hef" character was the inner superhero who lived the fantasy existence he imagined for himself. That is how I view the "Shawn Valentino" part of me.

Later that day, I was able to shake his hand and thank him not only for the entertainment, but for the education and the inspiration he has provided me. That night, I was having a party at my apartment, not too different from the swinging soirees Playboy was famous for, but obviously on a much smaller scale. I was talking to one of the weekly attendees of my gatherings and told him that I had met Hefner earlier in the day and how inspiring it was. I will never forget his reply. He told me that with my personality, mentality, and charisma, one day people would say they met me and it will inspire them.

I took that statement as motivation to do something really special in my life that has the power to influence and inspire open-minded individuals everywhere, similar to what *The Playboy Philosophy* did a half-century ago. It inspired me to write this book and express my own beliefs that I hope encourage people to live out their fantasies and not just dream about them.

Speaking of fantasies, while working on this book, I lived one beyond my wildest imagination when I was invited to the Playboy Mansion for Hugh Hefner's New Year's Eve Party. Of course, the very experience of stepping foot in the Mansion is something every boy dreams of while growing up. What made it sweeter is that I was born on the first of January, so I not only rang in 2009 in the world's most famous pleasure palace, but celebrated my birthday there as well.

Obviously, not just anybody can drive up to the Mansion like it is some drive-through at McDonalds, so I want to give you all an illustration of my unforgettable night at the Playboy Mansion. You can attend one of Hef's private parties by invitation only, and they instruct you where to park. From there, you are shuttled to the home. I cannot even describe the anticipation that overcame me when I sat in that shuttle. As we entered the gateway to the legendary home and I saw the glitzy lights that illuminated the manor, it may as well have been the doorway to heaven itself. All of a sudden, I was in the presence of everything I had dreamt of my whole life, and I walked into the house with awestruck eyes. Even though I have been all over the world and have seen more beautiful women in my life than almost anyone alive, I must say that nothing can prepare you for the dreamlike atmosphere of this extraordinary locale.

It is a man's paradise on earth. There are beautiful women decked out in unbelievably sexy outfits surrounding you everywhere, and there are about two girls to every guy on the premise. This is definitely not your Thursday-night happy hour where fifteen guys are hitting on every girl who moves. Waitresses in bunny outfits are constantly serving you impeccably delectable food. All of the people in attendance are friendly and in impossibly festive spirits. There are multiple bars with free alcohol all night. The electricity in the atmosphere is so thick you could cut it with a knife.

As I wandered through the storied hallways of the legendary palace and looked up at the pictures of Hefner, it was as if a myth had come to life. When I stood in the legendary grotto by myself, I was overcome by emotion and had tears streaming down my face realizing I was in the presence of history. Putting my hands in the pool, I felt that I had taken a dip in magic waters. Playboy models came up to me all night to wish me a happy birthday, and I shared a few memorable birthday kisses to say the least. And how do I even begin to explain what it was like kissing a beautiful blonde on my birthday in the grotto of the Playboy Mansion? When you are there, it is essentially every-thing exciting in the world captured in one mesmerizing environment.

To describe it further would be fruitless because you have to be in the setting of the world's greatest erotic fairy tale to comprehend the mood it creates. It is more than a home, but the symbol of a dream and a lifestyle, one that I believe in, and one that millions of people fantasize about. All of this has been possible due to one man who had an extraordinary vision, and fittingly, the centerpiece of the party was none other than the emperor of eroticism himself, Hugh Hefner.

Hef sat in one of his famous robes in a white harem-like canopy, surrounded by dazzling women, surveying the center of the empire he has built. When I shook his hand and thanked him for the party and everything he represents, there were chills down my spine. I could not get a picture of this magic moment because we were not supposed to have personal cameras there, but it will be embedded in my mind forever.

All I can say is that I hope that all of you are fortunate enough to experience the glory of visiting this astonishing place. If you never receive this opportunity, please take time to read Hefner's *Playboy Philosophy*. Perhaps it will inspire you to create your own Playboy lifestyle that others will clamor to be a part of. I am thankful to Playboy for its continuing influence on my own life, and I only hope that this book will be similarly influential in making your fantasies a reality.

CHAPTER 15
In God We Trust?
☆ ☆ ☆

"When I do good, I feel good; when I do bad, I feel bad. That's my religion."—Abraham Lincoln

People often ask me what my religious background is, and truth be told, I am just not a religious person. I am not educated or interested in religion enough to intelligently discuss the subject so this book will not spend much time exploring it. There is a huge history of religion doing both terrific and horrific things to this world and it is all far beyond the scope of this work. To put it simply, I feel that one's religion should be their personal relationship with whatever they believe in, so long as they are not using it to hurt other people.

The Playboy Philosophy discussed religion and its influence on society at great length, and I again recommend that you read it no matter what your convictions are. It is a very in-depth and intelligent account of how religion affects many of the topics I cover in this book. I will say that I do stand by the same ideals as Hugh Hefner in that a person should enjoy both freedom of religion as well as freedom from religion. In other words, people should be free to practice whatever they believe in, but these institutions should not be intertwined with our governmental organizations and be forced upon the masses. The separation of church and state was one of the first things we learned in law school and I firmly believe in the importance of that strict boundary. Religion should be a personal belief, not a political influence.

Personally, I feel that as long as people are not preaching to me or judging my lifestyle based on their own religious stance, I am willing to respect their faith. The hypocritical judgment that often comes with one's religious sentiments is something I cannot tolerate. Thankfully, nobody has ever tried to judge my actions based on this reasoning.

What I really hate is when people use their beliefs to make excuses for their own misbehavior and bad decisions, or when they wait for a higher being to solve their problems instead of taking responsibility for their own actions. No matter what you believe in, do not use your convictions as a substitute for sound judgment and using common sense in making smart life decisions.

I am going to keep this topic short, but before you make your choices based on a higher power, make sure you ask yourself these questions. Does God want you to be happy doing what you love? Does God want you to maximize every moment you are on this earth? Does God want you to be with a partner for life that you are not sure you want to be with? Does God want you to have children you're not ready for and cannot take care of? Does God want you to make decisions based on your own principles or those that others attempt to thrust upon you? Does God want your convictions to bring you closer to others or to separate yourself from them?

I am not saying I have the answers to these complicated questions, and I will not even attempt to answer them. You should be free to believe in any religious ideals that give you strength and shape your moral compass. Trust in whatever God you believe in, but at the same time, do not forget to trust in yourself to make smart decisions in life and pursue a path that will lead to personal happiness without harming others. It has always been my belief that the standards of being a good human being should cross universal boundaries and that religion should bring people together, not cause separation and judgments. After all, the very purpose of religious ideals is to bring you inner peace and to love others. Do not let your convictions cloud your judgment and complicate your common sense. Having faith can be a beautiful thing, but make sure it includes having faith in yourself that the life you are leading makes the most of every day you are blessed with in this world.

CHAPTER 16
Unlocking Your Inner Superhero
☆ ☆ ☆

"Our deepest fear is not that we are inadequate. Our deepest fear is that we are powerful beyond measure. It is our light, not our darkness that most frightens us. We ask ourselves, 'Who am I to be brilliant, gorgeous, talented, fabulous?' Actually, who are you not to be?"—Nelson Mandela

By now, you are aware of my love of movies and how they have influenced my life. In recent years, some of the biggest box office attractions have been movies about superheroes. The stories about these mythological men have struck a chord amongst viewers all over the world. What makes these films so popular is not only that these characters are so larger than life, but the fact that they also have very human emotions and sensibilities as well. Would Superman be so appealing if his love for those he cared about did not make him vulnerable? Would Spiderman be so familiar if he was not an insecure young man trying to fit in? Would Batman really be the Dark Knight if it were not for his internal conflict between doing what is right and what makes him happy? My favorite "superhero" movie in recent times was not about these comic book legends, but a tale about a man with less apparent heroism. M. Night Shyamalan's *Unbreakable* is about an "ordinary" man who slowly discovers that he may have hidden abilities to perform extraordinary acts. It is a fascinating parable about the inner superhero who resides within all of us.

We have learned the only limitation that makes a man "ordinary" is his inability to unlock the chains he constructs around his mind and heart, chains that constrain his freedom and his power. By now, we have covered a variety of topics that will hopefully give you the confidence to break free of those restraints and live the extraordinary life of your dreams. If you have developed this confidence, you are ready to unleash your own inner superhero. Of course, in doing so, you should sustain strong ties to the people who care about you. Do not lose touch with the underlying traits and morals that make you who you are.

Uncovering this hero who lies within you will allow you to feel larger than life and showcase your confidence and zest for life to the world. It is not so much about performing life-saving acts, but more about exhibiting your phenomenal skills at doing what you want, when you want to do it. In a world where the vast majority of people are repressing their true desires, the ability to live the way you want without fear can be construed as superhuman. Don't forget that Hugh Hefner was a regular guy from a conservative Midwestern family who became Hef, playboy extraordinaire.

My inner superhero is "The Hollywood Showstopper," Shawn Valentino. When I am in this mentality, I feel anything is possible. Not only is no girl too beautiful, but no challenge is too difficult and no goal is unobtainable. I may not wear a cape, but when I am in this state of mind, I feel as if I can fly. If I am out in public, I reveal these powers by simply going up to the people I want to meet without fear, and by doing the things I want to do without hesitation. I might as well be flying because my confidence is soaring.

Similarly, when you are encompassed by self-assurance and happiness, you will no longer be apprehensive about seeking out the pleasures you are passionate about. You may give your inner hero a nickname, but the overall presence that your excitement for life generates will not need a label. Summon up all of your positive powers and harness them to create a supreme being who lives out all of your fantasies. Proudly reveal this ability to live your dreams to the world, and if in your mind you are a superhero, the world will see your extraordinary powers.

CHAPTER 17
It's a Small World After All
☆ ☆ ☆

"The world is a book and those who do not travel read only one page."—St. Augustine

A primary reason I was able to pass multiple bar exams is that I have a bit of a photographic memory. This sometimes applies to things I learn in my studies, but especially to the events of my life. Many memories of my childhood are still firmly entrenched in my mind, and I can still recall little moments that most people tend to forget as they age. One of those early unforgettable recollections is of a peaceful summer day when I was in the front yard throwing a baseball around, imagining that I was a Major League pitcher trying to strike out the side to win the World Series. My dad was watering the lawn, and my mom was sitting on the porch, and the skies were as blue as the ocean. It was one of those magical days that made kids look forward to the ringing of the last school bell, signifying summer was here. As the sky darkened into night, my parents went inside, but I still immersed myself in my own world, tossing pitches as if it were a night game at Yankee Stadium while my mom yelled at me to get in the house.

I should have listened because soon my precious baseball had rolled onto the other side of the street. Keep in mind that I was about eight years old at the time and had never crossed the street on my own, so the ball may as well have been dumped into a shark-infested sea. I stood at the edge of my lawn, staring at it, so near yet so far away, wishing I could summon up the courage to make the journey. Unfortunately, that would be the last time I would see the treasured memento that brought me so much joy because I never could bring myself to cross that street. I now look back at that symbolic moment and smile at my irrational terror.

I have now traveled to more than forty countries on five continents. I have been touring the globe at such a rapid rate that I now have a difficult time being in one place too long. If somebody asks me about my background, I merely tell them that I am a citizen of the world because I have such a multicultural outlook on life. I now reminisce with amazement about the little boy who was so apprehensive about crossing the street because now I journey around the world by myself without the slightest bit of worry. Thankfully, although my parents did not let me cross the street that fateful day, they did instill in my mind the importance of seeing the world. My family would go on frequent vacations across the globe as I grew up, and that mentality has stayed with me to this day. Everyone asks me all the time how I am able to travel so much, and I tell them it is just having the mindset that the earth is a beautiful place and that I want to see as much of it as possible. It is one of the tragedies of life that most people do not realize how short life is and how big the world is.

So far in this book, I have emphasized to you the importance of having the confidence to be your own person and to maximize life experiences. There is no greater experience that can help you grow as a person than taking the initiative to see as much of this glorious planet as you can during your lifetime. Unfortunately, when it comes to getting on a plane and going overseas, most people have that same frightened frame of mind that overcame me when I was a youth sadly staring at his baseball. Statistics show that most Americans have never left the country, and many have never even left their own state. I can tell you from personal knowledge that you are doing yourself an injustice if you are too scared to make the journey to some of the magnificent wonders our world has to offer.

When you travel, not only will you witness spectacular landmarks, but more importantly, you will become stronger as an individual. Your confidence will grow exponentially and you will become a more cultured, cosmopolitan person. This increased self-assurance will assist you in all areas of your life, from your career to your skills with women to your over-all attitude toward life in general. Circling the globe will take you on roads that give you the opportunity to meet people from all over the world. You will form social networks of groups from all walks of life and from a pleth-ora of backgrounds. The exposure to such diversity is the ultimate avenue to becoming a more open-minded person, and that is the key to living the Showstopper Lifestyle.

You may be wondering how "a regular guy" has been to so many places at such a young age. As I said before, it definitely is not the result of being wealthy, because sometimes my bank account may be as likely to be in the negative as in the positive. The most important characteristic of becom-ing a citizen of the world is to form the outlook that traveling is not just a luxury, but a necessity. My bank statement may be ordinary, but my mental-ity is extraordinary because I have it ingrained in my head that seeing the world is the greatest learning experience there is and I am not going to let my monetary constraints stop me. I do not have a steady job, but I search for temporary jobs and gigs where I can earn money without the long-term commitment of more permanent employment.

After saving up my wages for a few months, I will take a vacation. Sometimes, I will do the opposite and purchase an airline ticket for an extended trip a short while into the future, then use that as motivation to work extra hard in the upcoming days to save up to enjoy it. Although I may not have consistent paychecks, I am free to spontaneously come and go with-out worrying about being tied to an employer. Additionally, since I am single without my own home and have no children, I do not have the responsibili-ties and the attachments that inhibit me from just getting up and leaving as I please. I have an enormous circle of friends and a supportive family, but those do not require the type of accountability or create the type of limita-tions generally associated with a long-term relationship or raising kids. As I repeatedly point out, there is nothing in life that gives you more power and more options than the freedom to make your own decisions without having your life restricted by others. It is about knowing what makes you happy in life and formulating your lifestyle around the pursuit of that fulfillment.

If you are interested in traveling more than you are currently, let me give you some advice on how you can make it happen. I realize that many of you do have steady jobs or are in relationships, but that should not inhibit you from seeing the world. First of all, you must take the initiative to schedule a vacation, preferably overseas, each year. Once you have made that plan, then do what you need to, legally of course, to earn the money to pay for it without sacrificing your responsibilities. People often forget that one of the main reasons they exert so much effort working or studying is to get the opportunities for enjoyable experiences, and unfortunately, most fail to take advantage of these pleasures. Do not let your life pass you by without benefiting from the fruits of your labor. The destination is really irrelevant, as long as you are breaking out of your comfort zone and exploring new adventures and discovering different cultures. Once you begin traveling, you will find that the more you see, the more you will be interested in seeing.

If you are single, I highly suggest that you take at least one trip abroad, preferably alone, before getting into a permanent relationship. I will discuss the benefits of meeting foreign women in a later chapter. Right now, I want you to become acclimated to a way of thinking that will motivate you to travel in the first place. I realize that the prospect of visiting another country without any friends might be a scary proposition but it can also be an enlightening experience. There is nothing like journeying the world without a serious romantic attachment because you will not only be free to meet various women, but you will formulate the mentality to thrive as an individual without constraints. Traveling alone forces you to be outgoing and meet new people while simultaneously discovering how to take care of yourself in an unknown environment. It also allows you to view the exquisite marvels of a locality untainted by the opinions of others.

You may find it liberating to be alone in a mysterious setting where nobody knows who you are and you can be anybody you want to be. This freedom gives you a different perspective on life, while increasing your self-esteem and decreasing your fear of being alone. Once you broaden your scope and become witness to what a magnitude of joys our world has to offer, it may transform your outlook towards life. I am not saying there aren't benefits to having a significant other accompanying you, but it is beneficial to first experience a journey by yourself. It allows you to develop inner strength as an individual, and this will aid you not only if you choose to remain single, but if you choose to be in a relationship in the future.

Once you build the mental capacity to be able to journey the world on your own, you may find that no obstacle is too large to overcome and that all things are possible. When you view the world as your personal paradise and have the confidence to explore it with excitement and vigor, you have captured one of the fundamental principles of the Showstopper Lifestyle.

Of course, I also highly suggest that you take vacations with your friends and family whenever possible, especially when you are single, but continue to do so when you are in a relationship. In fact, if your partner inhibits you from traveling and spending time with the ones you care about, you should seriously consider whether they are somebody you want to have a long-term commitment with. If your loved ones are apprehensive about taking such a trip, take the initiative to plan it out and convince them about the incredible memories they will miss out on if they decide not to go. Traveling with your friends and family gives you a shared experience that bonds you closer together. It is fulfilling, not only because you are encountering something new and exciting together, but because each person you enjoy it with can enhance the event with their unique personalities. I am not saying it is better or worse than vacationing alone, but they are completely different voyages that are equally beneficial.

So when your parents are trying to convince you to take a trip with them, do not act like you are too cool to travel with them. Take the opportunity to grow closer to the ones who love you the most, and you may learn things about each other you never would otherwise. Being close with your family will make you a much happier and secure person, and there is nothing cooler or more attractive than that.

Additionally, do not miss out on spring breaks, road trips, and other excursions with your buddies, especially when you are young. As you get older, even if you are free to travel, circumstances may not allow your friends the same freedom to plan a vacation together. Responsibilities such as spouses and children start taking precedence over escapes with friends, and you may find it frustratingly impossible to schedule a time where everybody can make such a trip. When you have the opportunity, do everything in your power to make it happen because you will likely have the time of your life.

Finally, when you do decide to be in a long-term relationship, there can be nothing more gratifying than making a voyage with the one you love. There is a certain romance to exploring different parts of the world with a significant other that enhances the relationship. Too many couples settle into an apathetic routine where they lose the passion that brought them together in the first place. Instead of going through the motions knowing you have somebody there for you all the time, make each day a new adventure as if you are getting to know each other all over again. It goes back to my philosophy of living every day as if it is your first. When you apply that philosophy to a relationship, traveling together is one of the best ways to sustain some of the fire and the desire that make you love each other, while simultaneously growing together in a shared experience that keeps things new and exciting.

This all sounds wonderful in theory but unrealistic in practice you say? Well, never let reality get in the way of your dreams or your need to maximize each moment here on earth. Often, people think they cannot do things simply because they are too scared to or because others tell them it is a bad idea. As I told you, I am living proof that one can travel on minimal funds. You may not have the luxury of having the endless freedom I do because of your need or want for more steady employment, but almost everybody has at least a few weeks out of their year free. If you do not, you have bigger problems in your life than simply taking a vacation. If expenses are your concern, just budget yourself a certain amount of money each year that you set aside for travels. Unless you make really poor financial decisions, you should be able to save up for at least one overseas trip a year.

Furthermore, here are some hints from an experienced traveler that will make your trip as inexpensive as possible. If you purchase a budget traveling book such as *Frommers* or *Lonely Planet* or the *Let's Go* series, they will give you cheap lodging and dining options that are clean and convenient. Hostels are very economical places to stay when you are in a foreign country, and they generally have all of the accommodations you could possibly need. Best of all, they are a terrific spot to meet people from all over the world who love to travel. This will introduce you to new people you can enjoy your vacation with. You may soon find that you become friends for life and that you have a place to visit and a person you can stay with for your next vacation.

I also recommend that you enroll in a frequent-flyer program and take flights on one airline or its participating affiliates. This can result in all types of perks and ultimately free airfare all over the globe. I am enrolled in Northwest Airlines' World Perks program, and I have benefited enormously from being loyal to the company and its airline partners. Some of the advantages I enjoy include free baggage and free first-class upgrades, as well as access to exclusive lounges. Best of all, I have had multiple complimentary flights all around the world because I have saved up my mileage. Research which airlines fly out of your local airport and then register for at least one of these programs if you have not done so already. It will make your travel experience not only far more enjoyable but also much less expensive.

Most importantly, do not let others discourage you from seeing the world. Many times, people do not want you to experience something because they are too afraid to do it themselves. They will attempt to convince you of your limitations and the detrimental effects that taking such a journey will have on you. They may say it is dangerous or does not make sound financial sense. I am frequently told that I should get a steady job or that I should not travel until I am more economically stable. While I know they mean well, I also know that I will be making steady money when I want to, and I do not have any serious responsibilities dragging me down so this is the best time for me to be a globetrotter. Even if they have the best intentions, do not let others dictate how you conduct your lifestyle. I am not telling you to neglect your finances but to plan things in a way where you can take charge of your own happiness and make things happen. People may try to persuade you that you can't afford to travel. I am here to convince you that you can't afford not to.

I said before that most people do not realize how short life is and how big the world is. One of my main goals in life is to make the world smaller one day at a time. Out of all of the wonderful places I have visited in my lifetime, my absolute favorite spot is Disney World in Orlando, Florida. If you have not been there, you are missing out on one of the most captivating experiences on this planet. It is a place where even the most cynical adult can be transformed into an awestruck child. The highlight of the park for me is the "It's a Small World" ride, one of its oldest and grandest attractions, where you hop on a little boat that takes you through miniature replicas of some of the most famous landmarks on this planet. The mythical ferry trip has both sentimental and symbolic value to me. My parents were the first ones to take me to Disney and my mom tearfully told me it was her favorite ride because it reminded her of leaving her family to an unknown location halfway across the world. Additionally, the glorious perspective it gives you on cultures coming together and bonding in one unified paradise is my ideal vision of what the world should be like. In fact, I have structured my lifestyle to replicate this utopian environment where everything is spectacular and the wonders of the world are all within my reach. Just like my beloved attraction at Disney, in the Showstopper Lifestyle, it is a small world after all.

☆ SECTION 2 ☆
Becoming the Man of Their Dreams

CHAPTER 18
What Women Want?
☆ ☆ ☆

"A man is given the choice between loving women and understanding them."—Ninon de Lenclos

Many of us men have spent years attempting to solve the mystery of what it takes to become successful with women. As you will see, the answer doesn't lie in a list of pick-up lines or psychological mind games you throw at girls in an attempt to impress or allure them. There are numerous works of varying quality that outline strategies for seducing the ladies. It is not a skill that is acquired overnight, but comes from an accumulation of attributes you develop over a long course of time. The cover of this book highlights that it is a guide to getting ultra-hot women, and many of you may be reading it based on that assertion. As I stated in the beginning, however, my intention in writing this is not merely to create a manual for pick-up artists.

When I was interviewed on *The Tyra Banks Show*, they attempted to uncover the secret of my success with the ladies. What I tried to explain, however, is that the reason I am a "womanizer" is not because I am some Casanova that seduces women. My attractiveness stems from the confidence, honesty and open-minded mentality I have developed by accumulating a wide variety of life experiences.

There is a reason I have waited until late in the book to get into detail about strategies for luring the ladies. I wanted to demonstrate that it is important to concentrate first on developing into a well-rounded person who is independently happy and secure with himself. First and foremost, it is essential to getting the most out of your own talents and fulfilling the Showstopper Lifestyle mantra of maximizing life experiences. In addition, when you can present yourself as a self-assured figure who is multi-faceted, women will be naturally drawn to you.

For men, our mentality is often simple because most of us are always looking to get girls. As long as a woman is reasonably attractive to us and enjoyable to be around, then we aren't likely to turn her down if she offers herself to us. Hopefully, if you are looking for a serious relationship you are looking for more than that, but when we are just casually dating, our needs are generally not very complex. Unfortunately, as we know, figuring out what a woman is looking for and then attracting her to you is a much more complicated process.

Not only have I dated hundreds of women in various degrees of seriousness, I have also researched thousands of female subjects in my own quest to discover the primary characteristics in a male that spark their interest upon an initial meeting. The number-one trait by far was confidence. Other important factors that ranked high in the results were a great personality, a sense of humor, ability to engage in intelligent conversation, and a well-groomed personal style. Notice that, contrary to popular belief, money and looks are not the principal things that turn a woman on when she meets a man.

Of course, as a relationship becomes more serious, a sense of financial stability becomes more important, but you do not need to have deep pockets to appeal to women. Additionally, while you should strive to be in the best shape you can, girls look for more than male-model good looks when they judge sexiness. The point I am making is that you do not have to be wealthy or handsome to be successful with women.

Let us now analyze some of the primary features that women are attracted to so you can harness your own unique attributes to optimize your appeal. If you take the steps to present a total package, women will find you irresistible.

☆ *Step 1: First and foremost, women are attracted to confidence.*

Most of the book so far has discussed methods to develop your confidence. If you take those measures, you should find yourself ready to confront the challenges of the dating scene. In fact, once you attain this self-assured sense of independence, your personality will naturally reflect this when you interact with others and dating will not seem so challenging after all. Confidence is a quality that radiates out of your very being. When you exhibit this trait, you will not only be more outgoing with girls, your charm will make them feel good about talking to you. Women find a man who is secure with himself sexy, and the ease with which you approach life will make you smoother with the opposite sex. Most men are awkward or nervous when dealing with women, and this can be crippling no matter how hot or rich you are.

Just remember that to project an attractive personality, the best thing you can do is to showcase your strengths as a person. If you can do so in a charming manner, then they will be intrigued by you without finding you egotistical. Most of the girls I talk to are frustrated by how generic and boring the guys they meet are. Women come across so many bland men who are apathetic about their own existence that finding a man who exhibits an innate passion for life will excite them. If you can communicate your own happiness to her, it will make her want to be closer to you.

☆ *Step 2: Display a good sense of humor.*

A sense of humor goes a long way in communicating your sense of joy. Now I am not a comedian, and I'm not going to tell you how to make yourself funny. A good sense of humor is not just about telling jokes, but about showing your wit and that you do not take yourself too seriously. Although women are attracted to confidence, they may also be intimidated by it. As you build yourself up, mix in an amusing story that reveals your light-hearted side. It does not hurt to be self-deprecating. This gives you a balance that shows you are not arrogant. Not only that, it will you make you more at ease in the conversation because you will be entertaining yourself. When women find you interesting and funny, they will feel comfortable, and you will flourish in the dating world. I will elaborate more on how to convey a mixture of cool and comedy in my chapter about how to talk to women. For now, just know the cliché is true that a sense of humor is sexy.

☆ *Step 3: Smart is sexy.*

Just as sexy as being funny is being smart. In fact, there is nothing more attractive than being well-educated and exhibiting common sense in your everyday life choices. Unfortunately, sometimes those are mutually exclusive concepts because there are many highly schooled people who have no logical reasoning skills in their personal life. To be successful with women and in life in general, you should develop both types of intelligence. Obviously, getting a good education means making the most you can out of your years in school and taking courses that cater to your strengths and improve your weaknesses. Common sense comes from encountering a diversity of life experiences and learning from them.

The combination of those two skills will make you an alluring prospect for women. If you can speak intelligently about a wide variety of topics and exhibit world-savvy, then you will capture their interest. Again, the weakness of other men is your strength because there are so many guys who either are not educated or do not have a sound sense of logic. I am not saying that you need to recite the periodic table or quote Shakespeare. I am merely highlighting that when you are well-spoken and can communicate your own life experiences and world knowledge in a charismatic manner, you become much more appealing than the typical guy.

In my own experience, I have found that one of the main reasons I have been able to date a large number of girls is that I have so many years of schooling. Even though I was not taught how to meet women in college, the awareness of a multitude of social topics that I have obtained over the years has made me a more interesting person. Even if I am acting goofy or sarcastic, or raunchy and provocative, underneath there is a foundation of knowledge that nobody can take away. If you saw me on *Tyra*, you would have witnessed her shock at how eloquent and well-mannered I came across. That is because many people have yet to grasp that being smart is seductive.

It is the combination of my open attitude and outgoing persona with my educational background and vast amount of cultural experience that makes me desirable to women. Generally speaking, I have a higher educational degree and have seen more of the world than most women I meet, so that immediately garners their attention and puts me ahead in the all-important power dynamic which I will discuss later. When you amass knowledge from school and your experiences, you become much more fascinating. With intelligence comes immense respect from others and confidence in yourself, and females are captivated by those qualities.

☆ Step 4: Look your best.

Notice how many different attributes I have described that women find attractive without discussing appearance. Unlike males, who usually place a high value on a female's beauty, women do not place such a strong emphasis on what a man looks like. That being said, it is in your interest to make yourself look as appealing as possible, not only to get girls but for your own health and well-being. Not everybody is blessed with chiseled features or the metabolism to easily obtain a muscular physique. What we all can do, however, is take efforts to look the absolute best we can.

I have already stressed the benefits of having a gym membership and doing yoga and I cannot recommend those things enough. I know as well as anyone how hard it is to get motivated to work out at home. Becoming a member of a health club can be an inexpensive way to inspire yourself to get on a steady workout routine. Many of you already attend these places, and if you do, make the most of your money by regularly going there. If you have not yet done so, look into local gyms and get on a conditioning schedule. If this is not a feasible option for you, at least make time to exercise at home or do some cardiovascular activities outdoors. You will not only look better, but you will feel more active and energetic.

Even if women claim that looks are not the foremost thing they are drawn to, your appearance inevitably is the first impression they get when they meet you, and you want it to be a good one. I am not saying that you need to seek a bodybuilder physique, but on each day you should try to improve your form and definition. Soon your body will be an asset that captures a woman's attention, and you will feel sexy as a result. Additionally, if you are insecure about your face, working out will help strengthen your facial features, which is the first thing girls take notice of on a guy. Most of all, looking your best will boost your confidence, which as I have repeatedly said, is indispensible for your success in every avenue of life, including dating.

☆ Step 5: Develop a strong sense of personal style.

Almost equally as significant as developing your body is displaying a strong sense of personal style. This is something you have complete control of and you should showcase your creative flair. It is not necessary to go out and purchase expensive, designer clothing to do so. In fact, some of the coolest clothes that people have complimented me on were bought at bargain-basement prices at thrift shops. Dressing well is not so much about how much your outfit costs but how well you wear it. Your clothing should complement your features and also exhibit your unique personality.

Obviously, you want to feel comfortable with what you are wearing and not sporting attire that makes you feel ridiculous. At the same time, you should be unafraid to add a little panache to your everyday outfits when you are out looking to meet women. I recommend purchasing a variety of different flamboyant clothes that make you stand out in the crowd and make a woman take notice. Assess your features and go pick out some hats, sunglasses, and accessories that add excitement to your appearance. Muscle shirts, cowboy hats, sea-shell necklaces, big belt buckles, and leather jackets are all worthy additions to your arsenal. This is also where working out also comes into play because your body becomes your ultimate accessory and allows you the freedom to wear a wider range of styles.

In the book *The Game*, the study of pick-up artists that you may have heard of, they call it "peacock theory." The basic idea is that to attract desirable women, you need to stand out with flash and color. You may feel cheesy at first and feel as if you are on a Village People audition, but I encourage you to at least give this tactic a try. It may bring out a wilder side of your personality that you never knew existed. Your clothing can reflect your confidence. If you show a woman that you are unafraid to be risqué, she may gravitate to your courageous style.

Even if you do not like wearing flashy shirts or jewelry, at least have some classic suits and elegant shirts in your wardrobe. Casual but slick can be appealing and can give you the GQ appearance that many ladies love. Of course, I hope I do not even need to stress the importance of good hygiene and grooming, not to mention nice cologne to tempt their aromatic senses. Eternity is my scent of choice, and I suggest you find one that suits your tastes. Bottom line is to not show up on a date or a place where you know you will meet women looking shabby. Do not get me wrong. Wearing a baseball cap and shorts is fine in a casual setting, but if you want to improve your sexiness, then having a good sense of style can do wonders in wooing the ladies.

Those of you who have seen my pictures have observed that I have a very unique and showy clothing style. This is a reflection of my personality, which is flashy and charismatic, and it has been instrumental in attracting women. I realize that some of the outfits I wear many guys would not be caught dead wearing, but I am able to pull it off because I sport them with confidence. Women always tell me that they are impressed with how I dress because it not only looks sexy but it radiates personality as well.

In fact, when I know I am going to meet a woman on a date, I ask them what they are wearing so I know what type of outfit I should show up in. It sounds kind of metro-sexual, but when you communicate that you care about your appearance, women will appreciate it. Even though many of my clothes may make one question my sexuality, nobody does so because they always see me with a gorgeous girl on my arm. My unique fashion sense has been a large factor in my success with women.

☆ Step 6: Get a good set of photographs taken.

Once you have taken measures to improve your body and have discovered your sense of style, it is time to capture it. By that, I mean you should get a set of good photographs taken. Just like your wardrobe does not need to empty your wallet, gathering a good portfolio of pictures does not require hiring an expensive photographer. In fact, all it really takes is a tripod and a decent digital camera, and soon you can confidently show off your looks to the world.

These days, the internet has become the number-one avenue in the dating game, so you have the opportunity to make an impression and attract women without even meeting them. You literally have access to millions of potential partners at your fingertips, so it is essential to present yourself in as attractive a manner as possible. I have stated that women are not enamored by aesthetics so much as men, but when you are competing with millions of other men for women's online attention, it is your picture that will make the difference. It is amazing to me how many guys put themselves up on dating sites with awful pictures that are detrimental to their own appearance instead of complimentary. The majority of the women I have hooked up with were ones I met online, and the major reason I have had the opportunity to meet so many of them is because they gave me their contact information based on the appeal of my pictures.

If you do not already have a good set of images of yourself, you should get them done immediately. Get your four or five best outfits together and find a park or place that provides a nice background and get some pictures taken. With digital cameras, anybody can be an amateur photographer. You can have your friend take your pictures, or you can use the timer on your camera to do it yourself. These photos will be like gold, and their light will shine from the computer screen to capture a woman's attention. Women love pictures, but most men feel too proud or manly to take the effort to get good ones taken. I will discuss how you can maximize the information superhighway in a later chapter, but for now, get some excellent photos taken that show you looking your best; otherwise, that highway will lead to an immediate dead end.

Now you have some solid clues to that mysterious question that few men ever solve. After all, it is impossible to solve a mystery if you do not know what you are looking for. My dating experience and my studies have given me good indicators of what women want, and I have maximized my personality and looks to make myself as desirable as possible. Mastering the dating game is not a quick process as I am still learning new skills and concepts every day. Similarly, I hope your experiences teach you to improve your own talents. Before jumping into the game, however, make sure you follow the steps I have outlined above to make you as prepared as possible. Every attribute I have described that women look for, from personality to sense of humor to intelligence to style, will play a part in improving your confidence. The beautiful thing about it all is that developing the traits that will make you successful with the ladies will also make you happier and more capable of maximizing life experiences.

CHAPTER 19
The Myth of the Pick-Up Artist
☆ ☆ ☆

"Don't concentrate on finding the right woman. Concentrate on being the right man."—Unknown

For years, society has been fascinated by the myth of "the pick-up artist." In fact, when people hear about my talents with women, they often use this term to describe me. Although I am flattered by the description, I do not find the semantics to be very complimentary. I have great respect for the men who have mastered the skills of the "pick-up" and feel you can learn a great deal from them, but I have always disliked the term pick-up artist. In fact, what has made me successful with the ladies is my inner belief that women want men just as much as we want them. I realize that there is an artistry in talking to women, but the art form should not be all about men chasing them. That may seem presumptuous of me, but the idea of guys having to be the ones who "pick up" girls is detrimental to the dating dynamic because it puts men on the lower level of the totem pole.

For those of you looking to succeed with the ladies, you need to erase the misconception that it is the goal of men to be the ones who pick up girls. When getting girls is a small part of a larger picture that makes you a well-rounded person, you will not need to chase them. In fact, when you are successful in various aspects of life and you can communicate this in a confident, charismatic manner, then you will find it is the women who are the ones who seek you. It all boils down to the manner in which you portray yourself and displaying your strengths so that a woman cannot help but be attracted to you. Most men waste their time on chase mode instead of focusing on their own positive traits. I have described fairly thoroughly how you can become a self-assured, well-rounded person. If you accomplish this task of being a total package, your appeal will be magnetic.

The following chapters will explain in great detail how to emphasize your attributes and succeed with women in a variety of avenues. You should not rely on "pick-up lines" or have the misconception that getting women is a pursuit. Instead, showcase your excitement for every moment of your existence, and women will want to bask in your delight. The key is to create an impression that your life is so filled with different activities that women are pursuing you, and the ones you choose are lucky to be with you. With this aura of unattainability, you will find that the sport of getting girls won't be a game of pick-up at all, but a natural manifestation of your enjoyment of life.

CHAPTER 20
Winning the Power Dynamic
☆ ☆ ☆

"I have an idea that the phrase 'weaker sex' was coined by some woman to disarm the man she was preparing to overwhelm."—Ogden Nash

In an ideal universe, men and women would always have the same wants, needs, and interests, and they would intermingle perfectly. There would be no deception, manipulation, confrontation, and frustration when looking for a mate, and dating would always be a mutual pleasure for both parties instead of the tiring task it often becomes. Unfortunately, those ideal conditions do not exist, and there is an opposition that goes on between genders that resembles a warped game where each player is struggling for power. I personally dislike this struggle and wish that we could come to a consensus based on mutual understanding. There are obvious biological and emotional differences between the sexes, but even if men are from Mars and women are from Venus as the book says, it should not be a war of the worlds.

Since that peaceful galaxy where we all share perpetual bliss is not our present reality, you must enter this scene prepared. Just as you do not want to enter a chess match without your strongest pieces, you do not want to enter the dating sphere without the mental strength and tools to be as powerful a player as possible. Now, I am not saying that this is a competition where the object is to defeat the opposite sex, but it is a metaphorical way of saying that you should not end up feeling like a loser in your efforts to become successful with women. Even though I have experienced numerous failures myself, I feel that the skills I have developed over the years in attracting large amounts of women has given me a bit of expertise in the area, and I wanted to share what I have learned. Because I have obviously only explored the dating world as a guy, I wanted to provide you some insight on how men can attain the success we all crave, but few ever achieve.

If you really want to enter the dating scene with the power to make your own choices, you will already have taken some of the steps I have outlined in the previous chapters that will make you a more well-rounded person. By that I mean you will have sustained strong ties with a set of friends and family that provide you balance, and that you have developed yourself educationally, culturally and physically to the best of your abilities. When you become a cosmopolitan person, you will gain a strong sense of confidence, and that is the most attractive quality women are drawn to. I realize that I have repeated the emphasis on confidence often, but I want it ingrained in your head. If you are putting yourself out there you need to make yourself as marketable as possible.

As I have stressed multiple times, before everything else, you need to know what you are looking for out of the women you date. Make sure your dating habits coincide with your lifestyle and do not inhibit your responsibilities, interests, and your relationships with those you care about. Above all, make sure you are content with who you are, and that you are looking to meet women to complement your happiness, not to complete an emptiness that lies inside. By now, all of this should be obvious, so don't complicate common sense!

Now that you are a versatile man with a variety of passions who is excited about life and knows what he wants, you are ready to maximize your powers to attract women. Let us step back for a moment and look at the broader scope of gender dynamics in American culture. Although inequalities are diminishing as the years pass in nearly every aspect of society, from the workplace to the political sphere, men remain dominant. Ironically, when it comes to dating, it is generally women who have the freedom to choose who they are interested in and who they will sleep with. It is a puzzling contradiction that flies in the face of logic. In order to make sense of it, we must attempt to comprehend why men are so limited in their choices and so frustrated in the pursuit of their desires.

Much of the reason goes back to hypocritical social standards when it comes to sexuality that I will soon discuss at length. The fact that women are judged by both males and their fellow females about their sex life makes them especially guarded, and often insecure, when it comes to their dating habits. While this is harmful to a woman's psyche, it also limits the options of men who are interested in them because they have to jump through hoops to get what they want. Even if she is interested in a guy, a girl often puts up a false front because she is worried about her reputation or her own sense of security. It is up to all of us to help erase this double standard. Social standards aside, the major factor in why women enjoy the power in the dating circuit is because most men simply do not know how to confidently attract women to them.

It is amazing that the male gender, which as a whole is so obsessed with appearing macho and strong, is so weak and cowardly in its dealings with females. A primary reason, as stated, is that many lack confidence in life in general and that extends to their interactions with the opposite sex. On the other hand, there are countless men who are successful and self-assured in almost all walks of life, but who spoil it all because of their inability to handle their relationships with women. It is because most guys enter the dating scene with a loser's attitude, thereby voluntarily relinquishing their power to attain what they desire from the women they pursue.

Let me discuss a series of guidelines on how to retain this power. If you follow these tips, you may find that you will acquire the sought-after ability to make women pursue you. Keep in mind that you will tweak some of these skills depending on the woman and what you are looking for out of her, but this basic advice should aid you no matter what you seek.

☆ Rule 1: Assert your individuality.

So now imagine that you meet a girl you are interested in and you want to showcase the characteristics that will attract her to you. The best way to analogize your quest to display this attractiveness is to think of an artist painting a portrait. You want to make this picture as unique and alluring as possible so you can show her the value that you bring to her life. Emphasize your strength and disguise your weaknesses to convey the idea that you are a man of the world who has a multitude of things going on in his life and does not need a girl to make him happy. There is nothing that reveals weakness more than appearing needy or desperate.

☆ Rule 2: *Let her know that you regularly date attractive women.*

The main thing to remember is to never feel intimidated by a woman, no matter how beautiful she is. When you meet a girl, you need to make it clear that you can regularly get hot women. This way you neutralize her strengths instead of reinforcing your weakness, which for men is usually that they are frightened of good-looking girls. When she sees that you are accustomed to attracting beauty and not enamored by hers, she will lose her superior position and become curious as to what other women find interesting about you. The more you get comfortable with relaying this message, the more you actually will be relaxed around women and find them attracted to you.

Don't hesitate to talk about how you have been exploring the dating scene, but have yet to find somebody up to your standards. When I start speaking with someone I am interested in, I make sure to explain that there are so many women in my life that I have a hard time making time for all of them. This sets off their insecurity because it renders their powers obsolete, and it often makes them want to go the extra mile to show why they are good enough to be with a guy who gets so many girls. It helps that in my case, what I am saying is true, but even if you are not dating a bunch of people, get across the idea that women are after you, and that you pick and choose who you spend time with. Getting men is easy for women because men are always chasing them, but if you present the idea that you have girls chasing you, it gives you an aura of unattainablity that many women find appealing.

☆ Rule 3: *Show that you are a well-rounded person.*

At the same time, make it clear that you are a well-rounded person. Talk about how you would rather spend quality time with your friends and family than waste it dealing with nonsense from women who do not satisfy your needs and interests. This may give you power points because it often hits a sore spot with girls. Many of them lack real friendships and that is why they are often needy for companionship from a man. Exhibiting that you are surrounded by good company erases any image of loneliness, which could translate into apparent neediness.

You should also enthusiastically share your passions. Get across that you would love a female companion to share these interests with, but would rather do them alone or with friends than be with a girl who is not worthy. After all, since you do have such a plethora of hobbies, she needs to realize that it would take somebody special to capture your attention. It is instrumental that she does not arrive at the conclusion that your whole life centers around searching for a woman to spend time with.

Matter-of-factly discuss your successes in various walks of life, and explain how important it is to you to improve your career and travel the world. Make sure you express all of these topics passionately so she understands that you are a man who is self-assured, secure with himself, and thrilled with the very idea of being alive. Hopefully, all of this comes naturally to you and you actually do feel this zest for your own life because if you do not, then you have bigger problems than merely attracting women to you.

When you are describing yourself, do it in such a way that you are subtly hyping yourself up without appearing too arrogant or self-centered. If you can do so, you will demonstrate your value to a woman and she will be so impressed that she will feel the need to do what you want to prove her own worth to you. This is a skill you will develop over time as you practice these tactics with an assortment of women.

By giving a similar description to the one I have outlined above, you will have illustrated an image of a man who is successful in a myriad of ways. She will know that you have no problem attracting women and she will be curious as to what other women find so appealing about you. Since women are turned on by more than just looks, she may be enamored by your ambition in your career and the pursuit of your passions. Additionally, the fact that you have ties to close friends and family proves that you are a man of depth who values the truly important people in his life. Most of all, the fact that you are able to honestly and excitedly describe yourself with such enthusiasm will reveal your confidence, which is, again, the ultimate trait that women are drawn to.

☆ Rule 4: Do not appear too sappy or complimentary.

Unfortunately, most men do not approach the game with such self-assurance. They fail to showcase the characteristics that make them attractive and do not paint the picture of a man who has so much to offer that a woman should feel lucky to be with him. Instead, they make the mistake of incessantly giving out compliments and putting the woman on a pedestal from the beginning. Women are accustomed to hearing praise about their looks, and they are constantly bombarded with lame pick-up lines and advances. By doing this, you are merely putting yourself in the same category with all of the other guys over whom women feel the power to reject. An occasional flattering comment is fine, but do not create a lopsided power dynamic for yourself where you are on an uphill struggle to compete with other men's affections. Again, your goal is to present yourself in a manner that makes her desire you.

Additionally, do not appear too sappy in the early stages of meeting a woman. As I said before, there is nothing that is more pathetic than a man who appears in need of a woman's approval or companionship. You should definitely enjoy every moment when you are fortunate to meet someone who strikes your fancy, but do not push things too fast or make grand assertions. Tell the girl that you enjoy her company, but do not immediately tell her that you "can't live without her" or "are in love with her."

First of all, you should never be in a position where your happiness in life is completely tied to your relationship to another person. Even if you are in a serious relationship or have children, you should still have a sense of inner joy independent of your loved ones. Second, real love for another human being, whether romantic or not, takes a long time to develop and is not something that magically overcomes you overnight. I cannot begin to count how many women have complained to me about how clingy men become and how every man they meet tries to desperately attach themselves to them. Hearing things like this make me ashamed to be a man because there is absolutely no reason for guys to present themselves in such a feeble way. If you really want a quality woman to remain in your life for a long time, then display your own strength as a person, and don't be a pansy.

☆ Rule 5: Make sure each party contributes equally.

While I am on this subject, let me address another dichotomy that is completely befuddling. Tremendous advances have been made in gender inequality over the last few decades to the point where women now generally enjoy similar salaries and opportunities for employment as men. With the feminist movement and women wanting to be recognized as equal to men, it makes no sense why it is still often expected that men be the ones who pay on a date. Let me make it clear that I completely understand this is not always the case, and there are many women who are more than happy to split costs or even pay for the couple on occasion. Still, there remains a bit of a social expectation that it is the "gentlemanly thing to do" for a guy to pay, and I feel it is wrong in this day and age.

Don't get me wrong. If you get to know a girl who you find genuinely likes you, and it is established that both parties are contributing equally to the relationship in some way or form, then there is nothing wrong with buying her dinner here and there. Even giving an occasional expensive gift is completely fine if there is a real connection and you know you are not being used. What I have a problem with are situations where a guy first meets a girl and then immediately takes her to an expensive restaurant or empties his wallet on lavish gifts. Even if you can afford to do so, it is not a good idea because it shows that you are trying to buy her affection. It exhibits a sense of insecurity. Any woman who is worthwhile will not be offended by sharing costs on your initial dates, and if they are, you should question whether they are the type of girl you want in your life.

Personally, I do not allow myself to get into scenarios where I am put in the position to pay for a woman I am not sure I am interested in. Unless I've already realized that I really like a woman, I don't want to take her on a potentially expensive rendezvous. Obviously, my first choice is to meet at my place or her place, but if we do meet in public, it will be a relaxed setting like a park or a coffee shop. The reason I bring up this topic is that so many men complain about women being money-hungry or spending too much of their cash on their girlfriends, etc. I cannot tell you how many men have told me that they need to work extra hours or are having trouble affording being in a relationship. To those men, I have one thing to say, and that is that you have nobody to blame but yourselves.

When you enter a relationship, you need to understand your financial situation so you can make your own decisions as to how you spend your money on a woman. There is no gun pointed at your head forcing you to take the responsibility. Therefore, there is no reason to set the precedent for you (and indirectly for other men) that it is the guy's job to pay for the girl. It should not be a prerequisite for sleeping with a girl or getting her to love you. If you feel it is, you need to become more secure with your traits as a person. I have had many women want me despite not spending a dime on them, and it is because they are attracted to my personality and the fun I bring to their lives. If you do feel as if you are wasting your cash on a lady who may not be worthwhile, don't complain about it because it's your own fault.

Let me explain to you an extreme example of the severe ramifications of not establishing equal contributions to a relationship. For about a year, I was living with a couple in an apartment in the Hollywood Hills. The guy was a close friend of mine, and I got along well with his girlfriend as well. That being said, the nature of the relationship was baffling to me. They had been dating for more than five years and he was paying for her rent, her education, and all of her various expenses. He was not financially stable himself and was struggling to make ends meet for the both of them. The girl seemed like a fairly nice person but did not take any effort to be an equal contributor to the relationship. She did not cook or clean or do much of anything to help him out. They supposedly had a mutual understanding that when she finished school, she would take charge of their finances as he returned to school.

As you can see, the whole premise was a setup for disaster. I saw the bitter ending from a mile away, and when I heard news of it, I could do nothing but shake my head. After I moved out, she was completing her final year of school. Sometime after he made the final payment for her university, they broke up. Not only that, she became bitter and angry and blamed him for not taking proper care of her, despite the fact that he was essentially her caretaker for years. On the surface, it looks like completely ungrateful, emotionally unstable behavior on her part and that my friend was taken advantage of. While all of that may be true, we need to examine why this terrible situation happened in the first place.

The reason he was exploited in such a manner is that he mistakenly established at the start of the relationship that he would take financial responsibility for her. As it continued, it became assumed that he would continue to do so until it was finally just taken for granted. By the time their relationship fell apart, he had wasted thousands of dollars on her and did not get his return on their deal for her to return the favor in the future. Understandably, he became depressed about the situation.

There is a lesson to be learned here, and that is to set the tone for your relationship early on after you meet a woman. Do not deliberately dig yourself an unnecessary hole by making irresponsible and unintelligent decisions that put you in a disadvantageous position. It is not even about being a good person, but is more about being smart. My friend was a really nice, charming guy who could get all kinds of girls who would not take him for a ride. Unfortunately, he put himself in a position to be exploited. Scarily, it could have been much worse. When you create this type of expectation, if you eventually get married, then all of your assets may be at stake if things go bad, and you could be legally obligated to give them up. Why make things difficult for yourself just out of a false sense of heroism or your quest to prove that you are a gentleman? Many men can attest that being chivalrous does not feel so honorable when you are broke or miserable.

Going back to what I was saying at the start of the chapter, the best way to be successful with women and avoid unnecessary hardships is to present yourself as a strong, independent person. I do not have a degree in psychology, but the dynamic makes complete sense. If you put a woman on a pedestal from the beginning and act as if you are pursuing her, then obviously she will feel that she has power over you. In contrast, if you can make it apparent from your initial conversation that you are above and beyond the average man, then she will be the one fascinated by you. Remember to create the impression that you have so much going on in your life that she will need to earn your attention. You may be amazed at what she will go through to do so.

This will be valuable on dual levels. If you can describe yourself charismatically and passionately, then it will reflect that you are an appealing person who is sought after by women. Not only that, if she is convinced by your description, then she will feel special herself for having the opportunity to have such an attractive man in her life. Women revel in their status of being the object of a man's affection. When you can turn the tables and become the object of their desire, then you will have successfully won the power dynamic. The Showstopper Lifestyle is all about maximizing your power and your freedom. When you attain this power, you will soon realize that you are the one who has the freedom to choose which women you want to be part of your life.

CHAPTER 21
3 Billion
☆ ☆ ☆

"We delude ourselves with the notion that somehow there is only one person out there who is a soul mate waiting for you."—Hugh Hefner

Three billion. That is a number that should be ingrained in your head just like twenty-four hours in a day, seven days in a week, and three hundred and sixty-five days in a year. If you have a short memory, you should etch it on a plaque and place it on your wall. Every man should always remember that there are more than three billion women in the world and not to be consumed with the illusion that there is only one person out there for everybody. The idea of a solitary soul mate who exists somewhere on this vast planet is a harmful myth.

There are too many people in the world caught up with finding "the one" when they should be enjoying "the ones." People often become brainwashed by the notion that when they meet that "special someone," they are irreplaceable. They miss the true beauty in life and that is the freedom of choice we are all born with. This applies to every aspect of our lives and is especially true for our dating life. In fact, I feel that everybody should explore various partners before settling down, if they choose to do so at all. When you get attached before that, you may find that you will want to satisfy those curiosities and hurt somebody you care about. One of the primary reasons there is so much cheating in marriage and relationships is that people do not maximize their single lives and regret it later. When you are free from the constraints of a relationship, instead of being obsessed with locating someone to fulfill that role, enjoy your freedom and meet women of all types. Obviously, this abundance of choices is enjoyed by women as well, and this advice applies similarly to all of you female readers.

Just remember that no matter who you are, there are more than three billion options who are all unique and may offer something to enhance your happiness. Why not take your time and discover what you really want? You will be more likely to find the woman you are really looking for, or you may even conclude that a permanent relationship is not for you.

If you are in a serious relationship, make sure you have chosen somebody with whom you share chemistry and have plenty in common with. If she does not live up to what you are looking for, just move on. There is no reason to limit yourself for any reason. There is always a plethora of beautiful women on this planet with whom you can mutually enjoy your wants and needs.

Just make sure you do not delude yourself into believing that there is only one woman out there for you. It may be a romantic vision, but it belongs in a fairy tale, not in the reality we live in. If you are suffering from a break-up, it does hurt, but after the pain wears off, you'll have the opportunity to find others upon with whom you can explore your needs and desires.

If you are stuck in a bad relationship because of some fantastical misconception that your mate is irreplaceable, you need to realize that you are each doing yourselves more harm than good. A miserable relationship is like an awful disease that tears away at your heart and mind and can ruin your life. All of us have been through these difficult situations. What makes us stronger is how we handle them and learn from them. When the writing is on the wall, it is better to appreciate the good times you shared and move on. Do not forget that there will be many lovely ladies out there waiting to meet you who will make you happier.

If you do not believe me, take advice from the master himself. I believe Hef said it best in his *Little Black Book*. "We delude ourselves with the notion that somehow there is only one person out there who is a soul mate waiting for you. Emotionally, you don't fully believe that you can ever have those feelings again for someone new, that you'll ever find someone comparable. That's an illusion." When you have the number "three billion" entrenched in your head, that daydream will fade away and you will realize that your heart is something you can share with many and be the better person for it.

CHAPTER 22
The Aura of Unattainability
☆ ☆ ☆

"Make like you don't need any girl, then girls will want you."—Paris
Morgan (Love Don't Cost a Thing)

There are a myriad of characteristics that can make a man appealing to women. I have done years of research, both personally and studying others, to understand what these qualities are. As I said before, success with women, like anything else in life, depends on knowing what you are looking for and making yourself as complete a person as possible so you can attain it. Many men yearn to uncover the secret of how to attract multitudes of women to them. I have discovered that the men who truly succeed in luring the ladies convey an aura of unattainability.

It is a fundamental part of human psychology that we always crave what we cannot have, or at least perceive is difficult to attain. There is a reason that so many people are fascinated with celebrities, beauty, fame, and fortune. If everybody was rich or famous or beautiful, then these qualities would be common and would lose their special appeal. It is because of the general perception that glamour and wealth are out of the realm of their reality that so many people are awestruck by them. The same principle is true in the game of getting girls. After all, why are so many women fascinated by famous men? These stars may be no more attractive, nice, or fun to be around than a guy who lives outside of the spotlight. It is because they are portrayed as being larger than life that they are appealing.

Just speaking from personal experience, when I appeared on *The Tyra Banks Show*, hundreds of women from all over the United States began emailing and calling me. These same girls might not have given me a second thought if I had approached them at a bar. It was the fact that I had been on national television that made me appeal to their fantasies.

I realize that not everybody can be rich or famous, but the good news is that you do not have to be to create the impression that you are something special. It is about developing the mentality that you are extraordinary, and then communicating it with those you encounter. Remember the importance of inventing your inner superhero. It can give you heroic magnetism with the women. When you can illustrate that not only are you attractive and interesting, but you do not need to have anybody in your life to be happy, then more women will want to be with you.

Let me give you an example that illustrates this theory. A group of my guy friends and I were together on a Saturday night watching a World Series game. Some of their girlfriends as well as their female friends were there as well. I had recently put together a photo album of some of my adventures with women that I brought to show my buddies. These pictures showcased me with some of the most beautiful girls in the world. One would imagine that it would be the guys who would be drooling over the shots of these sexy sirens. On the contrary, it was the girls, most of whom were in serious relationships, who were absolutely captivated by these images. I am not saying they were interested in me per se, but they found my lifestyle exciting and exotic. My friend asked one of the single women there if she would like to be one of the girls in the album and she responded that she would. The truth is that the idea of the single playboy living every moment to the fullest is one that is fascinating to women. Hugh Hefner does not need to be the only one who reaps the benefits of this fascination.

I have been enormously successful with women by exemplifying this elusive vibe. They see my pictures with all types of gorgeous girls. They hear me talk about being happily single and casually dating a multitude of women. Those who date me see that I am not intimidated by them and am immune to their manipulation. I pay little enough attention to them that they are happy with any contact that they get. All of these tactics aid in sustaining an unattainable aura.

The character Paris Morgan says it best in the movie *Love Don't Cost a Thing*, a charming film about a nerdy guy trying to get the girl of his dreams. She explains to him, "Make that you don't need any girl, and girls will want you." This is excellent advice for those of you who similarly want to date the women of your dreams. Let me emphasize again that nothing conveys weakness to a female like neediness. On the other hand, if you radiate the energy that you are a man completely comfortable alone and only allow those who are worthwhile to be close with you, women will clamor for your consideration. Like confidence, this is not something you learn overnight but rather is developed from the sum of your experiences. If you can follow the principles of the Showstopper Lifestyle that are illustrated throughout this book, you will exude this vibe. If you want to attract masses of women to you, just engrave the phrase "aura of unattainability" in your mind or write it down and post it on your wall. It is vital because it will be the very fact that you are unattainable that will make women want to attain your company.

To help illustrate, let me paraphrase a famous quote to sum up my attitude when dealing with the ladies. "Most men see the beautiful woman on their arm and ask why. I see the lovely ladies on each arm and ask why they deserve to be seen with me." George Bernard Shaw would be proud.

CHAPTER 23
Three Types of Connections
☆ ☆ ☆

"There are three things men can do with women: love them, suffer for them, or turn them into literature."—Stephen Stills

After you have taken measures to make yourself a confident, powerful person, you are ready to enter the dating universe. Anybody who has been in the dating game knows that it can result in deception, confusion, manipulation, frustration and ultimately, depression. One of the biggest mistakes people make in their dealings with the opposite sex is that they send mixed messages about their intentions. Part of the reason may be that the person is unsure about their feelings and what they want out of the relationship. Even if someone knows how they feel, many are afraid to express those sentiments, chiefly because they are worried that these revelations will result in rejection. Unfortunately, others know exactly what their feelings are but choose to disguise them to manipulate or deceive the other person. I have learned from my own personal experiences as well as my studies that the best way to approach a relationship with a woman once you get to know her a bit is to choose which direction you plan on pursuing, and then communicating your intentions to her.

Generally, a relationship with the opposite sex can go in three different directions. You may experience a strong emotional and physical bond with the person and explore a serious romance. On the other hand, you may feel that a committed relationship is impossible, but you share tremendous body chemistry. In that case, perhaps you may want to keep things mainly physical with no strings attached. Finally, you may find that you care deeply for the woman and that sex would merely complicate matters. In that case, a platonic friendship would be advisable, and for you smirking men out there, there are benefits to having a close female friend. Of course, the line between these three categories may be a thin one, as emotions and physical yearnings often create complex feelings for the other. Complexity aside, however, in order to minimize drama and lies in your dating life, once you discover what role a lady you meet plays in your life, choose one of these paths and make sure you are both on the same page.

Let me illustrate to you with a personal experience the potential disaster that may occur if you are not clear with yourself or the other person about what you want out of a relationship. When I first moved out to California, I met a gorgeous Czech model who was sweet, smart, fun, and with whom I shared incredible chemistry. When we first met, we hooked up here and there but ultimately decided that we should remain just friends. As the months passed and we became closer, I realized that she was falling in love with me. Admittedly, I had some feelings for her myself and gave her signs that our friendship would soon blossom into a romance. Even while I gave her those hints, I had no real interest in commitment, as we lived a few hours away from each other and I wanted to date other girls. I was flattered that I had a woman who cared so much about me and I did not want to lose that connection, but I also wanted to keep things uncomplicated and drama-free.

Eventually, we reached the stage that every relationship seems to arrive at when there is mutual attraction involved. Difficult questions arose that tend to complicate matters. Where is this going? How do you really feel about me? Isn't it time to take this to the next level? At the same time, we became intimate without any clear answers to these issues. After the intimacy began, she naturally assumed that she was my girlfriend and she had every right to believe I felt the same way about her. Unfortunately, while I deeply cared for her, I was not ready to commit to her and treated her desire to do so as a silly joke. The beautiful friendship we had built for nearly a year was shattered, and she was heartbroken. When we were no longer so close and I did not have that steady woman in my life who told me she loved me at the end of the night, I realized that it left a pretty big hole in my own heart as well.

This illustration may seem familiar to you as well as the hurt feelings associated with it. Notice that there was no cheating or lying that destroyed our bond. Rather, the hurt was a direct result of mixed messages. The main reason things fell apart between us is that I was wishy-washy about how I approached the relationship and sent deceptive signals instead of being clear to her or myself about how I felt. Although I felt some pain over losing a girl I cared about, it was even worse knowing I had hurt somebody who loved me. Ever since then, I have made it a point to be completely clear that I am not looking for a commitment and to steer things toward pure friendship or intimacy. Ideally, in rare situations, I have met a woman with whom I could enjoy a bit of both.

Similarly, when you get to know a woman, I advise you to know in your heart how you feel about her. Use your mind to make intelligent choices in your relationships that coincide with your lifestyle. If you want to date multiple people, that is fine, but do not string along the one you feel is most likely to stick around by pretending you are interested in monogamy. If you want to keep things purely physical, you do not want to tell the person they are not good for anything but sex, but you also do not want to mislead them that a physical relationship is a stepping stone to something more serious in the future. If you have a friend you have romantic feelings for, use your common sense in expressing those sentiments to them. It is better than repressing your emotions and always wondering if they feel the same way. Most importantly, if you have a platonic friendship you value greatly, do not try to sleep with that person unless you are completely sure the sex will not diminish your special closeness.

I completely understand that all of this sounds much simpler than it really is. When you factor in all of the complicated emotions that arise when dealing with the opposite sex, deciding what you want out of a relationship may not be so easy. We are not robots and feelings may often cloud our judgment, but do your best to control them and use your common sense to make good decisions about how you manage your relationships. Be intelligent about your own pursuits and be considerate of the other's feelings to minimize both of your chances of being hurt. Once you know what you want, make sure you communicate that honestly with the person you are dating. While it may be oversimplifying things to categorize emotional matters, my main point is that you should not unnecessarily lose people you care about due to your own confusion or deception of the other. Of course, if you are secure with yourself and happen to meet someone who is as well, then you may be able to blend these categories and form a unique relationship that is mutually beneficial…which brings me to my next topic.

CHAPTER 24
Friends With Benefits
Can Be Beneficial to All
☆ ☆ ☆

"Between men and women, there is no friendship possible. There is passion, enmity, worship, love, but no friendship."—Oscar Wilde

It is just about every man's dream situation. It is the type of woman most of us strive to discover because she brings us the best of both worlds. You have the companionship and closeness of a friendship as well as the physical pleasure that is generally associated with a relationship. Best of all, there is no commitment or drama or jealousy attached. So why is it so difficult to find "friends with benefits," and why is there a stigma attached to that concept?

Of course, the description I gave above regarding the classic "friendship with benefits" scenario is one that is idealized and sounds terrific in theory, but is difficult to develop in reality. A primary reason that this type of friendship is hard to attain and sustain is people's general close-mindedness toward sexuality, especially when it comes to women. The outdated attitude that sex should only be practiced between romantic partners or has some higher level of fulfillment in the context of a relationship is one of the reasons that most women are uncomfortable with this situation. That is not to say that sexual attitudes have not progressed over the last few decades, but it is still frowned upon for women to enjoy casual sex. It is impossible to make a sweeping change to people's mindsets overnight, but it is up to each of you to open your minds to the idea that sex is a beautiful thing and that being in a relationship should not be a prerequisite to this enjoyment.

I realize that for the men out there, I am likely preaching to the choir because most of you would love nothing better than to take pleasure in a drama-free relationship. It is usually women who are not open to this type of friendship. As a man, the best way to make them feel more comfortable is to be honest with the ladies you are dating about what you are looking for. Obviously, if you get along with her, a woman at the very least should be open to listening to your feelings. Tell her that you value her companionship and are attracted to her, that you do not want to ruin your friendship with the drama that often accompanies commitment, and that she is free to date other people. Make it clear that you will not get jealous or question her about her actions when she is not with you, and also stress the fact that above all, you are friends and will continue to be whether the "benefits" take place or not.

The advice I am giving is obviously generalized. Each case is a unique situation, so you need to get a good feel for your friendship as well as what you want out of it before proposing such a relationship. I am assuming you are friends because otherwise you are seeking a pure casual sex partner, which is fine, but is less complicated than when there is established caring involved. I am also assuming that there is some form of physical attraction, or the issue of sex would not even arise. Obviously, the first thing you need to do is gauge your own feelings about this friend you are attracted to. Figure out if you see her as somebody you view as a potential long-time girlfriend or if she is someone you want to become intimate with but not as part of a serious relationship. You also need to have an idea as to whether she is similarly attracted to you.

Once you come to terms with your own desires and discover whether the woman you're interested in shares them, it is imperative that you also consider how sex could complicate your friendship and whether it is worth potentially sacrificing somebody you care about. We have all had female platonic friends that we have had secret yearnings for, but there are reasons why we haven't always expressed those feelings or acted out on them. The fact is that when a man and a woman are friends and there is physical attraction between the two, there is always tension under the surface. How we handle those emotions can mean the difference between remaining friends for life and having your relationship dwindle to an awkward mess.

If you feel that your friendship will be endangered if you add sex to the mix and the thought of losing her bothers you, do not pursue a physical relationship. There are plenty of other women out there with whom you can enjoy this pleasure without the risk of losing a girl you care about. I have been close friends with some really beautiful women and have encountered internal conflict, as well as external pressure from some of them, about becoming physically intimate. As I mentioned in the previous chapter, I have unnecessarily lost women I cared about when we became sexually active without confirming the status of our relationship. Part of it may have been because I was unclear about my intentions, but some of it is because sex often changes the nature of a relationship and both parties need to be able to handle it. It is important that you do not feel weak or unmanly about being "just friends" with a girl because there can be an immense value to having a platonic female friend in your life. I will expand on this in the following chapter, but just remember to not let your ego or your libido ruin a valuable friendship.

Additionally, take into account the fact that physical intimacy may draw you so close to your friend that you may want a serious relationship with her. After all, women are not the only ones who frequently attach strong emotions to sex. Be sure that you are ready to confront this passion and not let personal jealousy or frustration arise if she does not develop similar sentiments.

That being said, if there are signs that she may be open to a "friends with benefits" situation and you are not worried, or do not care, about the possible negative ramifications sex may have on your friendship, then take steps to communicate your feelings. It is possible that this woman is one you do not know that well yet, and while you can see a friendship developing, you want to establish early in your relationship that you want to become sexually intimate. This is preferable to trying to get physically involved with somebody you are already close friends with because there is not so much at stake if things go bad.

Ideally, the potential "friend with benefits" is really cool and open-minded herself, and becoming sexually active with you will not change the genuinely enjoyable companionship you share. I know from personal experience that it is a rare case to find a female friend who is open to a drama-free casual relationship, so if you find her, enjoy every moment and make sure you do not complicate things yourself. I have dated hundreds of girls over the last few years and met only an extraordinary few who were secure enough to handle the benefits of a relationship without the serious commitment. When you find one, it is like striking gold.

Let me tell you about one of these exceptional ladies. I met her after she responded to a dating post online and told her that I was looking to meet a cool female companion who I could hang out with occasionally and enjoy physical affection without any drama attached. She was coming off a divorce and was looking to have fun with a free-spirited guy without any head games. I conveyed to her from the start that she could date whomever she wanted because I would do the same, but that when we were together, we could have a blast.

Soon we were together nearly every night and living out every fantasy imaginable. We would go to strip bars together and she would pay to watch me get lap dances. Eventually, I introduced her to the swinger scene and she absolutely loved it. It was not long before she became open to all sorts of hedonistic pleasures. So for all of you men out there who feel you are the only one who have these erotic dreams, think again. Many women are just waiting to meet somebody who is secure and open enough to share this type of excitement. She even went so far as to book a ticket to Portugal to meet me on one of my international escapades.

On the surface, it may appear that I was the beneficiary of meeting a vulnerable woman coming out of a bad situation. If you look at the entire picture, however, she was equally as fortunate to meet somebody who was open-minded and non-judgmental as well as full of amazing life experiences. I unlocked the doors to a whole new world that she had never imagined she would be interested in. While it is evident that she had always craved adventure, she told me that it took the right person to bring it out of her. She remains thankful that I broadened her horizons -- not just sexually, but for life in general. I am similarly appreciative for her true friendship and the fact that she was open-minded enough to understand my lifestyle.

The Showstopper Lifestyle is all about maximizing life experiences and eliminating unnecessary complications, and we were both lucky to share the excitement together. Although we drifted apart because I moved back to California, I am friends with her to this day, and that is because I was honest and unambiguous with her from the beginning about what I was looking for. The lesson here is to be unafraid to explore your wild side when you meet a friend who is open to it because sometimes she has the same fantasies and is yearning for a guy to share them with.

Again, remember the three types of connections I described in the previous chapter. The principles of knowing what you want and being truthful to yourself and your partner remain the same even if you attempt to blend these categories together. This goes back to you being secure with yourself and understanding your own place in life enough to know how to communicate your intentions to the ones you date.

If you are a woman reading this, I completely understand that it may not yet be deemed completely socially acceptable for you to enjoy sex outside the context of a committed relationship, but the "benefits" of this do not merely go to the man. After all, what makes a serious commitment work is a strong friendship anyway. Sometimes, however, two people enjoy a strong connection, but circumstances make a serious relationship unfeasible or undesirable. Who is to say that you cannot enjoy physical pleasure with someone you care about without labels or judgments? Just as sex can sometimes complicate a friendship, sometimes drama and jealousy can ruin the companionship of two who are attracted to each other but are not suited to a long-term commitment.

I know women are more prone to being judged for their sexual liaisons than men and I will elaborate on how we can begin to erase this double standard in a later chapter. As a woman, one of the first steps in eliminating this hypocrisy is to be secure with yourself as well as your sexuality and not worry about how others may perceive you. My research showed more than seventy-five percent of single women said they were open to having a friend with benefits under the right circumstances. Unfortunately, the results also revealed that a majority of them felt worried about how others would perceive them. If you give it a chance, you may find that you can have a terrific time with a man you care about without any labels or boundaries. You may find this type of freedom both refreshing and illuminating. If people are going to unjustly criticize you for your personal decisions, then they are not the type of friends you want anyway. There are too many women who get into bad relationships just for the sake of being socially acceptable. They succumb to the myth that women can only enjoy sex if they are a girlfriend or wife. This false ideal is sustained because there are also too many men who lie to a woman about being monogamous just to sleep with her because they feel that is what she wants to hear.

When you are "friends with benefits," you do not need to create this illusion of monogamy nor do you need to put on the pretense that your sexual relationship is a precursor to something more serious in the future. If you are comfortable with having a close friend whom you happen to be in a sexual relationship with, then it is best to not feel pressured to conform to anybody's moral standards other than your own. As long as you are honest with each other and enjoying physical pleasure while sustaining your companionship, then becoming friends with benefits can be a mutually beneficial situation.

CHAPTER 25
The Value of the Female Best Friend
☆ ☆ ☆

"Sometimes you put walls up not to keep people out, but to see who cares enough to break them down."—Unknown

They say guys and girls cannot be just friends, and this is often the case. All too frequently, when a man and woman become really close, some type of romantic attraction develops in at least one of the parties and it complicates and eventually ruins the friendship. There is a thin line between friendship and desire and crossing that line frequently causes a breakdown of the unconditional love the two share for each other. Often, one party, usually the man, secretly wants to sleep with this "platonic" companion. At other times, one party, usually the woman, secretly has an emotional craving to date the other. Unless there is absolutely no physical attraction involved, a relationship that can be simple and special can get really complex and dramatic.

While women commonly announce that their best friends are men, guys will, on the contrary, testify that they have no need to have girls who are just friends. In fact, it is often taken as an insult or a blow to the ego when a lady tells a man that she wants to be "just friends." There are times when you meet a girl and realize she will only play a role in your life in a dating situation. If you have an intense physical desire for her and cannot imagine enjoying your time with her without sexual pleasure, then I would recommend that you end it if she tells you she just wants to remain friends. There are times, however, when a close girl friend can be an extremely valuable addition to your life.

Let us assume that you meet a girl under circumstances where opportunities for dating or casual sex just do not arise or would make things awkward. For example, I have a personal rule that I will not sleep with anybody I go to school with or work with, simply because I do not want to mix my business with my pleasure. In those types of instances, the satisfaction you may feel by having sex with that person is outweighed by other factors that make it undesirable for you to do so. That gives you an opportunity to formulate a friendship with this woman without the topic of intimacy arising. Sometimes, you will meet girls who are so cool and fun that you can be completely happy with just hanging out with them minus the drama or desires. These women are a rare breed and should be treasured.

As cheesy as it sounds, when you can find a platonic girl best friend, no matter how attracted you are to them, you should resist those temptations in favor of sustaining the friendship. This girl may end up being the most valuable woman in your life. This is especially the case if you are dating a large assortment of women. Sometimes, when you are playing the field, you can get frustrated by the flakiness and the lack of logic in the game. Having a close female companion who really understands you and cares for you provides a good balance to counteract that irritation. She prevents you from becoming jaded and will serve as a constant reminder that there are many quality women in the world. You cannot underestimate how special it is to have a lady like that in your life and you should treat her accordingly.

To illustrate, let me use an example from a movie that many of you may have seen, *Ironman*. Tony Stark, who wears the costume, is a complicated figure. He is a cocky, obnoxious, womanizing Hollywood playboy who probably could not even remember the names of most of the women he has been with, but at heart he's a good guy. His assistant, Pepper Potts, is a sweet, loyal woman who cares for Tony in a way that the random women he sleeps with never could. She understands him and loves him enough to look beneath the brash exterior to see the caring person he really is.

The dynamic between the two is fascinating. She really likes him, but she knows him too well to get more involved with him and get her heart broken.

He likes her too, but he knows himself too well to allow a girl he cares about to get too emotionally involved with him because he knows he is unable to return those feelings. When I saw the movie, I thought Pepper Potts was one of the sexiest females I had ever seen on film. She is, in many ways, every man's fantasy: a pretty, loving, loyal woman who accepts her friend for who he is and is willing to do anything to make the guy she cares about happy and safe.

If you become fortunate enough to encounter a similar woman in your life then do not make the mistake of trying to sleep with her unless you are sure that both of you can handle taking that step. Instead, enjoy every bit of the companionship you share with her. I know from personal experience how exceptional it is to share such a bond. Although I have been casually dating for a long time now, even during those escapades I have always had some type of really devoted female friend I could hang out with minus the nonsense. Unfortunately, in the past, I was not completely clear about my intentions with them, partly because I was not sure, and also because I did not want to close the door to hooking up with them by telling them that we would never be more than just friends. Consequently, they would usually develop strong feelings for me and things would get complicated, shattering what brought us together in the first place. As you remember from the previous two chapters, if you send mixed messages, your indecision can ruin a friendship.

Having learned from my experiences, now I place high value on my female friendships. Thankfully, I have an especially wonderful friend in my life right now that is not only gorgeous but an incredibly sweet and loyal human being. She looks past all of the bravado and the bedroom adventures to see the caring person on the inside. She has the patience and understanding to comprehend that I live the lifestyle I do because I have a different outlook on life than most people, not because I am arrogant or strange or misogynistic. I am grateful to have my beautiful blonde buddy Amanda, and the reason our friendship works is that it is clear that we are going to be platonic friends, so there is no illusion of anything else. I call her my real-life Pepper Potts. And while I am on the subject, I wanted to share my appreciation for some of my close lady companions over the years. Pav, Tam, Kit, Cheryl, Genny, and Monica, if you are reading this, I want to express my thanks for caring for me and being such wonderful friends, and if I was not always the easiest guy to deal with, I apologize.

If you are fortunate enough to have a special female friend in your life, you must make sure you appreciate her and keep things as uncomplicated as possible. So here is my advice for all of you men reading this, especially the ones who plan on dating a multitude of partners. When you become close friends with a girl who is basically like one of the guys, laid back and pleasant to be around and without drama or jealousy, take a page from what girls do all the time and draw the line in the sand and make it clear to her that you want to remain friends. You will then have a person in your life who will provide a sweet voice and a listening ear, someone you may feel comfortable telling things that you may be too macho to express to your closest guy friends.

Not only that, she can be a partner in crime you can go out with, who will help make you more appealing to other girls. It is no secret that women get turned on by men who are surrounded by sexy women. Other girls will be more attracted to you because you have a companion on your arm. Because of the nature of your relationship, she should be more than willing to assist you in hooking up with these random ladies you come across without getting jealous. In fact, having a girl best friend can become a key component in living the Showstopper Lifestyle. So the next time anybody tells you that guys and girls can't be just friends, don't listen to them, because you may be missing out on some of the most extraordinary friendships you will ever have.

CHAPTER 26
Honesty Is the Best Policy
☆ ☆ ☆

"If you tell the truth you don't have to remember anything." —Mark Twain

The previous chapters discussed different avenues you can pursue in the dating game, but knowing what you want out of a relationship is not enough. I have stated this many times already but I want you to ingrain in your mind that you need to communicate these intentions truthfully to each other. When you are in the game of meeting women, no matter where you want an encounter or relationship to go, the best way to get what you want is to simply be honest. It sounds cheesy and oversimplified, but the fact is, if you are truthful about your intentions when you meet a woman, then you eliminate the pretense and the deception that can not only hurt the other person, but yourself as well. I have always thought that it is too much effort to lie about what I am looking for, and it is better to illustrate my actual intentions. Reliance on this principle has made me enormously successful with women. If you are to enjoy similar success, both in casual and serious dating, you must understand that honesty is the best policy.

One of the major reasons people have so much trouble with the opposite sex is that they are trained to tell the other person what they want to hear. Men are supposed to say that they want to get to know a girl for an emotional attachment, and that at the end of the day, they really only want to be with one woman. We all know the reality behind that, but society feeds that delusion and too many women buy into it. If you are a guy looking to date multiple women, it's not a good thing that women are vulnerable to your lies. In actuality, if you have no further desires with a girl you meet other than to sleep with her or become friends with benefits, it is better that you tell them that. Many of them may be turned off, but you will be surprised at how many women are looking for the same type of fun without the drama.

After all, women are also socially trained to say that they do not sleep around, are against casual sex, and are also looking for a man who only has eyes for them. In actuality, there are millions of women who are tired of the nonsense and the deception that men put them through, and are simply looking to have a good time without being committed or judged. If you are honest with each other, you may discover that you share more common ground in your beliefs and intentions than you would imagine.

Over the years, I have dated hundreds of women and although I have not been able to enjoy the experiences I desired with all of them, most of them have been pleasantly surprised by my frank discussions about my motives. If you are not looking for anything serious, this does not mean you immediately tell them about your sexual fantasies in graphic detail, although some are opening to hearing that as well. It simply means that you start off by sharing with them that you have a multitude of things going on in your life, and that your lifestyle does not allow a committed relationship. Obviously, frame it in a way that makes you sound like a bit of a cosmopolitan person, not simply one who is emotionally vacant. There are countless women out there who enjoy the idea of living for the moment, but are unable to act on those desires because it is socially unacceptable. I will expand on how to talk to a woman as well as discuss this double standard in ensuing chapters, but for now, I am stressing that the way to make them feel comfortable is to honestly explain that there is nothing wrong with having fun without the commitment.

When I say "honest," do not get me wrong. I am not urging you to instantly reveal everything about yourself to the other person when you meet her. We discussed three ways to approach the type of connection you want to make with a woman. Of course, if you see a girl as a potential serious relationship or a friendship, then it is good to let her get to know the real you over time. If you see somebody as merely a potential sex partner, however, then it may be better if they know little about you other than the things that may detrimentally affect them. (I am not advocating concealing information if you have a disease or something potentially harmful to them.)

I have told girls I only saw as potential physical partners some wild tales about what I do as well as things I have done. I have said that I am everything from a barber to a professional wrestler, mainly to entertain myself more than anything. When you realize that you do not want to be emotionally close with somebody, there is no reason to give your biography. What you should not do is give her an illusion that you want a committed relationship with her. It will cause you unnecessary stress trying to sustain the lie, and it will mislead her, possibly resulting in a broken heart. The benefits of the physical pleasure you may receive are not worth the negative effects deceit will have on your conscience. As I explained, you are more likely to meet women for casual encounters if you simply are straightforward about your intentions. Furthermore, you will find that no matter what type of relationship you want with a woman, honesty is the best policy.

CHAPTER 27
The Brotherhood of Man
☆ ☆ ☆

"The mystical bond of brotherhood makes all men brothers." —*Thomas Carlysle*

One of the most famous urban phrases is "bros before hos," a slang expression signifying that a man's guy friends always take precedent over any woman he might be dating or sleeping with. Although it is intended to be a fun bonding catchphrase amongst males, there are actually some very real sentiments behind the statement. A primary advantage of being men is that there is generally some type of brotherhood that unifies us and allows us to understand each other in a manner that generally does not take place amongst women.

This connection men share is one that indicates eternal friendship even in the face of adversity or instability from a female counterpart. This camaraderie should be cherished because it is much more consistent and stable than that of a dating partner. If things go bad with a potential significant other, then you can always rely on a stable of friends who will always be there for you. In fact, I would suggest that you do not even get into a relationship unless you have a solid set of guy friends. Otherwise, you may be entering into that relationship out of loneliness, instead of finding a companion who complements your own life and can blend in with your buddies.

When you have a strong circle of friends, they are likely people who share your likes and dislikes. You can enjoy your time with them without the complication of a committed relationship. As you become closer, you will realize that these are the people you can rely on through your trials and tribulations. Your relationships can end at a moment's notice, but friendships are generally much less fickle and more significant in the long run. The familiarity that accompanies this attachment provides you with people who understand the way you think. They can support you in times of trouble and can share with you your times of joy. Thankfully, guy friends generally do not get jealous of each other or backstab one another, but usually provide support in each other's endeavors. These will be the people who will help form your foundation of strength and can help you recover from any obstacle in life. As I said before, when my father passed away, I was fortunate to have loving friends who came to my assistance through that difficult period. It is because of them that I was able to minimize the struggle of that distressing experience and move on with my life without becoming depressed or lonely.

If you are already lucky enough to have a collection of comrades who will be with you through good times and bad, then you should always make efforts to stay in touch with them and keep that connection. I have seen too many close friends drift apart for no reason other than pure laziness on the part of each person. They will neglect making contact with each other, and eventually might be waiting for the other person to take that step. The price they pay is the loss of valuable shared memories due to inertia and stubbornness. You should never underestimate the value of a person who cares about you, and if the other person is not sustaining the ties, then you should go out of your way to do so.

To make things clear, the advice I am giving applies equally to the female readers of this book, but I am addressing the men because they often share an alliance with their fellow man that women do not. So do not let apathy ruin a friendship that you value. Additionally, and women are generally the worst at this, do not let a relationship become ruined because of something petty or unimportant. Life is too short to hold grudges over such matters. The reason these silly arguments get prolonged is because people often like to add unnecessary drama to their life. If this person is really valuable to you, then their companionship is much more meaningful than the complication. If you do not reform a bond with them, you may regret it forever. In fact, if there is a person out there whom you once shared a strong friendship with but lost touch with or held irrational resentment toward, put this book down and call them right now or attempt to find their phone number. Not only will you feel fulfilled when talking to that person, they will be excited as well that you decided to contact them and show you care.

When you sustain long-lasting friendships, you will not rely on a relationship to ease your isolation. As I have explained, being alone does not mean being lonely, so you will be much stronger as a single person when you have great friends. If you do decide to get into a long-term commitment, this camaraderie is something consistent that will always be there even through the often rocky path of a long-term romance. Just make sure you do not make the mistake many men do and lose track of your priorities when you are dating somebody. You must take the initiative to schedule extended time with your guy friends, and remain in contact with them even when you are "in love." You do not want to make your girlfriend the center of your universe, or even worse, your only source of companionship and enjoyment. When problems arise with your lady friend, then you will have people to talk to who will keep you positive. I will explain more about how to intertwine your friendships and relationships in a later chapter, but I am stressing right now to never underestimate the bond that brings the boys together.

As you can see, I believe a strong circle of friends is absolutely invaluable. The obvious reasons are because of the social and emotional benefits of having loved ones who share your interests. Moreover, this alliance will be an enormous source of power that will boost your self-esteem and your confidence. Even if you don't see your friends all the time, just knowing in your heart that you have people who care about you will provide you with tremendous inner strength to confront any challenge that life has in store for you. Additionally, you may be more inclined to do things on your own, knowing you have this foundation. One of the reasons I am able to travel so much by myself is the knowledge that I always have loved ones to come back to. My strong ties with my male buddies also make it much easier for me to remain single and date a multitude of women. Even if I am frustrated by the girls I am dating, companionship is never an issue for me because I have such a wide variety of people to enjoy my time with. I am not dependent on having a significant other. You will find the added self-assurance that encompasses you when you enjoy a strong closeness with your male contemporaries will help you meet females as well. I will elaborate on that in the ensuing chapters. For now, just ingrain it in your mind that the brotherhood of men will be one of your principal sources of strength in living the Showstopper Lifestyle.

CHAPTER 28
Women: Their Own Worst Enemy
☆ ☆ ☆

"The loneliest woman in the world is a woman without a close woman friend." —George Santayana

"All of my best friends are guys." I am sure you have heard the statement from many women. I can't even count how many times I have heard a girl say this to me and each time I shake my head. Not that there is anything wrong with a man and a woman being close friends. I have often enjoyed very close platonic friendships with ladies. The problem lies in the subtext of that assertion, and that is the fact that women often have a difficult time getting along with each other. While there is generally a brotherhood amongst men that creates a strong support circle, with women, that camaraderie isn't as commonly found.

In my research for this book, I studied thousands of subjects, and one of the questions in my surveys asked women if they had trouble trusting each other. More than sixty percent of women answered that they often found their female counterparts untrustworthy. Nearly half of them said they were the victim of backstabbing or gossip from a close girl "friend."

These statistics reveal a disturbing glimpse into the nature of interactions between women. Because women often have so much suspicion regarding each other's motives and there is so often a good deal of cattiness and jealousy involved, they frequently depend on men to be their companions.

As I mentioned, inter-gender friendships are perfectly fine, but if women turn to men because of their inability to befriend women, that is a problem. Don't get me wrong. A genuine, uncomplicated friendship between a man and a woman is a wonderful thing. Unfortunately, this alliance often is fleeting because one party develops romantic feelings for the other. There is also the additional dilemma that often arises when a guy becomes close friends with a girl as a pretense for his desire to sleep with her. This is the reason why so many women require a serous relationship to avoid loneliness. If you are a woman reading this, I hope you appreciate your female friends and do not let petty conflicts or drama complicate matters.

A few years ago, I was at a convention where I met former teen singing sensation Tiffany, who had hits songs such as "I Think We're Alone Now" and "Could've Been." We were discussing the current teen idols at the time such as Christina Aguilera, Jessica Simpson and Britney Spears, and I asked her what she thought about Britney's recent marriage to Kevin Federline. Her response was fascinating, especially coming from such a wealthy and famous woman. She said, "No matter how rich or successful a woman becomes, there will always be a part of her that is dependent on having a man in her life for stability."

While this is not always the case, unfortunately, it is a common scenario. It is the classic case of one getting into a relationship because they need somebody in their life for happiness. This is an awful premise upon which to enter a commitment, and generally will spell failure. There are obviously many reasons why women, and men for that matter, want to get into long-term romances, but one of the primary ones is loneliness. If women felt more comfortable in their friendships with each other, then perhaps there wouldn't be such a need for a man to provide emotional support and companionship. While the inability of women to be friends with each other is a distressing trait, it can also be used to a man's advantage if he is interested in casually dating a variety of women.

As we discussed in the previous chapter, a man generally has the luxury of other male friends who provide the friendship and caring that women often do not receive from each other. Since this closeness usually is not accompanied by drama or commitment, it is much more stable and long-lasting than the erratic nature of a serious relationship. Accordingly, guys can date a variety of women without heavy emotional involvement but still not experience the emptiness and lack of close companions that plagues so many women. I am not telling you to emotionally take advantage of these women who are looking to satisfy their desire for support, but merely warning you to not get trapped. If you sustain your comradeship with your buddies, and are just honest to girls that you are not looking for commitment, you can be happily dating a multitude of ladies and still have your own emotional needs met.

The mistake that so many men make is that they attempt to fulfill a woman's need for stability in her life. As a result, they often lose the strength of their brotherhood of men, not to mention their own autonomy, by letting their life revolve around making sure their girlfriend or wife is happy. Now there is nothing wrong with a long-term relationship if entered into for the right reasons and under proper circumstances. However, just as you should not *need* to have a significant other, you should not become the person that the other person *needs*. By this I mean if you are just filling the emptiness in a woman's life, then she may be too dependent on you to the point where you are her sole source of stability. Consequently, you lose your own power and your freedom because your own life will be so attached to her requirements.

I will discuss the steps to analyzing whether you are entering a good relationship later in the book, but right now I want you men reading this to make sure you are not compensating for a woman's inability to get along with her female peers. If you do, just as women are so often their own worst enemy, you will become your own worst enemy. For all of my female readers, make sure that cattiness or jealousy does not interfere with your bonds with other women. If you do, you may find that most of the friendships you form will be built on unstable grounds, and no man can give you the stability you desire.

CHAPTER 29
Getting Lucky
☆ ☆ ☆

"Sex isn't something men do to you. It isn't something men get out of you. Sex is something you dive into with gusto and like it every bit as much as he does." —Nina Hartley

One of the most frustrating things I have encountered in my studies of relationships and interactions between genders is the concept of "getting lucky." The idea that if a man "achieves" sexual contact with a woman it is because he is "lucky" enough for her to allow him to do so is ridiculous. A woman is not doing a man a favor when she decides to have sex with him. The misconception that a man needs to chase a woman for pleasure and that he is fortunate if she responds in kind is a primary reason there are so many sexually frustrated people out there. In reality, women enjoy the physical activity just as much as men do, and both genders need to become comfortable enough with this fact to fully enjoy one another.

From the moment that men enter the dating game, most approach it with a loser's attitude. It is ingrained in their minds that they need to pursue women for what they want, and that if they get it, then it's purely a matter of luck. If you are a guy reading this, erase the notion from your mind that having sex with a woman is some type of victory over her. This is a game where both parties should be winners because you are each enjoying the ultimate in human pleasure. You should have the self-assurance both as a person and as a lover that your partner is lucky to be with you.

The key, as always, is to have confidence in your attractiveness and your self-worth, and to challenge the erroneous beliefs that inhibit sexuality in American society. You should not approach a woman like a desperate hound dog, but should have it in your mind that she wants to be with you. This will make her more comfortable with you as well. If you are a man who is sexually attracted to a woman and feed into the false premise that you need to win her desire for you, then you will voluntarily lose the power dynamic between the sexes. I will go into much greater detail about how to become more successful with women as you keep reading, but it is imperative that you first form the mindset that will allow you to become more comfortable with getting what you want out of dating. Just remember to have the confidence that she wants you just as much as you want her and to not let social standards, or your own inferiority complex, prevent you both from having a good time.

If you are a woman reading this and are manipulating men by using sex as a reward to get what you want, in the end you will likely find that you are unhappy and sexually frustrated yourself. There are many women out there who are trained to act as if they are not interested in intimacy. I am not advising anybody, men or women, to recklessly sleep around without regard for your own or your partner's personal interests. I just want you to embrace the fact that sex is a wonderful thing and not to repress your fantasies for the sake of pretense or a power play.

I refer to what Nina Hartley said when she was addressing a group of women, "Sex isn't something men do to you. It isn't something men get out of you. Sex is something you dive into with gusto and like it every bit as much as he does." You should be at ease with the fact that being sexually liberated does not make you a slut. Instead, it indicates that you are a woman who is comfortable with herself and unashamed of what makes you happy. If you truly want to be empowered in your relationships and your life, then a healthy sex life devoid of games and manipulation will make you a much stronger person

All of that being said, I completely understand that a primary reason why the concept of men having to "get lucky" to have sex with a woman exists is because of social restrictions. American society represses a woman's sexual desires and teaches her that it is not okay to embrace her sexuality. I will soon discuss how all of us can help eliminate this double standard that inhibits sexual pleasure for each gender. What about the idea of getting lucky? Just remember that as long as you are doing so safely and consensually, each of you is fortunate to experience erotic bliss.

CHAPTER 30
Embrace Your Sexuality
☆ ☆ ☆

"The only way to get rid of a temptation is to yield to it."—Oscar Wilde

The United States, in many ways, sets the tone for the rest of the world. The country is on the cutting edge of economic relations, technological innovation, and popular culture. For such a progressive society, however, Americans are extremely closed-minded in their sexual attitudes. The foundation of the country was based on the Puritanical belief that sex should only be enjoyed in the confines of marriage. Although in actuality the Puritans may not have been living so "pure" a lifestyle after all, the lingering effects of those ideals can be felt to this day. It may be much more progressive than many other regions of the world, but American culture still has not yet become comfortable with sexuality. Many people are obsessed with suppressing the pleasure others enjoy in the privacy of their own home. I am sure I am not the only one who feels it is ridiculous that people who are so comfortable with seeing guns and violence on a television screen are embarrassed and offended when they see a private body part. It is an immature, hypocritical outlook that is harmful on various levels.

This sexual repression is a large reason so many people are unhappy and frustrated in their personal life. Studies have shown that an unhealthy sex life can lead to lack of self-confidence, low self-esteem, depression, suicidal tendencies, and more aggressive behavior. It is also a factor in divorce rates being so astronomical. People now have more avenues than ever through which they can fulfill their desires, but this fulfillment is still frowned upon. In order for people to be happier and for relationships to flourish, then people have to learn how to embrace their sexuality. Here are some rules to remember when enhancing your sex life.

☆ Rule 1: Practice sex safely and intelligently.

Let me make it clear that before one even considers being sexually active, they should be educated in the matter and know about protection, diseases, birth control, etc. I firmly believe that a person should always, without exception, use protection when they are sexually active, unless it is in the context of a long-term relationship. It is absolutely inexcusable to not be as safe as possible. If you cannot practice sex responsibly, then you should not partake in it at all. There are too many unplanned pregnancies going on that unnecessarily ruin the lives of people who are not ready to take care of a child. Even worse, it is the child who most suffers the ill effects of their lack of preparation. It is inexcusable for you to be in this position, considering the wide availability of condoms and birth control.

Being unsafe also leaves you susceptible to all types of diseases. I am not going to explain them all here, but why take that chance when using protection can help prevent a large portion of them? Sex is supposed to be the highest form of pleasure, but a transmitted disease can transform it into an extreme source of pain, or worse. You do not want to put yourself or your partners through such suffering. Again, if you are not going to be as safe as possible in your sex life, then you should remain celibate.

☆ Rule 2: Wait until you are ready before having sex.

I am also an advocate of waiting until you are older before becoming sexually active. If you are more mature and have more life experiences, then you will be more educated and prepared to enjoy these pursuits. Research indicates that children are exploring sexuality much younger, and they are often not ready to tackle the responsibilities that come with these actions. I am not saying that you should wait until you get married. On the contrary, I feel people should not see sex as something that can only be properly enjoyed in the context of marriage or even a relationship. You should not, however, just do it for the sake of curiosity or acceptance.

As I mentioned before, I waited until after college, and I do not feel as if I missed out on anything. Quite the opposite, it was because I spent my youth developing a broad range of interests and forming strong ties to friends and family that I did not become dependent on having a woman in my life to fulfill my need for pleasure. Many hormonal teenagers become so obsessed with feeding their sexual appetite that when they get older, sex loses its meaning. It is a reason many people get married younger than they should. They may feel they have already lived out their erotic pleasures and are ready to settle down with one person. They often find out differently later and end up cheating. When you wait until you are well-rounded as an individual, then you become smarter in your life choices and the fruits of your passions will be more gratifying.

☆ Rule 3: Approach sexuality with an open mind.

I hope I have made it clear that I do not advocate practicing sex unsafely or irresponsibly. Once you have reached the stage when you are mature enough to handle it, you should be open-minded and creative in enjoying your sexual fantasies. Don't worry about what others may say about you. Those who choose to be judgmental of another's sexual enjoyment generally have some type of insecurities and issues with their own. If you fantasize about being with many types of women, you should explore your various desires and date an assortment of partners before settling down. If you are overcome by temptations, instead of holding them inside, freely seek partners who have similar interests. One of the major reasons that marriages are falling apart is that parties go into it without having satisfied their sexual cravings in their single life. They want to make these wet dreams come true after they are already tied down and look to do so elsewhere. This causes deception between the spouses and eventually the destruction of their relationship.

Even if you choose to settle down with one woman, make sure you sustain the passion and creativity in your sex life. Trying new things to spice up your relationship will not only bring you closer together, but it will make you less likely to look elsewhere behind your partner's back. During the ensuing chapters, I will cover various topics that will explain how you can maximize your sexual enjoyment. For now, I just want to encourage you to become comfortable with the idea that sexuality is a wonderful thing. Of course, you should understand your personal comfort level, but as with everything else in life, approach your sexual options with an open mind. This liberated attitude can enhance your happiness in all of your existence.

CHAPTER 31
The Double Standard
☆ ☆ ☆

"If you men only knew!"—Alice Hartford, Eyes Wide Shut

One of the most fascinating examinations of sexuality that has ever taken place in a film was Stanley Kubrick's final masterpiece, *Eyes Wide Shut*. It is not your typical formulaic Hollywood thriller, but an intense study of sexual lust and passion created for a more sophisticated audience. If you have not seen the movie, I recommend that you do so because it will open up your eyes to complicated attitudes towards sex. The film also showcases the social double standard that exists between men and women when it comes to sexual behavior and desires.

The most revealing scene in the movie is when Bill and Alice, the married couple played by actual husband and wife at the time, Tom Cruise and Nicole Kidman, are having a bedroom discussion that turns into an argument. As Bill describes why he was talking to two models the night before, he also brushes off the sexual implication of Alice's slow-dance with a handsome European gentleman. He ignorantly dismisses her possible physical interest in other men by stating that women "basically don't think that way."

Her response may as well have been an anthem for millions of women, tired of having to repress their erotic rumblings. "Millions of years of evolution, right? Right? Men have to stick it in every place they can, but for women... For women it is just about security and commitment and, ah, whatever the fuck else... If you men only knew!" In her frustration with Bill's obliviousness regarding a woman's sexual mindset, she unveils that she fantasized about a young sailor she had met in passing a few years before. In this naked glimpse of her innermost feelings of lust, Alice tells him that at that one fleeting moment, she felt she could risk her marriage to enjoy just one passionate night with the sailor. This revelation shocks Bill to his core, and his innate feelings of insecurity set him off to do some exploration of his own desires.

The scene is a fabulously insightful depiction of the social double standard that inhibits a woman's sexuality while celebrating a man's prowess. While a guy is encouraged that bedding multiple partners is a showcase of his virility and his manhood, when a girl does the same thing, she is considered a slut. My research revealed that more than eighty percent of women were worried about the criticism of others regarding their sexuality while less than twenty percent of men shared the same concerns. Speaking from my own personal experience, most men, and even many women, have found my open-minded attitudes toward dating multiple women refreshing. Many who have seen my pictures or heard my tales with various gorgeous ladies have seen me as a heroic stud. If you were to reverse roles and a woman were to showcase her free-wheeling mindset toward sexuality with equal vigor, I am certain the reaction would not be so positive.

This perplexing dichotomy is a major reason why there are so many sexually frustrated men and women in our society. Most men want to be free with their sexuality and explore multiple partners. Unfortunately, since women are so often vilified for their own lustful desires, they are not as willing to satisfy those fantasies. The result is a vicious circle where most people of each gender are disguising their true intentions and are unable to satisfy their wants and needs.

If you truly want to be a cosmopolitan, open-minded man who dates multiple women and lives life to the fullest, you cannot be judgmental of a woman's sexual attitudes. In fact, even if you are seeking monogamy, you should not be offended that there are ladies who are not. This closed-minded, hypocritical thinking is ingrained into the social psyche and is harmful to all types of inter-gender relationships. In order for things to change for the better, people need to be more open and understanding of one another's needs and actions.

Since I assume most of the readers of this book are men, I implore you to take the initiative by being more secure with yourself and less critical of women. If you want to casually date women, you should not refer to the ones you sleep with as "sluts" or "whores." As many of you know, I had a bit of role reversal scenario myself in front of a studio audience of women and millions of viewers at home on *The Tyra Banks Show*. Being chastised by a group of females and referred to as "a male slut" by Tyra because of my free-wheeling attitudes toward dating gave me a glimpse of the type of judgment women face all of the time.

Instead of being condescending, you should be thankful that there are women out there who have similarly open attitudes toward sexuality. If you are in a relationship where you actively seek multiple partners but expect your partner to be faithful, you may be in for a rude awakening if you find out she is acting on her own cravings. Women tend to be more secretive about their escapades, and discovering that you are not the only one who acts out on them may be a shattering blow to your own obviously thin sense of security. Although it is not a mainstream lifestyle as of yet, if you love somebody emotionally but want various partners physically, there are ways to do this without lying to your mate that can bring you both more pleasure. I will expand on the swinger scene later, but first develop the outlook that sex is a wonderful thing that both men and women should have the leisure of exploring to their own content.

It starts with the attitude that there is nothing wrong with a woman being sexually promiscuous as long as she is safe and honest with her partners about her lifestyle. The reason so many females are confused about their sexual identity and often behave in such a flaky, unstable manner is that they are sent mixed messages. It is almost like a double-edged sword. If you sleep with too many men, you are a slut, and if you do not sleep with enough, you are a prude.

Sadly, unless widespread societal perception toward female sexuality becomes more progressive, this confusion will continue. I am focusing on women because they face criticism not only from men but also from others of the same sex. If you are a woman reading this who wants to act out her sexual fantasies, you must not be judgmental or jealous of other women who do the same. You should support your fellow women who actually have the courage to live the way they want to live and respect their choices.

It is the responsibility of both men and women to be more frank and open-minded in their mentality, not only toward their own sexuality, but of others as well. Who is one to judge what another person does in the privacy of their own home if they are not hurting others? Even more importantly, who makes the decision that the behavior which is acceptable for men is unacceptable for women? If we are to become a more sexually sophisticated culture, instead of one where divorce, misery, rape and repression are all too common, then every one of us needs to become more understanding of the fact that sex is a beautiful thing that should be enjoyed evenly by all without discrimination. When people become more equally accepting of the erotic yearnings of both genders, then this double standard will slowly disappear and people will be much happier and sexually satisfied.

CHAPTER 32
Women Need Security,
but They Crave Excitement
☆ ☆ ☆

"A pessimist is a man who thinks all women are bad. An optimist is a man who hopes they are."—Chauncey Mitchell Depew

It is amazing how people never cease to surprise you. During the creation of this book, I spoke to hundreds of men and women. When I described the theme, I told them it would be a self-help book geared mainly for men that will help them become more open-minded, self-confident, and success-ful with women. One of the most fascinating things I came across was that the women I discussed this concept with were equally as excited about the subject matter.

Perhaps it should not be surprising because the principles of the Showstopper Lifestyle are not specific to gender. After all, self-assurance, open-mindedness, and inner peace are attributes that almost everyone strives to attain. What really generated enthusiasm amongst the women was the ideal of living an exciting life without worries or restrictions. They felt that learning my "secrets" of how to live to the fullest would not only help their own lives, but also that the men they date would become more in tune with their desires. Even the ladies who desired a more traditional life often agreed that it would be more fulfilling if each party went in with more life experiences. This goes back to what I have discovered during my years of dating a large diversity of girls, and that is the idea that women need security but they crave excitement.

It is a well-known biological fact that men and women are designed differently and have varying physical and emotional wants and needs. Numerous studies have outlined these basic variations. Men are generally more logical thinkers who are ego-driven and who place a higher value on achieving goals, attaining power, and displaying their independence. Women tend to be more nurturing creatures who seek strong emotional attachments, relationships, and love and understanding. Although these surface differences may indicate that women require close companionship more than men, they also yearn for an escape from their everyday existence.

In my surveys on dating and relationships, an overwhelming amount of women revealed that they felt most men do not understand how to keep things fresh and exciting. During my own dating escapades, I have repeatedly encountered women complaining about how bland and unoriginal most of the men they talked to were. This boredom is a large reason an increasing amount of women are cheating in the context of relationships and are thirsting for adventure in their single life. I must admit that other men's weaknesses have been my strength because it is the very fact that my life appears so thrilling that so many women have been attracted to me.

Of course, this goes back to the fact that so many people aren't making the most of every moment and are not genuinely happy with themselves. Even many of those who are content have a difficult time conveying this to others in a manner that piques their interest. For men on the dating circuit, I cannot stress enough how important it is to passionately present yourself to a woman so she does not see you as just another vanilla face in the crowd.

If you are looking to casually date, be honest that you are not looking for anything serious and let a woman know how sensational your single life is. Present the scenario that she will be happier in a casual relationship with you than a serious one with another guy. Appeal to her need for escapism by keeping the conversation on the level of fantasy. Women are intuitive and can sense the passion in a man's voice. Since they also appreciate good communication, expressing this joy will spark their curiosity. The underlying theme of the Showstopper Lifestyle is maximizing life experiences, and you want them to realize that being with you is an experience that will benefit them and that they will regret it if they do not choose to accept it.

As I said before, American women are bored and frustrated with living in a society that represses their desire for adventure. There are millions of women living a monotonous existence simply because it is socially acceptable. The majority of men are creating this social climate because of their insecure need to keep women "pure" while they engage in their own philandering. Not only that, there are too many men lying to women and portraying themselves in a false manner to make a woman attached to them. The irony is that if you are a man who really wants to explore his fantasies with a variety of women, you will be more likely to do so if you can truthfully depict the advantage of drama-free fun. There are many women who do not want to be in a committed relationship, but are not meeting open-minded men who seem interesting enough to share time with.

If you can be the man who can provide women an escape from the ordinary, you can enjoy some extraordinary experiences of your own. Let me show you how you can do this by sharing with you how I generally describe my lifestyle to the women I am interested in dating. I tell them that I am traveling the world and focused on my career and do not have room in my life for serious emotional attachments. I separate myself from other guys by saying that most men are too closed-minded and dishonest about their intentions. Then I get philosophical about how society is too judgmental toward women and that they should be allowed to enjoy the same freedom I do. I candidly talk about how I am dating plenty of women and that I encourage the woman I'm speaking with to do the same because I do not get jealous.

In my initial conversation, I am painting a picture of a man who is circling the globe, ambitious, honest and nonjudgmental. It seems natural to me, but there have been so many women who found it a revelation that a guy was so ecstatic about being alone and free. This type of open-minded, free-wheeling attitude appears so exotic and exciting to them because most guys are not so passionate or forthcoming. When women want to be with me, they often tell me they want to "experience" me, meaning they feel that meeting me will be not just a date but a memory they will have forever. In the process, these women have given me some unforgettable memories of my own! If you can similarly present yourself as a passionate person, then the ladies may lust after your excitement. It does not matter if it is a day at

Disneyland or a night in your bedroom, giving a woman an exciting encounter that is out of their everyday realm will make you much more fascinating than the men they are accustomed to dating.

Many women who want this pleasure are still scared to break out of their comfort zone. One way you can do this is to present a situation that will spark their interest. I have stressed the importance of honesty, but here is where you can be a little creative with the truth to captivate her attention. Do not get me wrong. You should not manipulate her emotions, but do not be afraid to create a situation that will force her to break out of her shell.

My friend has brilliantly employed this tactic to attract women for years. He lives in Los Angeles, where there are frequent special events and award shows. He is one of the more talented artists in town so he gets many invitations to these gatherings. When an event is on the horizon, he will tell a variety of girls that he is looking for a date for the occasion and needs someone who is cool and fun to party with. This produces a sense of urgency because there is a potentially entertaining evening that takes place on a fixed date. As a result, in their desire to accompany him, many of them will go out with him right away instead of agonizing over the decision. He has had a long list of hook-ups over the years from this technique. My friend may or may not actually take the girl to the event, and sometimes he may not even have had an invite in the first place, but the fact is they were drawn to the allure of the situation. The existence of the event is actually irrelevant because even if a woman hooks up with him it is because she is attracted to him. Sometimes, women need some type of excuse in their head to do what they really want to do. If you share a special connection, then you will continue to see each other, regardless of what brought you together.

You can use this method as long as you are comfortable with what you are doing and not hurting the girls you are dating. As I said before, women are emotional beings, and their need for stability may make them desire something more serious, even if you are dating casually. In that case, it is up to you to evaluate your own feelings and make an intelligent decision about what you want and communicate it to her. If you decide you are not ready for commitment, just tell her that and move on. Neither of you should see it as a failure because each of you enjoyed a good time while you were together.

If you do decide that you have similar needs and you are absolutely sure you want to settle down, then continue to take the relationship to the next level. Just make sure that you do not lose the sense of excitement that attracted you to her in the first place. It is when things get monotonous and uninteresting that a relationship begins to crumble. Share activities that are new and enjoyable to keep things fresh for both of you. Additionally, you must not lose touch with the passionate part of you that makes you desirable. When you understand that women crave excitement and you can satisfy those yearnings, you will become successful both in casual dating as well as in serious relationships.

CHAPTER 33
Nice Guys Finish Last...Sometimes
☆ ☆ ☆

"A true gentleman is at a disadvantage in dealing with women... Women admire gentlemen and sleep with cads."—Louis L'Amour

There seem to be two conflicting schools of thought on the type of persona it takes to attract the ladies. Some people think that it is best to be a chivalrous gentleman who is romantic and takes care of her wants and needs. Others have the idea that "women love assholes" and the way to get girls to want you is to act like an arrogant jerk. In actuality, the truth lies somewhere between those two extremes. To really be successful with women, you need to give off a cocky, unattainable edge but also have an underlying layer of charm, sense of humor and sweetness. Of course it is most important to be yourself, but it is this combination that will make you a hit with the ladies.

When we are growing up, boys are taught to put girls on a pedestal. We are supposed to believe that if you are kind and caring, then when you grow up, women will appreciate these qualities and like you. As we get older and interact more with the opposite sex, we learn things are not so black and white, but that the real trick to luring ladies is to develop a shade of gray.

Unfortunately, most guys adjust to one side or the other, thus never really capturing that ability.

I will be honest and say that I started out as a naïve, "nice guy" who would pay for dates, buy gifts, and be someone girls came to for help. When I did this, instead of having women flocking to date me, I usually ended up being someone they either saw as "a friend" or someone they could go to complain about their troubles with the other guys they date. There is nothing wrong with having platonic female friends, but when you are looking to casually date a multitude of women, the last thing you want to be is the sappy good boy who caters to them or is a shoulder to cry on.

Thankfully, I learned pretty quickly and with minimal damage to my psyche that I would be much more successful with women by showcasing some swagger and attitude. My own extensive dating experience after discovering this has taught me that women are tired of dealing with clingy, overemotional men. In fact, one of the main reasons that so many women are frustrated is that many American men act like pansies who get attached too quickly. My studies revealed that more than half of women find a man who is too nice and accommodating to be weak and needy.

If you are a polite, pleasant guy who is always paying for a girl's dinner and attentive to all of her demands, ask yourself how that is working for you. Are you really getting the type of attention you really want from her? I have seen friends try to portray themselves as some type of chivalrous hero with the girls they date, and many of them become doormats who get stomped on and tossed to the curb. The majority of the men I studied came out hurt and disappointed when they played this role. Women quite simply are not aroused by excess adoration, but are more intrigued by a man who is bit of a challenge. They may not say it in public, but girls prefer a man who exhibits some strength and individuality to somebody who is merely a servant constantly trying to impress them.

At the same time, I am not advocating being an arrogant jerk who is outwardly mean or hurtful to women. This is not only wrong on a humane level, but it is also not going to attract the type of women you are looking for. If you are constantly rude and nasty to the girls you are trying to date, you come across as an insecure, bitter human being who is unhappy with life. The only girls who will be turned on by this type of maliciousness are the ones with such extremely low self-esteem that they will not even be enjoyable to be around.

You want to strike a balance between being a good guy who is caring and understanding of what women want and the bad boy with a cocky attitude. When I tell guys that they should not be too nice to girls, many misinterpret it by thinking I am convincing them to be cruel. What I really mean is that you should not be such a pushover that women will feel that they can walk all over you.

So how do you exhibit this mix of sweet charm and sexy danger? It is not so easy to explain because in order for you to use that cocky edge to your advantage, it must come naturally to you. You also want to exhibit it with a wink and a smile so as not to appear smug or conceited. It is important to be confident because otherwise your swagger comes from a false sense of self-worth. Having confidence is not enough, however, if you do not know how to communicate it. There are many self-assured guys who are still unsuccessful with women because they do not know how to convey this assurance in a sexy manner.

You need to create the vibe that it is dangerous for her to get too close because you do not get tied down to just anybody. Talk to her as if you are in a position of strength and take charge of the conversation. Women are turned on by powerful men who take action and make decisions. Tell her what you are interested in and say it so convincingly that she cannot help but be looking for the same things you are. Understanding how to set a tone is paramount, and I go into extensive detail on how to communicate power in my chapter on how to talk to women. For now, remember to showcase a bit of an attitude which suggests that all-important aura of unattainability.

You could actually be a really nice guy, which is fine and dandy, but do not let her translate those qualities into thinking you are a patsy. I am not telling you to be a phony either, because the last thing you want is to lose track of who you really are. I am, at heart, a very caring and compassionate person, but in the dating game, I only unveil this side of my nature selectively. Psychology comes into play because if you are always endearing and complimentary, it is no longer special. Instead, if you are brash, flirtatious, and even a little bold, while mixing in some occasional flattery, those sweet remarks will have much more impact.

Nina Hartley described me really well when I was introducing some of my friends to her. She smiled slyly as she told my pals, "Be careful. This guy is dangerous. But you know what? Hanging out with him will lead you everywhere good." This is precisely the type of image that will get you plenty of women. Truth be told, I am about as dangerous as drinking a bottle of spring water, but what she meant when she said this was that I do the things most people want to do, but are afraid to do. Her "warning" was that spending time with me will make them stretch the boundaries of their imagination to such a limit that they will question everything they believed in before. I do not do any drugs nor engage in any crimes, but just being a self-assured, free spirit who lives by his own set of rules has given me the "rebel" image that women love.

Contrast that to portraying the bland, safe guy who will be a good friend but not really add any type of excitement to a girl's life. In essence, if you want to attract large quantities of women, you want to create the impression that you are so sexy and individualistic that you are irresistible. This will make you tremendously appealing to women, and they will be much more willing to hook up with you. If you are looking for something more serious and can blend that edgy sex appeal with loyalty, caring, friendship and love, you can attain her devotion without being considered a pushover. While nice guys might not necessarily finish last, they likely will not get first choice in the dating life they desire.

CHAPTER 34
The Art of Talking to Women
☆ ☆ ☆

"Lots of people act well, but few people talk well. This shows that talking is the more difficult of the two."—Oscar Wilde

Traveling the world has allowed me to see some of the most famous and beautiful paintings in history. I am not even an art lover, but you cannot help but be in awe when you stand before the works of da Vinci, van Gogh and Picasso. These creative geniuses used their paintbrushes to express their emotions, and left us all timeless treasures to behold and interpret. Just as painters draw an image they hope others will admire, when a man talks to a woman, he should create a portrait of someone she will be attracted to. You need to illustrate an attractive representation that will leave her in amazement. I said before that I did not like the expression "pick-up artist," but talking to women truly is an art form that you need to master if you are to be successful with them.

Just as the average person cannot draw a masterpiece without ever having taken an art class, displaying artistry with words when communicating with females is not something most people are born with. It took me a few years of dating girls of all types to understand how to portray myself in a way that maximizes my appeal. First of all, you need to a date of diversity of women and practice different techniques that you are comfortable with. By doing so, you can analyze their reactions and see what captivates them. As you gather this experience, you should naturally develop an approach based on your own personality that showcases your attributes.

Don't forget that women are attracted to men who can convey a strong sense of power and independence. Mix those traits with some charm and humor and you will generate a sexy air that will be alluring to a girl's senses. I'll explain how you can demonstrate this power when you are speaking with someone you are interested in dating. First of all, your tone of voice should reflect your confidence. No matter what you say, it will be ineffective if you sound nervous about how she will react to you. A man who appears self-assured will generally be more appealing than a guy who seems worried, even if he is not as sweet or respectful to her. Make sure you are not stammering or slurring your words because those are sure signs of discomfort. Talk in a clear, authoritative voice that not only commands, but demands her respect. If your voice whimpers into a Michael Jackson circa-1984 falsetto, she will deem you weak and you will lose the power dynamic from the start…unless you can do the moonwalk.

Once your speech exhibits an attitude that you are secure with yourself and not intimidated by a woman, what you say becomes as important as how you say it. Much of it comes down to intricate subtleties that make the difference between mutual pleasure and solitary frustration. When you speak to her, make sure you phrase things in a way that allows you to dominate the conversation. For example, instead of asking her, "Do you want to go out?" you should say, "So when are we going out?" When you read the two questions they sound the same, but when a woman hears them, they convey completely distinctive messages. When you are asking her if she wants to get together, you are leaving it up to her discretion to form a decision if she finds you worthy enough to meet. This gives her the idea that you are unsure of yourself, and it also gives her the opportunity to reject you. On the other hand, if you are asking when you are going out, you display authority and let her know that she will meet you, but it is just a question of time. This reveals a strong sense of confidence and belief that you will show her a good time. Most importantly, it is a question to which she does not have the option of answering with the almighty word that men are deathly afraid of: "No."

That is just a little example that depicts how to use your words to your advantage. Your main goal is to try to structure the conversation around your own life and what makes it so special. The more you can make yourself sound fascinating, the more she will be inclined to do what you want. Again, present yourself in a fun, light-hearted manner so that you do not come across as self-centered. This is where your humorous side becomes important. You want to keep her just as comfortable as you are.

Here is a model of how you can strike this cocky-funny balance when you are describing yourself. "I always have lots of stuff going on. I'm traveling and working hard to make sure I can keep my lifestyle going. I barely have enough time for my friends, let alone all of the girls that I'm dating. I know I deserve a spanking for being a bad friend and a bad boy for not keeping the girls happy, right? Ha ha! Who knows though…you seem pretty cool…maybe you might get lucky!"

Keep in mind that the example above is a very basic description you might give her to get her interest. Most of the art in talking to women is in the mood of the conversation and the context of the moment. This narrative may sound cheesy without it, but let us examine this for a moment. In a few sentences, you have accomplished many objectives. You have illustrated that you are a renaissance man with a diversity of activities who is focused on being successful. Women love ambitious, accomplished men because they are turned on by power. By giving a vague introduction that you want to sustain your "lifestyle," you have created a sense of intrigue about exactly what makes your life so exciting. She will want to know more about you and become closer to you, often literally, so your passion will rub off on her.

One response I give when a girl asks me what I do that makes my life so enjoyable is this. I tell her, "You are not old enough to hear about what I do." It is irrelevant how old she is as I have even used this line on women old enough to be my mother. When I respond with this answer, I am telling her that I have much more life experience than she does and my open-mindedness has given me adventures she could not possibly understand.

Let me explain how this is a brilliant reply. First of all, it is a challenge to her ego because a guy is calling her out on not being able to handle how exciting his life is. Usually, men are clamoring to be part of a woman's life. This turns the tables on them because a guy is questioning if she can be part of his. It also portrays you as a guy who has done so much in his life that you cannot even talk about it because she would not relate to you. In doing so, it makes them want to talk about their wild side because they feel they need to demonstrate that they are "old enough" to be with you. So in one fell swoop, you are painting yourself as a sexy, experienced figure while at the same time making her intrigued as to what makes your lifestyle so stimulating. Remember that women yearn for excitement in their lives because few guys provide it.

Now let us go back to that introductory statement I presented above. Not only have you made your daily life sound thrilling, you have also simultaneously communicated that you have plenty of real friends as well as women in your life. This shows that you are not lonely or needy because quality people already surround you. If she senses loneliness, this can be translated as weakness, and she may either not be interested in you or she will see you as a pushover. These are not traits that will enhance your sex appeal. Just to make sure you do not come across as conceited, you mixed in a humorous statement about needing a spanking. This reveals a self-deprecatory side that shows you do not take yourself too seriously. At the same time, it adds a naughty, playful element into the dynamic without being lewd, and it might lead her to reveal her kinky side. Finally, instead of asking for permission to enter her life, you demonstrated that she would be "lucky" if she can become part of yours. The last sentence indicates that you are accustomed to making the decisions as to which ladies you date, but it does so in a funny, nonthreatening manner. It even tosses in the all-important back-handed compliment that she *might* be "cool" enough to be seen with you.

In the course of about less than a minute, you have given her the essence of a well-rounded, ambitious man with a fun personality, great friends, and a healthy sex life. The initial steps you take when attempting to make a connection with a woman, no matter what your intentions are, become vital in establishing your power position in the relationship. You want to sustain this power whether you are looking for a one-night stand or a long-term relationship. If you do not, she may either be bored or feel she can manipulate you. As you can see, it all depends on your ability to create a compelling portrait of yourself.

Many people may have the misconceptions that focusing on yourself is wrong and that you should romantically seduce her with compliments. In fact, building yourself up as a larger-than-life figure psychologically appeals to her on multiple levels. First of all, it sparks her interest in getting to know more about you. At the same time, she feels she can benefit from the thrill that surrounds your lifestyle and can make her own life more pleasurable. Most importantly, when she sees you as a sexy, dynamic figure, it also raises her own self-esteem. She thinks to herself that if you are such an extraordinary person, she must also, by that token, be pretty special to get the opportunity to be part of your life. At the end of the day, that is what it is all about because we all want to be happy. Employing this technique can make each of you feel better about yourselves, especially when you meet and share your enthusiasm for life.

I have mentioned that you want to make her feel good about being with you, but notice I have not stressed that you need to incessantly compliment her. Remember that you do not want to put the woman on a pedestal and voluntarily surrender the power dynamic. You also do not want to shower her with the same hollow praise she is accustomed to hearing from other men. This is where the tactic of the back-handed compliment comes in. This is a remark that sounds like it may be a compliment but in actuality is a bit of an insult. It serves the purpose of throwing a woman off her mark and making her more vulnerable to your seduction. Simple examples of this would be telling her that she looks good for her age or telling a beautiful girl that you like pretty women, but feel that intelligence is more important.

This works because it neutralizes the strengths she usually uses to her advantage and that other men typically fall prey to. When this happens, she is thrown out of her comfort zone, but in a way where she questions why you are not susceptible to her charms. This separates you from the other apparently weaker men because you have given her an idea that you are not easily impressed. It is important that your back-handed compliment is not too obviously condescending, but that it is a subtle mix of praise and slight. If she is offended, just tell her a joke or make fun of yourself as well so that she does not think you are being rude or making fun of her. If you can employ this tool intelligently, then she will try to work hard for your attention and approval. In the process of this "work," you may mutually fulfill some of your hottest fantasies. Additionally, when you do give her a rare genuinely flattering remark, it will mean so much more to her because you do not throw out such praise flippantly.

Of course, many of you who are in the dating game are not looking for anything remotely serious, but want to enjoy fun for the moment's sake. As I have said many times, there is nothing wrong with that as long as you are honest with your partner about your objectives. So how do you express that you may not be looking for more than physical pleasure? I have found the best way to fulfill your erotic desires is to simply be honest about it. Remember that women need security, but they crave excitement. So if her mood is right, or you can present the right set of circumstances, it could lead to what you want. I have found that if you are just looking to sleep with the woman you are talking to, the best way to go about it is to keep the tone of the conversation mostly sexual.

There is a way to do this without being offensive. First of all, I suggest that if you want a purely sexual relationship with a lady, then the first time you call her should be after ten o'clock at night. If she picks up the phone this late, she is likely feeling a little lonely, and since it is near her time to go to bed, she is likely more in the mood for some hot topics than when she was doing the dishes a few hours earlier. Do not immediately go into sexual innuendos and remarks as it is not a phone sex line and she will probably not appreciate it. Instead, cover the introductory points I suggested earlier to create the impression that you are a sexy, desirable man. This caters to a woman's yearnings for excitement as well her longing to meet men who are strong and honest. Once she feels fascinated by your personality, then you can seduce her with your honesty about whatever fantasies you have. You may be surprised how many women love frank discussion on these matters and are turned on by it. Again, if you can present to her that sleeping together will be an unforgettable erotic experience and do so without being crude or threatening, then she may be comfortable with sharing this bliss with you. The key is to keep the conversation on a level of fantasy so her mind escapes from her everyday reality.

The art of talking to women encompasses such a broad scope that I could write an entire book on that one topic alone, and I am sure there are plenty of works out there that do focus completely on it. Since this book is not merely about seducing women, instead of going into significant detail, I wanted to give you a general idea of how you can develop this skill. The best way to illustrate this art form is to present real examples of how it is done, so I want to conclude the chapter by sharing a story.

One of the more memorable moments when I applied my artistry to perfection was when the superstars of the WWE were in my hometown for Wrestlemania week. A friend and I were at a store when we encountered one of the sexy "Divas" of wrestling out shopping with her mom. I will leave her name confidential, but this woman is a real-life Barbie doll with long blonde hair and a perfectly proportioned body. Unexpectedly, her mom was extremely attractive as well! As open-minded as I am, I generally draw the line at attempting to hook up with girls in front of their mothers, and I usually stop myself from picking up moms in front of their kids. Let us just say this was one day that the line was not drawn.

I approached them both with confidence and started schmoozing with the young one while also flirting with the mom. Of course, I threw out the tried and true, "Is this your sister?" line, guaranteed to make an older woman melt. The daughter began to laugh as the mom blushed and "informed" me that she was actually her mother. I have become excellent at reading people, and I could tell they were both intrigued by my charm and self-assurance. The next thing I said was one of the greatest lines I have ever delivered. I looked at the Diva and told her, "You do realize your mom is more beautiful than you, right?"

She gave me an awestruck, uncomfortable smile, not knowing how to react to the backhanded compliment. At the same time, the mom became completely infatuated and she stuck her hand out and said, "Well, hello handsome," with a suggestive smile on her face. The daughter, both uncomfortable and jealous at the same time that her mom was more a subject of my fascination than she was, gave her "the disapproving daughter look." "Mom!" she said with an awkward expression on her lovely face.

At this point, I was in the presence of two gorgeous ladies and was in complete control of the interaction. Let us rewind a bit and study how I attained this dominant position. There were two women whom I targeted with my radar. The first was a WWE Diva who was on television every week. Because I was highly experienced with beautiful women, I realized that she was likely insecure and vulnerable to my advances if I used the proper tactics. I also knew that she was familiar with attention and men building up her fragile ego with compliments. The second was a hot older woman who probably had been an absolute knockout in her day. She was now upstaged by her daughter, who was a star on a highly rated TV show. It would make sense that she probably just wanted to feel young and sexy again.

Now let us analyze that line. "You do realize your mom is more beautiful than you, right?" It sounds irrelevant, but that one simple sentence accomplishes multiple purposes. It suddenly sends the mother on a time capsule back to her youth, when she was surely a showstopping beauty. The fact that I called her more attractive than her television-star daughter was a huge ego boost for her and suddenly made me look like a young knight in shining armor. There is a reason so many older women like younger guys. They get to taste a drink from the fountain of youth.

Simultaneously, it fed off the insecurity of the young model and broke down the ego that sappy guys everywhere had built up. She could not accuse me of being mean to her because I was complimenting her mom! At the same time, I did not blindly do what most guys would have done in the same situation and talk about watching her on TV or how good she looked. Instead, I fed her a statement that accomplished the goal every guy should strive for when approaching a hot girl and that is to say something that throws her off her mark. Although she did not know how to react to what I said, she was completely fascinated by my presence. During the next few minutes, I had both women completely captivated as I wove between them and threw out suggestive propositions for a really fun night. My command of the conversation was masterful, as I had a sexy star of a cable ratings juggernaut and her hot mom completely glued to my every word. Unfortunately, since the Diva also happened to have an enormous boyfriend who was a professional wrestler, there was no closing. It did not matter to me because I had exemplified my confidence and poise by capturing their attention.

What you will learn as you become more experienced in the dating game is that sometimes the outcome of the interaction does not matter. I have had plenty of success with women, and I have also had lots of "failures," but it is really these in-between stories that I remember the most. After all, a hookup is a hook-up, but the real fun in the game is to understand the psychological principles of how to talk to women and master the art of seduction.

When I think of the story I described above as well as my goal every time I talk to a woman I want to date, I go back to when I was a young college kid in Paris. My parents took me to the famous Louvre Museum, where I had the joy of coming before the most famous painting of all time, The Mona Lisa. It may not have been the most beautiful portrait, but it had an aura that generated a magnetic appeal which made it appear even more magnificent than it was. As the years went by, I realized that if I can create that same aura about myself and illustrate that to the women I encounter, they may find me similarly irresistible. You may not be using a paintbrush, but by learning how to use your words to show that being with you will be an exciting experience, you will have mastered the art form of talking to women.

CHAPTER 35
Tips and Techniques
☆ ☆ ☆

"Did you promise to be a good boy...not to waste your time on girls?"—Angela Vickers
"I don't waste my time."—George Eastman (A Place in the Sun)

When you have followed the guidelines I have outlined over the previous chapters, you will have gone a long way toward establishing a successful dating life. There are various other skills that you can develop to optimize your appeal with women. The more you have to offer a lady, the more she will come to you to seek your company. Here, I will discuss some further skills to make you irresistible to the female population.

☆ Skill 1: Take a public speaking course.

One terrific way to become more comfortable with talking to girls as well as building your self-confidence is developing your public speaking skills. I recommend taking a course in speech to improve this ability. Studies have shown that public speaking is one of man's most terrifying fears. If you can be relaxed in front of a large crowd of people, then you will be more at ease with approaching a female. I was president of my high school and had to deliver speeches and hold council meetings every month. This greatly improved my confidence as well as my leadership skills, both attributes that convey power. Developing this talent will aid you in all aspects of your life.

☆ Skill 2: Learn how to host parties.

In addition to becoming comfortable with giving lectures to an audience, I also advise that you learn how to host parties. After all, what would Hugh Hefner do that could compare to his legendary parties at his mansion? Planning and hosting parties is an excellent way to meet women and create an illusion of power that she may find unbearably sexy. I invited people to weekly parties at my place when I was in school, and the majority of the women who attended were interested in being with the master of ceremonies. Of course, first you need to have a place that is suitable for soirees, ideally your own home, but a friend's place or a rented hall can do as well. Then you want to create a festive atmosphere and project a pleasant, charismatic personality so that all of your guests are having a blast and see you as the star. There is no more satisfying way of having a good time than creating a fun environment and bringing the party to you.

☆ Skill 3: Become a master of body language.

No matter what the locale, whether it is your own party or at a nightclub, one of the surest ways to showcase your sex appeal is to have a swagger in your step and sensuality in your body language. Walking with strong posture projects self-assurance and can capture a woman's attention. Additionally, when you approach her with confidence, your posture and body movements can enhance your attractiveness. Make sure your poses give off a strong, sexy vibe because it will show you are not intimidated by her presence. When you start talking to her and she expresses interest, give off subtle signals of your own attraction to her. Holding her hand, caressing her cheek, and gliding your palm against her arm are some delicate touches that can create a closer connection and stimulate her desire to do more.

☆ Skill 4: Make sure you can share in passionate kisses and give sensual massages.

When you ask women which physical acts of foreplay arouse their senses, two of the top answers are inevitably kissing and receiving massages. Nothing will turn a woman on more than a warm, passionate kiss. They say practice makes perfect, so the more you share these adoring lip-locks, the better you will become. When you are first talking to a woman you can discuss what a great kisser you are and how much you love a good embrace. As you become more at ease with approaching women, you can use it as a "reward." Tell her that if she promises to be nice to you, you will give her a sweet kiss. You can say it with a charming laugh so she will not find it offensive if she is not interested. It is an innocent, playful way of striking her interest no matter where you meet her, and it may arouse her curiosity about whether you can back up your words. Whether she is looking for romance or a one-night stand, a good kiss can be the key to her heart, and more. Make sure you do plenty of kissing in the buildup to more intimate activities because it will get her fires burning and make her much hotter by the time you get closer.

While I am on this subject, let me explain one of most successful strategies of seduction, the mid-sentence-make-out. It is when you can feel sexual tension and chemistry with a woman you meet, and in the middle of conversation, you slowly draw closer to her and kiss her. This is something often seen in movies, but many feel does not work in real life. I have discovered on numerous occasions that it works brilliantly in bridging the gap between pretentious small talk and the physical pleasure that both parties desire. Of course, this tool has to be employed carefully and intuitively. You obviously should not just randomly go up to girls and kiss them. As you gain more experience in interacting with women, you develop a natural sense of how attracted they are to you. When you are talking to a woman and can feel the attraction intensify by reading her body signals and hearing the tone of her voice, you know you are ready for the mid-sentence make-out. If done perfectly, this first kiss can set the stage for a night of passion.

Equally as appealing to women as a splendid kiss is a nice massage. This is one of the most sensual pleasures that you can share together. I highly recommend either taking training in massages, getting a book or video on the art, or practicing extensively with a female friend or partner. If you can learn how to rub a woman's body tensions away, you will find that she will be willing to do just about anything for you. It is an incredibly erotic experience that will turn you on as much as her. If you really want to satisfy a woman and have her come back to you repeatedly, this is an immeasurable skill for the bedroom and beyond.

I have utilized the "massage angle" countless times to meet women. First of all, I have become really good at giving them. Furthermore, it plays to the power principle I discussed in an earlier chapter. I will often bring up the idea that she needs to relax more and that a good massage will help her body and mind feel better. This demonstrates I have a unique skill that will benefit her, and it creates an impression that makes her seek "my services." Additionally, it is not necessarily a straightforward sexual request, but it is a seductive scenario that she may not resist and can often lead to much deeper desires being fulfilled. Remember the importance of creating an illustration that is attractive to her senses, and the idea of a sexy massage is one that can drive any woman wild.

Apart from the physical acts that can stimulate your fantasies, you should also employ some psychological principles based on common sense. If you are looking for one-night stands with little connection, follow these four simple rules. You should minimize time wasted, money spent, and emotion invested, and maximize pleasure experienced. It sounds shallow, but when neither of you are looking for depth there is no reason to expend your energies pretending that the situation is more than it is. Keep things as simple and uncomplicated as possible and have a mutually enjoyable experience.

☆ Skill 5: Do not immediately shower her with attention.

When you are looking for something more than that, whether it is casual or serious dating, make sure that you are intelligent about how you portray yourself to maximize her fascination with you. One surefire way of appearing weak and pathetic is immediately getting attached and professing your love for her. As I explained before, women are tired of men becoming too possessive early in a relationship, so it is better to give her space and let things flow. I am someone who hates telling anybody I love them. When those emotions truly exist between two people, you should not have to say it in words. It should already be understood. Nonetheless, if you do want to express this deepest emotion, do not do it until you have known each other for a long time and have developed mutual respect, trust, communication and friendship with one another. Otherwise, the phrase becomes hollow because not only is there no substance to back it up, there is nothing to build your relationship toward if you immediately take it to its highest level.

One way to appear too clingy and obsessive is to call her too often. Be very selective about how often you call. If she really wants you, giving her a little less attention will make her crave you a lot more. It goes back to the psychology of wanting what you cannot have. If you are calling her every few hours, then you become common and boring. It is better to have her telephone you, and ring her only on occasion. That way every time you project your interest, she appreciates it much more, and you sustain your special quality.

You also do not want to shower her with gifts or immediately take her to expensive restaurants you cannot afford. Understand your budget and save those expenditures for when you become closer, and even then, only on special occasions. If you do it all the time, it becomes expected and you create a sense of entitlement. Not only that, she will not find it exciting because the expectation is that it is the norm. When you form a bond and occasionally do something really thoughtful, it will mean that much more.

☆ Skill 6: Give her unique, personal gifts.

Although I am obviously not seeking a serious relationship, I have dated women before and have had really close female friends. I've discovered that what really touches their hearts is when you give them something that is unique and personal. That need not be expensive. I have had much more gleeful reactions to a homemade card or a framed picture than a piece of jewelry because it indicates that you actually put some thought into showing you care. In theory, anybody can spend money for a lofty gift, but when you use your creativity to give her something special, she will treasure it and remember it forever.

☆ Skill 7: Make each meeting special.

When serious emotions do get involved, I suggest not ruining the situation by seeing each other so often that your entire lives revolve around each other. I will get into further detail on how to have a fulfilling long-term relationship later, but you do not want to be going through the motions. There are so many couples who are together for the sake of convenience and lack the passion and spice in their lives that likely brought them together in the first place. I suggest that when you begin a serious relationship, you build up to your meetings. That way, every time you see each other, it will seem special and you can sustain the electricity that fills the air when you are together. That is difficult to do when the person is there all the time because you start taking them for granted or become overly dependent on their company.

These are merely some suggestions to spice up your dating life. As you accumulate experience, you will discover what makes you happy and maximizes your success while minimizing your drama.

CHAPTER 36
The Superhighway to Your Dating Dreams
☆ ☆ ☆

"For those of us who want a change from the dating status quo…we are the internet generation and at the click of a mouse, we can find just about anything, including that elusive date."—Amy Fisher

You have to love technological advancement. Thanks to the wonderful innovation called the World Wide Web, your dreams are at the tips of your fingers. Nowhere has this breakthrough felt more impact than the dating scene. Without leaving your home, you have access to millions of women who are searching for somebody to fulfill their wants and needs. It boggles my mind why anybody would want to expend time, energy and headache going to bars and clubs to interact with women who will likely act like they are not interested, even if they are.

Those hours could be much better spent in front of your computer screen exploring the countless females who are readily seeking company. If they are on some form of dating site, you already know that they are searching for someone and it may as well be you. Just think of yourself in a car and having to choose from multiple roads to reach your destination. One of them is a one-lane street full of potholes and roadblocks and usually reaches a dead end. The other is a multilane high-speed freeway that has its traffic, but has plenty of other lanes to travel on to arrive at your goal. When you master the skill of finding women online, you will be riding the superhighway to your dating dreams. Let me take you through a step-by-step process on how you can utilize this tool to its full capacity.

☆ Step 1: Get a great set of pictures of yourself.

I mentioned this before but the first thing you need is a set of great pictures. These do not need to be professional images. Well-lighted, crisp shots that highlight your best features will be sufficient. I recommend showcasing a variety of different looks, from professional to casual to athletic. Obviously, if you have a nice build, take some pictures that show off your physique. Do not feel egotistical or cheesy getting photographed at your best because having a good portfolio of portraits will be your primary asset in introducing yourself to the women of the web.

Remember that not only are there millions of available women online, but you are also competing against enormous quantities of men, and you need to stand out. The good news is that the vast majority of men do not take the effort to post quality pictures on their profiles. When you do so, you are already ahead of the curve.

If you do not have any good images that highlight your physical attributes, that is your first step. If you really want to attract attention, then you will take some pictures of you surrounded by luscious backdrops and beautiful women. When you can show that not only are you attractive, but you also live an exciting lifestyle, then the woman you're interested in will really take notice. Ideally, you live in a place that is within close distance of a postcard-like locale. If so, go there with a camera and get some photographs with magnificent backgrounds. If not, when you are on vacations or daytrips, make sure you capture some images with whatever landmarks you come across. These pictures will spruce up your profile and give off the impression of a man of the world who appreciates traveling, nature and the aesthetic pleasures of the earth.

Even more of an eye-opener is when you have images of you with other beautiful women. Remember the psychology of women being fascinated by men who are attractive to other lovely ladies. Just like being accompanied by gorgeous girls makes you more alluring in bars and clubs, pictures with them make you more appealing on a personality profile. If you have nice shots with a pretty female friend or ex-girlfriend, then place them on your site. This also goes back to the importance of attending events where other sexy females will be and bringing a camera to those places. These photos do wonders in creating the all-important aura of unattainability that women find mesmerizing.

☆ Step 2: Construct an intelligently written, provocative description of yourself on your profiles.

Once you have a series of images that showcase your looks and your lifestyle, take the time to write an illustrative description that makes you sound as interesting as possible. In a few paragraphs, you can demonstrate what makes you special and why a woman should choose you above the rest of her infinite options. Make sure that it is well-written with no spelling or grammatical errors. Draft it first on a word -processing program so you can ensure it is error-free. Do not forget that a smart man is a sexy man, and it is inexcusable to present yourself to the world in a less than intelligent manner.

Additionally, provide a provocative illustration that makes you appear like a diverse, well-rounded person. I have already demonstrated how you can do so in my chapters on the Power Dynamic, as well as the Art of Talking to Women. Take those conversational tips and translate them to a compelling written description that showcases your attributes. You do not have to be humble in doing so. Just as most men do not bother getting good pictures done, they also do not take the time to compose a worthy description of what they have to offer to a woman. Even if you are living an exciting life, if you cannot convey this on your profile, a woman may not consider contacting you in the first place.

Once you have an attractive profile with excellent images and a gripping description, you are ready to enter the internet dating sphere. This profile will be the equivalent of a resume when you are searching for a job. All of us know that those who are truly successful in that market are the ones who have employers seeking them. Just like the prospective hotshot employee who is sought after by companies, having a stand-out profile will capture a woman's attention so she will make the effort to contact you. That is the ideal scenario because most dating sites are flooded with excess amounts of men, and women frequently receive more proposals than they can handle.

☆ Step 3: Create an intriguing introductory email.

Even men with the most spectacular profiles, however, will need to exert some effort to contact the women they are interested in. Here is how I recommend you do so. Formulate a generic introductory email that provides some interesting information on who you are and what you are looking for, and save it on your computer. You can cut and paste it and then make subtle changes to that template so the woman assumes it was personally written for her. This way you do not have to spend needless amounts of time writing personal emails to all of the women who catch your eye. Speaking of all of those women, in internet dating, there is power in numbers. You may need to send out hundreds of emails in order to get only a few responses. That is why it is essential for you to create an appealing, well-drafted letter that you can send out in minutes and which will generate as much interest as possible from those you send it to.

☆ Step 4: Use the Instant Messenger on dating sites.

An even better way to utilize dating sites than blasting out mass emails is to use the power of the instant messaging system that most of them come equipped with. The IM tool works brilliantly because you already know that these women are online browsing through emails and other profiles. An instant message can capture their attention faster than an email and can be more immediately interactive. It is true that many of the women may already be chatting with a guy and others may not want to be bothered with it, but there are also plenty of girls who are lonely and seeking to make that instant connection. My strategy has been to log on at night and attempt to IM as many women as possible that I am attracted to. Usually, at least a couple of them respond, and then I illustrate a fantasy situation that builds up their anticipation to meet me. By the end of the chat session, I ask for their number and then transfer this fantasy to the phone, and eventually in person. It is a highly effective usage of this medium.

☆ Step 5: Post ads on internet classified sites.

While I recommend starting out your online dating escapades by sending out emails and instant messages to measure the response you receive, eventually you will want to learn how to make the women come to you. This will happen if you have a nice profile, but the best way to do this is to find an internet classifieds site, whatever is popular in your region, and put up a posting in the dating section. The way these sites generally operate is that you click a category of what you are looking for and then browse through headlines that link you to a more in-depth description. That is why coming up with an eye-capturing tagline is paramount when you are using these sites. Then follow that up with an exciting description of yourself and the type of women that you seek. This is one area of online dating where you do not want to post a picture. That is because you may be putting up a variety of different ads and you do not want to limit yourself. Once you discover which depictions attract their attention, you may find a stream of women contacting you.

Posting in the classified sections has been by far my most successful method in meeting girls on the internet. I tried mass emailing on the dating sites and it worked to an extent, but it is far easier to create a generic ad you can repost daily that women respond to. Additionally, when they are emailing you, they cannot deny that they are interested. It gives you the power to pique her interest and then meet to see if you have a connection. Even the online dating game has its levels of effectiveness, and you might as well maximize pleasure and minimize exerted effort. Obviously, your ad should correspond with what you are looking for, but it should also be written with the idea in the back of your mind that it needs to grab their attention.

I would suggest creating a headline and a description that caters to a niche. For years I have used an ad searching for women over thirty-five years old. I realize that many of these women generally have wants and needs that are similar to my own, so I draft a posting stating that I am a smart, sexy, and successful young man who appreciates the glories of dating a mature woman. Just like your personality profile, a concise, compelling, well-written ad will captivate their attention and separate you from the majority of lazy guys who post the same uninteresting nonsense. I have also made ads looking for Eastern European women, Hispanic women, and a variety of demographics. When you are searching for something specific, you are more likely to get a response from your target market. Just remember that the description of yourself must convey intelligence, sex appeal, and success.

If you are looking for some fun casual pleasure, I would suggest writing a playful ad that is subtly suggestive. I have created ad templates searching for "nice girls with a naughty side" as well as "friends with benefits." These are actually the ideal women I am looking for because they are fun to be around but do not add drama to my life. That is what I say in my posting along with some flowery language about how these types of women are rare and should be celebrated. Do not forget that women are raised to be insecure about their sexuality and are hesitant when they hear a man wants to keep things casual. By framing it in a way where they not only think it is okay, but they feel that they are special if they are open to such a relationship, they will be more inclined to respond favorably.

☆ Step 6: *Get her phone number as soon as possible.*

Once a woman responds to you, it is important not to get caught up in an endless series of emails. As I've said many times, much of what captures a woman's attention is appealing to their sense of fantasy. When they have too much time to think about what they are doing, they may be apprehensive about meeting you. That is why you should reply to her response with a short email saying how busy you are and that you do not have time for endless emails. If she hasn't sent a picture, request one immediately. I have a general rule that I will not meet a woman unless I see what she looks like, and I am surmising that physical attraction is important to you as well. This succinct note not only tells her that you have plenty going on in your life, but it also creates a sense of urgency for her to give you a phone number. Once you have her digits, you can employ your artistry in talking to women to take it where you want to go. Just remember that your first phone call to her should generally be after ten o'clock when she is likely to be home in bed and more attentive to your seductive skills.

☆ Step 7: *Create a sense of urgency by presenting an exciting situation.*

Let me further elaborate on the importance of a sense of urgency. This goes back to the crucial step of knocking a woman off of her mark and making her more vulnerable to your desires. One way to illustrate such a scenario is putting up an ad that states you are looking for a date for an upcoming event. This works brilliantly in Los Angeles, where there are all types of festivities going on monthly that will draw a woman's interest. For the majority of you who are not living in Hollywood, I would suggest either researching special local events or making one up. This sparks a feeling of excitement that creates an escape from their reality and makes them want to do something out of their comfort zone.

The idea of dressing up for some type of glamorous gathering is intriguing to them, and many women will respond. Again, once a woman contacts you, give her the quick request for her phone number and the game is on. The fact that the event is on a specific timeline will motivate her to give out her number more quickly. When you speak to her, try to steer the conversation away from the event itself, whether it is legitimate or not. Refocus on setting the stage for an exciting time between you two, which is likely what she is looking for anyway. This may sound contradictory to my advice that honesty is the best policy, but I feel that rule mainly applies to major emotional matters. There is no harm in generating a little buzz in her mind to get her attention. If there is a true connection there, the initial contact will become irrelevant over time.

As you can see, the internet is a spectacular tool that provides you access to an endless supply of women who are just waiting to meet a man who will fulfill their wants and needs. If you are single and searching, you need to employ the power of the World Wide Web. If you use the techniques described in this book, soon you may discover a whole world of wide-eyed women tangled in the web of your desires. Hop on this superhighway and make all of your fantasies come true!

CHAPTER 37
Raising the Bar
☆ ☆ ☆

"Don't even think about it and just do it. If you don't, you'll be regret-
ting it the rest of the weekend."—Neil Strauss

If the internet is the superhighway to your dreams for meeting the women
you want, then the American bar and club scene is the alley of nightmares
in comparison. I realize that some guys enjoy success in picking up ladies at
these places, and at times I have been one of them, but it is a small percentage. In fact, there are times when I would rather study for the bar again than
go to a bar. It boggles my mind why so many men waste their time exploring
the nightlife scene in hopes of hooking up with a girl, then come out frustrated when it does not happen. Going to a bar expecting to take home a girl
is like going to Burger King expecting to take home a lobster. You are going
to the wrong place for the wrong thing, and you likely will not get things
your way.

Most women do not hit the night scene to find a guy, and even if they
secretly want to hook up, extraneous factors will likely marginalize your
chances of success. I do like to dress up and go enjoy the local nightlife once
in awhile, but I do not enter with the expectancy that I will meet a girl who

will fulfill my needs. If you are going to spend your precious time in bars and nightclubs, make sure your main goal is to simply enjoy the atmosphere and have a good time, either with friends, or entertaining yourself if you are on your own. That being said, I wanted to outline some guidelines so you can make the most out of your nightlife experience, and maximize your chances of meeting women in this tough environment.

If you are a guy who has tried to meet women at bars, you probably already know this from experience, but let me go through some reasons why it is their home court advantage. First of all, the prime factor, as always, is the social double standard that does not allow women to freely express their sexuality. I have explained this pretty thoroughly already, but it is their mentality that it is not okay to just randomly hook up with men. Additionally, their fear of being labeled a slut makes them apprehensive about their actions.

Obviously, a typical guy is not going up to a girl at a bar thinking that she will be a really great friend. If you are one of those rare men looking to meet close friends in the nightlife scene, there are far better venues to do so. Let us face the facts that when most men approach women in clubs, it is because they want to hook up with them. Because of the reasons I have discussed, a woman's natural inclination is to reject them.

In theory, it is easy for a woman to hook up if she really wants to. This is because guys are more outwardly sexual beings and are always looking to do so. Women generally prefer to be more secretive about their erotic pursuits than sleeping with a guy they meet at a bar. Even if a woman is looking for a good time, her fear of judgment, as well as the other obvious dangers may prevent her from pursuing it. That is why the internet is a far better place to meet girls than a disco.

Women simply go to bars for different reasons than the men who are looking to meet them. They are generally there to drink, dance, soak in the atmosphere, and hang out with friends. Keep in mind, those are the same things I advise you to do as a guy going out in that scene. The vital distinction is that, as a man, you are unlikely to reject a woman's advances. If you have tried talking to a girl at a bar, you know that her response may as well be a recorded message on an answering machine, because you hear the same things over and over. "I am here to hang out with my friends." "We are just here to dance." These are such carbon-copy responses that you would think that women were trained to say them since birth. Just like Burger King is not going to be grilling lobsters on their broiler any time soon, it is unlikely that girls will suddenly start going to bars with the mentality that they will not be leaving without a guy they meet there. I frankly feel that if girls want to dance with their friends so badly and are going to be so irritated by the guys who talk to them, they should just have a slumber party with music and boogie away.

Another reason why women are so unresponsive to men's desires in the nightlife setting is quite simply that so many of them are extremely insecure. It amazes me that even when we nicely approach a girl in a bar they often react rudely. This is a sign of their natural insecurity and low self-esteem. After all, shouldn't you be flattered when a guy expresses interest in you? I understand that they need to protect themselves and their image, but if they are out to have fun, they should at least be friendly. On the other hand, when a guy doesn't talk to them, girls wonder why they aren't getting any attention. It is simply ridiculous that so many ladies make the effort to dress up and look their best to attract the opposite sex but act frustrated when they are shown signs of this attraction. I firmly believe that many women go out just so they can get hit on so they can feel the power to refuse the men who do so.

To make things worse, even if a woman is genuinely interested in you, you may have the added obstacle of her jealous or overprotective friends. We all have heard the term "cock-blocks," and having to overcome the gauntlet of women that obstruct your path can be a formidable proposition. First of all, they all came to the bar together, and they do not want their friend to take off with some stranger -- understandably so. This protective attitude does make sense, especially because obvious biological differences make women more vulnerable to something dangerous happening, and they do not want to feel the guilt in case their friend gets hurt. There are also social reasons that make them want to safeguard their companion's reputation as not being "easy." This goes back to that infamous double standard.

Being protective of their girlfriend is reasonable, but not all of their intentions are so noble. A large reason that women are uncomfortable with one of their own talking to a guy at a bar is because of their inherent catty attitudes. This bizarre sense of competition does not really exist between men trying to meet girls because we understand each other's purpose. With guys, it is generally a friendly struggle because we do not want to get in the way of each other's success. When a girl sees someone in their group flirting with a guy who is interested in her, they often get jealous. They may feel inse-cure about why the man is not interested in them, or they may be envious that their friend is having more fun than they are. Even if you do feel things are going well with a girl, it is not unusual for her friend to pull her away. Why put yourself through these unnecessary difficulties when there are far better avenues where these obstacles do not exist?

I analogize these friends to an offensive line on the football field, where you are the linebacker and the woman you want is the quarterback you are trying to get to. Even the best at the position rarely break through the line to get a sack. Similarly, it is highly difficult to break through the barrier of friends who shield your desire to get her in the sack.

If you have not already experienced all of these difficulties yourself, I hope I have adequately described why bars and clubs are not the ideal venues to meet women. If you have been highly successful in these settings, I commend you because it is not easy, even for the best of us. I hate the term "pick-up artist" and I am not going to claim that I am an expert at picking up girls in bars, but I will share some strategies that I have utilized that allow me to have a great time, whether I am there alone or with my friends. I talked about creating your inner superhero. When you decide to go out to meet women, unleash these powers and exhibit your confidence.

☆ Rule 1: Develop a camaraderie with the other guys there.

It may sound unusual, but the best way to optimize your enjoyment in your nightlife is to first attempt to get in good with the guys in the place. Earlier in this book, I described the brotherhood of men, and you can use this to your advantage. When you can formulate camaraderie with the other guys at the establishment, you appear to be a popular figure there. Women are turned on by power, and this popularity can boost your image in their eyes. Simultaneously, when the guys feel comfortable around you, they will likely encourage your success. If they have girls in their group, it opens the doors to meeting them. Most men do not have the jealous inclinations that plague so many women, so working the scene and gaining the support of the men there can make you the life of the party. If you can project a charismatic image, then the women there will be fascinated by you.

☆ Rule 2: Approach her without hesitation.

When you do decide to talk to a girl at the bar, employ the methods I described in the Art of Talking to Women. The usage of those techniques differs according to the setting so here is how to use your skills in the nightlife scene. First thing is to make sure you approach them without hesitation. Women can sense awkwardness and discomfort so when you convey confidence, it immediately grabs their attention. If you are too cautious, you may overthink things and psych yourself out. I understand the prospect of approaching girls can be a chilling one for many men, but there is no room for nervousness in the game of meeting women. If you can train yourself to go up to women in a smooth and outgoing manner, you are way ahead of most men. Just remember to not take things personally if it does not go well. You are happy with yourself anyway and if she reacts well, it is a bonus. The absolute worst thing she can do is reject you, and if that happens, you're simply in the same position you were before. Too many guys look at the word "no" as a bullet to their heart.

☆ Rule 3: Do not constantly buy drinks for a girl.

There is one thing you can say to a girl that will almost be guaranteed to be met with approval and that is when you offer to buy her a drink, but I urge you not to make this mistake. As a general rule, I recommend that you never purchase beverages for a woman at a bar or club, unless she is a good friend of yours. On rare occasions, getting her that one extra drink may make the difference between taking her home and saying goodbye, but those are rare instances. On the whole, however, it is not a good idea, and is more likely to result in you having an empty wallet than a full bed. Buying girls drinks shifts the all-important power dynamic to her favor. When I talk to women about men who buy drinks for them, they usually talk about how pathetic these guys are and how no amount of money they spend on them will make them more interested. Remember that you want to present yourself in a manner where she is intrigued enough to prove her worth to you. To do this, you are better off showcasing your appealing personality than attempting to buy her attention. Buying drinks is an introductory tool, to be sure, but it is also a pathway to frustration that you should avoid.

☆ Rule 4: Say something that throws them off their mark.

After summoning up the courage to approach someone you are interested in, your initial statements are of vital importance and may make the difference between a night of passion and a night of rejection. When you open your mouth, make sure it is not a lame pick-up line or cheesy compliment. As I have mentioned repeatedly, any halfway-decent looking woman has heard every compliment imaginable, so do not waste your time flattering her and putting yourself in the same position as these other men, who likely failed in their intentions. Instead, tell them something that catches them off their guard and does not give them an opportunity to reject you. If you simply ask them how they are doing or if they want to talk, then they can easily blow you off. On the other hand, if you say something off-beat or funny, it not only knocks them out of their comfort zone, it intrigues them at the same time.

As I mentioned before, you can avoid opening the door to rejection by saying something where "no" is not a potential answer. For example, you can begin by asking if there are any cooler places to hang out that night of the week. This is a very innocuous statement that will not only be unthreatening to her or her friends, it will force her to stick around and give you an answer. Her answer is irrelevant, but it is the impact the statement makes on her that is important. It gives her the impression that you are accustomed to being in hipper places, and by that token, you must be a pretty cool guy. Once that initial exchange is complete, you can gauge her tone and body language. If she seems receptive, then you can take the conversation where you want to go.

Much of what comes out of your mouth upon meeting a woman depends on your personality and what you feel comfortable saying to get a favorable reaction. Tailor your game to your strengths. For example, I love pictures, so one of my favorite lines when I approach a girl is pulling out my camera and saying, "Hey, do you mind if I get a picture with you? I want to prove to my mom that I'm not gay." That one has worked brilliantly because it plays into a woman's psyche. You are indirectly complimenting her by asking for a picture. Most women love to be in front of the camera so you are appealing to that instinct. At the same time, you are showing your sense of humor and wit. It takes a confident guy to say something that ridiculous, but at the same time it makes her comfortable because it shows you do not take yourself too seriously. You may have seen me employ this technique on *Tyra*, and it enjoyed varying degrees of success, but it really works better in a more natural setting without the mechanics of a television camera filming. Most of the time, women become intrigued by my confidence as well as get a good laugh, and those are great icebreakers. Come up with your own unique approaches based on your persona. The key is to make the art of meeting women fun, instead of an endless game of frustration.

I could write an entire book on different things you can say to a girl upon meeting to capture her attention, but the underlying theme is that you want to say something that separates you from the rest of the men who have approached her. Additionally, you want to keep things light-hearted and funny. That way, at least you are entertaining yourself. Keep in mind that no matter how witty or charming you may come across, you face a high chance of rejection. Do not take it personally by getting angry or upset about it. As I explained earlier, various factors go into the reason so many girls turn down guys in a bar. It does not necessarily mean that she is not interested in you because if the setting were different, that same girl might give you a chance. If she is not receptive to your advances, just laugh it off and say something humorous or self-deprecating and move on. This will make her feel foolish because she is giving up an opportunity to meet a cool guy she could have had a great time with.

Now let me briefly address you female readers who are interested in a man's thought process when he is at a bar or club. It is true that many of them may be primarily concerned with sleeping with you when they talk to you, but above all, most guys simply just want to have a good time and enjoy the night out. For many men, the prospect of talking to women is a terrifying one, and they base their confidence on your reaction. That being said, unless someone is outwardly offensive to you, I think girls should be a little nicer when a guy makes an effort to talk to them.

Personally speaking, I am secure enough with myself to not worry about rejection. There is a chance you may encounter a shyer guy, and if you just blow him off, you may ruin his self-esteem to the point where he will be apprehensive about approaching another girl who may be more interested in him. I am not saying that you should engage in extensive conversation with somebody you have no attraction to, but at the very least show that you are flattered and kindly tell them you are there to have a good time with your friends. This will be much easier on him and will allow him to use his charms on somebody he eventually shares a connection with. Additionally, there may come a day when men no longer find you so attractive, and you will look back and wish that guys would hit on you. When you act bitchy or aloof about a guy's advances, you are really making yourself look like a miserable, insecure person, and I believe you end up having less of a good time as a result.

My mentality when I am rejected by a woman is that she is not good enough for me anyway, and I genuinely believe that. It may seem arrogant, but it is this belief that has enabled me to achieve a high degree of success in getting girls without getting flustered or feeling dejected. I just know that no matter how skilled you are at seducing women, there is no logical pattern that will guarantee you success at a bar. On the same night, you can walk up to a supermodel who is really nice to you, and you can approach an overweight, bucktoothed girl with an oversized mullet and meet refusal. Women are bizarre creatures when it comes to reacting to a man's advances, and much of their reaction depends on their mood and the environment. That is why I do not take things that seriously if they don't go well.

☆ Rule 5: Do not be intimidated by a beautiful woman.

While I am on this topic, let me address those of you who get scared to speak to women who appear too attractive to be attainable. One of my number-one rules is to never be intimidated by a beautiful woman. You should never feel that any girl is too good for you. Generally speaking, she will not be any more or less inclined to give you a hostile response than an average-looking girl. As I explained previously, beautiful women are usually more insecure because they are so used to being judged by their looks. Sometimes, they may overcompensate by being friendlier than normal. Since most guys are too scared to talk to them, if you can go up to a hot girl without fear, then you should garner her respect and her attention. Additionally, the more you practice talking to gorgeous girls, the more comfortable you will become around them and the more confident you will become as a person.

When you decide to approach a woman, you want to give off the vibe that it would be her pleasure to be with you. Give her a back-handed compliment that neutralizes the importance of her looks. If women are going to be so insecure about a man's advances, you might as well play off that insecurity and use it to your own advantage. Go up to her and tell her that she looks "really intelligent" or like "a nice person." This will throw her off her mark because those are not usually the traits immediately associated with beautiful women. She will wonder if you are serious for one thing, and at the same time, she will question the status of her own appearance. This moment of vulnerability may cause her to lower her guard and try to find out what you really feel about her. This gives you the window to work your magic.

You can even take a more indirect method in bringing out this insecurity. Sometimes I go up to a sexy lady and ask why every girl I have spoken to in the place is so superficial and obsessed with attractiveness. This makes it appear as if I am above those shallow motives and am looking to find a more complete person. Since I am not drooling over her looks, she may want to demonstrate her depth of character, thus giving me a chance to highlight my own strengths. When you are attempting to meet a woman, a large part of your success will depend on making yourself so interesting in the opening moments that she is fascinated enough not to reject you. Most men do not get past this early stage, but if you do, anything can happen.

☆ Rule 6: When approaching a group, start by talking to someone you find less attractive.

While it is imperative that you not be too scared to speak to good-look-ing girls, another strategy in getting to them is to approach the friends you are less attracted to. This is a classic tactic that really confuses and frustrates the type of women who are used to being the center of attention. Generally speaking, hot women often go out with friends who are not as attractive as they are. We have all seen the perfect specimen that looks like she stepped out of a Vogue magazine out with her overweight friend who looks like she has been cleaning out the Hershey's catalog. I am not going to be completely cynical and say they do this to avoid competition and reinforce the spotlight on themselves, but it is sometimes the case.

Whatever the reason may be, if you begin talking to the girl who is not expecting to be hit on, it not only catches her off guard, but it also sets off the insecurity of the one who is accustomed to the adulation. As you work your charms, the one you are really interested in may compete for your interest and you can gradually refocus on her after she is already knocked off her high horse. I realize that all of this sounds really shallow, but, as I said, the bar scene is not exactly an ideal place to make genuine connections anyway, so you may as well have fun basking in the superficiality of the environment.

☆ Rule 7: Find parties where the theme involves beautiful women.

Now that you understand some techniques that will make your outings more spectacular, make sure you choose the proper venues to exploit your skills. If you are insistent on going to bars, you might as well go the places where your chances at success are maximized. Research the local papers that detail the nightlife scene and the special events that are taking place. Try to find parties hosted by models or with some type of theme involving sexy sirens. These types of gatherings are good on multiple levels. By being in this environment, you become more comfortable with being around beautiful women, and soon you will be more relaxed in approaching them. The girls who are normally used to standing out in the crowd are in a setting where others look equally as good, so they will not have the advantage of being the focus of every man's flirtations. Additionally, models are generally trained to be social and friendly, so they will likely be more amicable than a less attractive girl just hanging out with friends.

I have been spoiled in this regard because I live in Hollywood, where the majority of the women in the country who want to become models reside, so occasions like this take place regularly. If you happen to live in Los Angeles or are visiting the city, you have an even more exciting opportunity, and that is to party with the porn stars. Yes, the very women whom men around the world drool over on their television and computer screens almost all live in Southern California. As you can imagine, these are some of the most exciting women in the world to party with. I am friends with a number of girls in the industry and often attend these events, which occur frequently in L.A. I have hooked up with more girls at these parties than going to the generic local taverns. The majority of these girls are the absolute epitome of the hot, insecure but friendly goddesses who can cater to all of your fantasies.

Porn starlets are usually really nice and fun-loving and are not so consumed by the pretenses and cautions of a typical girl at a bar. Because they literally put it all out there, they are less prone to judgment. They love attention, but are not as guarded about that desire. Moreover, they will play off the most outrageous things you say to them and have fun with it instead of being offended. If you are in the LA area, make sure you look up these adult industry events online or in the local guides, and do not forget to bring your camera because they can be the party experience of a lifetime.

I understand that the majority of you do not live in Los Angeles, but the general idea I am trying to convey is that no matter where you live, you should focus your nights out on locations that will have a festive, escapist atmosphere where girls will be open to doing something wild. Obviously, keep an eye out for bachelorette parties that are rolling through the bars you visit, and attempt to mingle with any of the ladies who are part of the group. These are prime occasions where women let loose and are much more inclined to do something out of the realm of their everyday existence. If you can show that you are an exciting person to be around, then they may look to you as their entertainment.

You should also look for special events where the theme is risqué, such as costume parties, Mardi Gras celebrations, and the like. There is a reason that women wear really revealing things on Halloween and feel free to kiss random men on spring break, and it goes back to their true desires being repressed because of social restrictions and their own fears. The ultimate institutions that display this type of escapism and sexual liberation are swinger parties and strip bars. I will go into greater detail about the joys of these settings as you read on. Being in a surreal environment where it is acceptable to be liberated allows them to unleash their fantasies. Just remember to be intelligent about where you choose to party because if you are at the right place at the right time, then you may share in their dreams and fulfill your own.

Another prime locale to meet women ready to have a good time is a singles bar, particularly those that have plenty of older women. I will dedicate a separate chapter to describing the advantages of dating these mature maidens. Look up what bars and clubs are known for a thriving singles scene because you know that there will be women eager to make new connections who are not ashamed to admit it. If you are on a dating website, they will generally have frequent singles events where you can mingle with other members. These are tremendous opportunities to meet the girls who spark your interest on your computer screen, and they cannot use the excuse that they are just there to hang out with friends or dance.

☆ Rule 8: Dressy sexy to showcase your best attributes.

Now that you know where to go and what to do, here are some added tips on how to make yourself as appealing as possible. I explained to you the importance of having some slick and sexy clothes in your closet, and when you are out to meet women, dressing nice will put you far ahead of most men. The average guy has no clue how to dress in a manner that maximizes his appearance. If you wear something cool that highlights your features and your personality, it will reflect in your confidence.

I also recommend that you always keep a camera in your pocket when you go out. I already discussed one of my favorite introductions with the ladies, and you may similarly find that this camera can be a valuable tool in breaking the ice. When you are interested in taking pictures, it shows women that you are excited enough about your life to capture the moment. They love the ego-boost of being in photos, and most men do not pay attention to such matters. Soon, not only will you have memories you can look back on and smile, there will be women who will want to be part of these joyous recollections.

☆ Rule 9: Create a memorable business card.

Another introductory tool that has worked wonders for me is my over-the-top business card that was specially highlighted on *The Tyra Banks Show*. You can see pictures of this card on any of my online profiles or websites, but if you have not seen it, let me explain. This is not the generic business card that I would hand to potential employers, but an attention-grabbing symbol of my confidence and excitement towards life. On one side is a picture of me with my shirt off showing off my physique as well as a list of the things I do, ranging from attorney to model to self-help guru to massage service. On the other side is a picture of me with two beautiful blonde porn stars, Jesse Jane and Carmen Luvana, with my contact information and the tagline, "Make all your fantasies come true."

Needless to say, this sparks a woman's fascination on multiple levels. I have even had women go out of their way to approach me just to keep the card as a souvenir. It showcases my strengths, such as my education, my body, and my ability to aid them in becoming happier with themselves. In mere seconds, I convey that I am smart, well-built, great at massages, and an all-around self-assured guy. The fact that I am pictured with two gorgeous ladies shows that I am able to get hot women and not intimidated or shy around girls. It accomplishes more than any pick-up line ever could. Even if you do not hook up with this girl, it at least makes you memorable and separates you from the bland characters she usually comes across. Remember, once you can get past the initial stage of grabbing a woman's interest, you have the power to take the conversation where you want it to go.

Having a card like this in your arsenal can be a terrific ice breaker for you as well. I would suggest putting a picture on it that showcases your best look and words that highlight your strengths as a person. This card can encapsulate your persona and elevate a woman's level of intrigue. You can get a specialized glossy business card designed by a professional and print out a thousand copies for less than a hundred dollars, and the benefits can be priceless.

☆ Rule 10: Learn to go out alone.

Obviously, if you are at a club with your friends, your primary focus will be to have a good time with those you arrived with, but I also suggest exploring the nightlife scene on your own. This goes back to the importance of building individual strength and being comfortable with the idea of creating your own excitement. When you are by yourself at a bar, you are forced to be more social and you may break out of your comfort zone by talking to people you normally would not when with your buddies. You are not subject to anybody's restrictions and are free to roam and talk to or leave with anybody you choose to.

Some girls may find you creepy for being out on your own, but when you are happy with yourself and can show that to others, that apprehension will disappear. Many women are intrigued by guys out on their own because they may appear mysterious and sexy. They may even feel less threatened by you because you are not accompanied by a group of hormonal guys. It takes a strong person to explore the nightlife by himself and when you can approach women like this, you will feel your self-confidence grow, as well as the amount of women who find you attractive. Personally speaking, I have hooked up with many more women at clubs going out alone than when I am with others.

☆ Rule 11: Go out with an attractive platonic female friend.

As important as it is for you to develop your comfort level by going out on your own to thrive in the bar scene, there can be no more worthy aid in helping you to meet women than having a beautiful platonic female friend with you. Women are usually fascinated by guys who attract other gorgeous girls. If you have one by your side, they may become interested in what makes you attractive to her. On top of that, when you have a girl friend with you, the women you approach will usually be more comfortable with talking to you. It makes you appear much less threatening because another hot girl is already out with you and having a good time. When I go out with a wing woman, I find that I have a much higher rate of success in hooking up with other girls. Also, remember that it is vital to make things clear with your friend that things are completely platonic so jealousy or unnecessary drama does not surface. If you have an uncomplicated relationship with a female best friend, then she may be instrumental in luring other ladies into your life.

Although I have outlined numerous strategies to maximize your enjoyment when going to bars or clubs, I still want to stress that the nightlife scene is not the ideal location to meet a woman. If you do choose to do so, however, I hope some of the techniques I have described will help you in finding what you want. I have included a summarized list of tools that can help you at the bar at the end of this book. Hopefully, it will raise the bar of your success in this difficult setting.

CHAPTER 38
It's Not All About the Money
☆ ☆ ☆

"I am not interested in money. I just want to be wonderful."—*Marilyn Monroe*

It is a place nearly every adult male has visited at some point or another. For some, it is a place where dreams come true, while for others it is a sad reminder of what a nightmare their personal relationships have become. For most, it is just a place to chill out with your buddies and have a great time. Whether you are there purely for entertainment or out of desperation, frustration, loneliness or depression, a strip club can be an outlet for a variety of emotions. What most fail to realize is that going to these bars can also be an educational experience. Yes, that is not a misprint. Now, I am not saying you are going to learn about quantum physics from getting a lap dance or discover the theory of gravity by staring at a girl hanging on a pole. What you can learn at a gentleman's club is how to become comfortable and confident with beautiful women.

The notion that you can gain knowledge on how to interact with the ladies from a bunch of girls who are eager to raid your wallet may seem absurd to you, so let me explain. While the regular bar scene is a woman's home court advantage, the strip bar is a place full of beautiful women where men are in charge. The girls are there for your pleasure, and they rely on you not only for their finances, but also for their enjoyment while they are there. First of all, while in regular bars women generally have their guard up, the best thing about these gentlemen's clubs is that the girls are trained to be social and friendly. Without that initial barrier, you can utilize your verbal flair with the ladies, and you shyer types can learn this valuable attribute from being surrounded by women who have no choice but to give you the opportunity to talk to them.

I have already explained numerous methods you can employ to attract more women, and strip bars are a perfect place to test these skills. Reading a book can help you, but confidence with women mainly comes from experience with interacting with them. Talking to gorgeous women in sexy clothing can boost your self-assurance and make you more outgoing when approaching ladies in other venues. Even if you are initially uncomfortable with women, these girls are accustomed to dealing with men who feel awkward around them so they will not look down at you because of it.

Since the strip club is already a sexual environment where the women need to intermingle with the men, you can be much more bold and risqué with your banter without being called rude or obnoxious. Obviously, you need to exercise restraint and walk that fine line by being outgoing and funny without appearing crude and belligerent. You can say some raunchy, off-the-wall things, but as long as you do it with a wink and a smile, you can keep a woman amused and interested. Showcase your charm and sense of humor without being rude or mean, and you may find that the women come to you for entertainment and not the other way around. Despite their tough façade, at the end of the day, these girls are only human, and they will be responsive and attracted to a man who presents himself with a charismatic, sexy personality.

While strippers have a bad reputation for being soulless, money-hungry sluts who are abused, insecure, and hate men, not all of these women fall into that stereotype. It is true that most of them have been victims of some type of childhood abuse, but many of them are really fun-loving, cool people who are actually much more enjoyable to spend time with than "regular girls." Possibly because they have been through so many tough times, they are more empathetic and responsive to a man's needs. Additionally, they tend to be much more open-minded and nonjudgmental than the average woman. Even though most of them have low self-esteem, somewhere inside of each of them is a girl who struggles for acceptance and yearns to meet a man who can understand them without being condemnatory. If you can connect with that piece of their heart, even if it is at her workplace, then I promise you that she will want you, not just your money.

Let me illustrate to you my own experiences at these clubs and how going to them has helped strengthen my skills with the ladies. If you recall my chapter on the Making of Shawn Valentino, I discussed a crucial turning point moment where my friend and I chose to go to a strip club instead of going to our favorite college restaurant. That day, a gorgeous Turkish belly dancer was all over me, and she was the one who begged for a date. This encounter provided me with a great confidence boost because here was a woman who men spent money on to satisfy their own fantasies, and she was fantasizing about me. It may seem silly or irrelevant, but sometimes it is just one event that can trigger your self-confidence and give you the motivation to explore your dreams without worrying about the consequences.

That day, I was with a friend, and I feel that going to a strip club with your friends can be an incredibly fun experience, but soon I discovered that I could have just as much fun going on my own. I would put on a flashy outfit that showed off the body I worked hard to maintain, and I would go in with an edgy attitude that fascinated the girls. As I have stressed from the beginning of this book, doing things by yourself may seem unusual or scary to you, but if you are comfortable with who you are and are able to create your own excitement, you will always be happy. When I was at these clubs by myself, I was forced to become even more outgoing than I already am, and I harnessed my charm and my wit when talking to women. Girls are obviously there to make money, but they cannot get paid if they do not approach men. Once they came to me, I made sure that my personality radiated such a magnetic excitement that they could not help but be attracted to it. Remember that women need security, but they crave excitement.

I consistently went to a variety of clubs every week for a few months straight, and I would practice my lines to the point where I could seamlessly talk to even the most beautiful women in any setting. Soon my confidence reached such a high level that I would literally go up to a girl on stage and smoothly ask her out on a date, and amazingly, many times it worked! Strippers like to tell themselves as well as the attendees that they do not cross the line and meet customers outside a club. The catch was that I was not a customer, but went to the club presenting myself as a sexy, fun-loving guy who loves women and was just having a good time. It got to the point where I was dating a few different dancers from various clubs. My main problem was making sure the girls I was dating from the same bar did not get jealous. With my newfound magnetism, I employed the tactics that made me so successful at these clubs in other places, and soon I had such a huge list of phone numbers that there were not enough days in the week to keep track of the women I could be dating.

You may notice there is one thing I haven't mentioned. It's what most men generally go to strip clubs for, and that is to spend money to get lap dances. Despite the numerous women I have dated who work at these establishments, I never spent any money on them. That is the golden rule, because once you start paying for lap dances, the women see you as a customer and the power dynamic shifts to their side. The idea of emptying my pockets just to get teased has never been very appealing to me, and I find it completely appalling that there are so many men who blow their hard-earned money on a cheap thrill. I know from personal experience that you are better off not spending your money at these clubs. Instead, use these places as a playground where you can enhance your game, and then utilize your skills to woo women and really fulfill your fantasies. Not only that, you can get to know some really fun, sexy girls who will see you as charming playboy, instead of just a personal ATM machine. You may even surprise yourself with the type of relationships you can form at a strip club.

They say you can make friends in the unlikeliest of places, and I must admit that I never imagined that the adult institutions young boys drool over would one day become places where I would meet some great friends. Being an open-minded person, I have become close friends with many of these girls, and they are some of the coolest people I have ever met. Since they live outside of everyday social boundaries themselves, they are generally open to all types of fun and are not worried about what people think of their actions. These friends have not only been incredible to party with, but also have stuck by me in tough times and have been loyal supporters through all my ups and downs. Since most of them have survived a rough life, they are more understanding of people's problems.

Of course, you need to use common sense and recognize that it may not be a good idea to make a heavy emotional investment with a stripper because these women usually do not have a lifestyle that is conducive to a serious relationship. The idea of falling for a stripper may sound ridiculous to you, but once you get to know these girls, you may find their allure enticing. They know how to look and dress sexy and live out the fantasies that other girls may be too shy to. At the same time, they tend to be much more fun and dynamic than a woman with a more vanilla background. What man doesn't want those things? Unfortunately, like any double-edged sword, that comes with a price. The very things that make them cool also generally make them mentally unstable and insecure about their self-worth, and those are not the traits of a woman you want to be serious about.

Believe me when I tell you that if you are looking to enhance your talent in seducing women, strip clubs are an excellent place to do so. Let me outline a strategy on how you can maximize your experience at these places. Look into that closet of flashy clothes you should have in your arsenal and pick out an outfit that looks sexy and cool to make you stand out in the crowd. You may even want to pull out the shades to give you the mysterious appearance that makes the girls intrigued. Remember that you are in a room where most of the girls are either nude or in lingerie or bikinis so you do not need to worry about them thinking your outfit is outlandish. Enter the club with a confident strut and study the scene a bit. Most of these bars have a set of tables or chairs where most of the dancers hang out when things are not busy. Find a seat in that area because every time the girls need to relax, they will come to you. Since it is a region of the club where they aren't hustling so much, it gives you an opening to showcase your magnetism and make a girl realize that you are there to entertain her, not to be a customer.

What works in your favor is that strip clubs are a classic place where other men's weaknesses are your strength. Most guys there come dressed as complete scrubs so when you appear well put together, it will make you stand out in the crowd. Not only will you look more attractive than the typical customer, the fact that you are not blindly spending money on these girls will actually earn their respect. As I said earlier, I have been close friends with many strippers, and they usually find the guys who throw money at them pathetic and lonely. I suggest that you go to the club with not much more money than you need for the entrance fee and a couple of drinks, and leave your ATM and credit cards at home. That way, you do not even have the option of wasting your cash. While some dancers are there just to make money and resent anybody not spending any, many of the girls will see you as a cool guy who has a charming persona and will go to you when they are not hustling for dollars.

I have already discussed numerous techniques for talking to women with confidence. You should use these tips, but also formulate your own unique persona that you are comfortable with and which draws women to you. As with anything else, the more practice you have, the better you will get at it, and soon it will be effortless. Just make sure you steer the conversation away from the topic of money. You can even mention how most of the guys who waste their paychecks there are dorks. This indirectly makes it clear to them that you are above that. One strategy I use is talking about how I spent the past weekend going to swinger parties, or I tell the girls about a hedonistic vacation spot I recently went to. It helps that I actually have experienced lots of wild adventures, but even if you spent the past weekend watching porn on your computer, give them a story that sounds exciting. This not only makes them recognize that a lap dance presents minimal value to you, it also makes you appear as a man who gets lots of women and goes to much wilder venues than a strip club. Once this power is vanquished, she may look up to you as the sexy object of her affection.

So the next time you and your friends decide to have a night at the strip club, go out and have a great time with the guys, but also utilize the experience to strengthen your skills with the ladies. Even though most people have the preconceived notion that strippers care about nothing more than taking your money, once they realize that you're not giving them that option, you may find there is more to them than meets the eye. As long as you keep your wallet in check and concentrate on developing and using your skills, you will discover that gentleman's clubs are not just all about the money.

CHAPTER 39
The Awards Show Where You Are the Winner
☆ ☆ ☆

"Las Vegas looks the way you'd imagine heaven must look at night."—
Chuck Palahniuk

One of my main passions is watching movies, but I have never been one that has been interested in the Academy Awards or the other prize ceremonies. The events are too pompous, political, and self-congratulatory for my tastes. Even worse are the gag-inducing pre-show specials critiquing the clothing and gossiping about the celebrities. There is one film awards celebration, however, that I enjoy enough to attend every year, and it does not contain all of the pretenses and contrivances of shows like the Oscars. This annual gala is the Adult Video News Awards, the most elusive and exclusive honor that one can receive…in the porn world!

Why is there a chapter on a festival commemorating erotic films in a self-help book? Let me explain. Everone knows that Las Vegas is a legendary party place all year round where debauchery, decadence and delight permeate the atmosphere. Just imagine the Vegas setting and mentality and add to it hundreds of sexy adult video stars who are completely accessible and ready to party. The women much of the world fantasizes about are in the flesh in front of your very eyes. The beauty of it is that anybody can attend the festivities, and I am recommending that any man should do so at least once in his life. I know just about every guy dreams of going to the Playboy Mansion, but getting an invitation to one of its exclusive parties is difficult. The AVN Awards is an event where you can capture a similar ambiance to being in the Mansion and it is open to the public for a reasonable price.

This event takes place around the second weekend of January in Las Vegas, and it is not merely an award show but a week of events. There is an expo that goes on all week, and it is simply an awe-inspiring experience. It is a man's fantasy come true. There are gorgeous women in incredibly sexy outfits surrounding you everywhere. The mood is jovial, as everybody is happy not only to be in Vegas, but to be so close to the women of their dreams. The adult video industry is a multi-billion-dollar business and they go all out in presenting an unforgettable spectacle. You quite simply have to see it to believe it. If you have a favorite pornstar, she will likely be there signing autographs and taking pictures. All of the girls are extremely friendly and in high spirits. Once you pay the admission fee, you get all of the photos, signatures, and free stuff you want. There are all kinds of complimentary adult gifts passed out at the expo, from DVDs to shirts and more.

Everybody knows about the world-famous Vegas nightlife, and there is no week where the clubbing is as thrilling as AVN week. There are adult industry-sponsored events going on all over the town, so you can literally party with the porn stars. These girls are some of the coolest and most fun people in the world so it truly is an opportunity of a lifetime. Unlike typical girls with attitudes you meet at bars, these women are trained to be social and are generally always cordial when you approach them. Additionally, since they are drinking and it is their biggest week of the year, if the cards are lined up right, you can redefine the phrase getting lucky in Vegas!

By the time you get to the awards show itself, it is almost an afterthought because there are so many other events leading up to it. Although you probably don't care who is going to win Best Actress or Best Anal Queen, it is an entertaining show where the performers are self-deprecating, and often deliver hilarious speeches as they pick up their trophies. It does not have the pretentious atmosphere of a typical awards show. The real attraction of the awards is the red carpet arrival. You just cannot imagine the surreal setting where sexy starlets in revealing evening gowns are everywhere. To describe it further will not do it justice—you simply have to witness it for yourself.

The photo collection you take home from this extraordinary experience is just unparalleled. You can literally get hundreds of pictures with some of the hottest women in the world, and given their line of work, they know how to pose in front of the camera. This is a week where you want to make sure you constantly have the batteries charged in your camera or you will miss out on something special. Your internet profiles will be spiced up so much that every guy will consider you their hero. As a bonus, the pictures you'll get with the hot women can be used to make other girls jealous. Remember the psychology of the game. When a woman sees you with other beautiful women, she will be intrigued by what makes you so attractive to them. You do not need to tell these girls where you took these pictures or let them know the secret that any guy can get them!

Let me stress that if you are a man who is happily in a serious monogamous relationship, then I do not advise you to make this adult pilgrimage unless you have a really cool, open-minded partner. If you are not, the major reason I want all of you to experience this event is because it will open your mind and expose you to a whole world of possibilities. When you are surrounded by such an enormous quantity of breathtaking beauties, you realize that you should never be obsessed or depressed over one girl. I'm not saying that you will hook up with a porn star there, but the sheer magnitude of lovely ladies gives you hope that there are always plenty of options for you. Those of you obsessing over finding a relationship will learn that being single does not mean a path to loneliness, but that it can be a celebration of freedom to live adventurously without deception or jealousy. For all of these reasons and more, you need to attend the awards show where you are the winner!

CHAPTER 40
Kross My Heart
☆ ☆ ☆

"Who's the fairest of them all?"—Snow White

Since I have been fortunate enough to meet so many gorgeous women in my life, you might be wondering who I feel is the most beautiful of them all. Beauty is so subjective, and somone who is attractive to me may not be so to another. It is true that I have been lucky enough to come across some of the most stunning females in the universe. A list of some of the more famous lovely ladies I have encountered include Pamela Anderson, Jessica Alba, Britney Spears, Jenna Jameson, Stacy Keibler, Tyra Banks, Kirsten Price, Jennifer Love Hewitt, Trish Stratus, Torrie Wilson, Sunny Leone, Jenny McCarthy and countless others. Additionally, after traveling so much and living in Hollywood for a few years, I have constantly come across hundreds of women who may not be so well-known but are no less beautiful. I am attracted to ladies of all ages and backgrounds, so to name one woman who stands out above all the rest is an extremely difficult proposition.

If I were to choose one who is perhaps the fairest of them all, however, it may have to be Kayden Kross. You may have heard of her, but if you have not, you owe it to your eyes to look her name up on the internet and discover for yourself. The aesthetic appeal of this captivating creature is simply unparalleled. The very sight of her luminous looks is enough to take your breath away. My favorite type of woman is the blonde-haired, blue-eyed, baby-faced beauty, and Kayden is the absolute epitome of this archetype. She is a Barbie doll come to life if there ever was one.

As good as she looks in pictures, to truly appreciate how stunning she is, you simply have to see for yourself in person. The camera simply cannot capture such perfection. You see that I am struggling to use various adjectives in my attempts to illustrate her appearance, but when you are in her presence, pure superlatives are rendered meaningless. I could say she is physically flawless, sensationally sexy, or breathtakingly beautiful, but none of those descriptions would be enough. I would not be exaggerating when I say that she makes Jessica Alba and Britney Spears look like your regular girls next door. Prior to meeting Kayden, I thought that Trish Stratus and Stacy Keibler would be the most gorgeous women I would ever meet in my life. Kayden combines Stacy's all-American beauty with Trish's sultry sex appeal so you can say she is a cross, or Kross, between two of the hottest women alive. So if I had to answer your question as to who would be my most magnificent fantasy maiden, it would be Kayden Kross.

Most amazing of all is that she is also an incredibly sweet and down-to-earth person in real life. This goes back to what I said about the lack of logic in the game of pursuing females. You can approach an overweight girl with missing teeth and she may blow you off. At the same time, you can meet somebody who is essentially physically flawless and she will be receptive and respectful. I have met Kayden many times, everywhere from conventions to clubs, and she is always extremely friendly. Not only that, this girl appears to be highly intelligent and well-spoken, traits you rarely find given her profession.

Oh, yes, I forgot to mention that Kayden Kross is an adult video starlet, or a porn star. If you read my description and didn't know who she is, you may have assumed that I was describing some fair princess from a fairy tale and not a woman who does adult movies. It just goes to show that you should never judge somebody by what they do or the lifestyle they live, but for who they are and the nature of their personality. The mainstream populace may consider her trashy, but one thing I have learned in life is that the line between "classy" and "trashy" is much thinner than people like to imagine.

In fact, people often see my pictures and hear about my stories and write me off as a shallow sleazeball. Some of you may have had preconceived notions yourself or have seen me called out on national television by the world's biggest supermodel. Those who look past the image and really know me understand that I am a very caring person who is really close to my family and friends. I do not really know Kayden well, but just from our brief encounters, I have found her much nicer and more well-informed than many people society would deem more acceptable.

The lesson here is to keep an open mind about not only the type of women you approach, but the type of people you become friends with, because you never know what quality people you are missing out on meeting. Do not let stereotypes cloud your judgment. That being said, because most of you are not lucky enough to live in Los Angeles and may never meet Miss Kross, I highly advise that you take advantage of modern technology and look her up, but also realize this astonishing creature is also an outstanding human being. After all, isn't that every man's fantasy?

Speaking of fantasies, you realize by now that one of my goals in this book is to convince you to live them out instead of just dreaming about them. The fact that I have met this girl so many times and not attempted to hook up with her may seem to contradict that that. On the contrary, sometimes your fantasies are equally as valuable if they remain that way. Just knowing that there are women like Kayden, who are beautiful, nice, and smart, gives me motivation not only to exercise and look my best, but also to reach a level of success where they will be fantasizing about me, not the other way around. So even if you do not hook up with the girl of your dreams, you can use that ideal to stimulate you to greater accomplishments. Kayden, if you are reading this, believe it or not, you have played a part in me getting this book published, Kross my heart.

CHAPTER 41
Older Is Better
☆ ☆ ☆

"A diplomat is a man who always remembers a woman's birthday but never remembers her age."—Robert Frost

For hundreds of years, men have enjoyed the luxury of being able to freely date younger women. It has been considered socially acceptable for guys to be with girls despite an age gap. In contrast, women did not enjoy the same freedom to be seen with younger men because it was deemed strange and not conducive to a long-term relationship. There are various reasons for this dichotomy in social attitudes that existed for so long. Primarily, it was because men were the dominant gender and many preferred to be with youthful, "more beautiful" women. Additionally, since women age faster aesthetically and have biological time clocks that men do not have, it became expected they would get settled earlier than their male counterparts. With societal changes over the past decades that have bridged gender inequalities, it has become not only accepted but fashionable for older women to date younger men. The myth of the "cougar" on the prowl has now become entrenched in our culture. Men should be thankful for these advances because dating older women may bring you more pleasure than you can ever imagine.

Now, I am not going be dishonest and tell you that I am not attracted to the appeal of a young fresh-faced beauty. At the same time, however, younger women generally lack the maturity and sex appeal that comes with experience, and their personalities often erase their attractive features. I personally prefer dating women a few years older than I am, and I have enjoyed my best experiences with them. When dealing with ladies that are more mature, you typically encounter fewer mind games and less nonsense than you might have to worry about with someone less experienced. Additionally, women typically reach their sexual peak in their mid-thirties and beyond; thus, they are not only more experienced, but they are also much more comfortable with their sexuality.

Women in their early to mid-twenties are often looking for a knight in shining armor who will sweep them off their feet and be "the one" who will eventually take care of them emotionally and financially. With these high expectations come added pressures that a man might not necessarily want to complicate their lives. Younger women also tend to be more insecure and unsure about what they want. Guys are endlessly trying to figure out exactly what it is women are looking for, and trying to date younger girls can become a frustrating task. I have already described numerous strategies to minimize the drama in your dating life and those apply for women of all ages, but when you are open to dating older women, you may find the experience much less complicated.

Let me outline the advantages of dating older women by describing the two major types that you may come into contact with. Just to illustrate my point, I am assuming that you are a man in his twenties not ready for a serious relationship and looking to meet women over thirty-five. The first major category is composed of the ones who are already divorced and have children. Women generally get married and procreate at an earlier age, so most of them may fall into this description. Since they have already been through the stability of a serious relationship, they are much more likely to want to enjoy the freedom and spontaneity of single life. They may not desire the drama that comes with commitment because they have already experienced it, and it did not work. Obviously, there was a reason they got divorced, and they may want to avoid the problems and the pain.

For a guy, that eliminates much of the expectations that come with a girl who may be looking to get married soon. It also means much less pretense and games to get what you want because an older woman may be looking for the same thing you are: drama-free fun. Now that these older women are newly single and in their sexual peak, they may be much more apt to want to live out the fantasies they did not experience when they were younger. Those dreams could include you, so you should not be turned off by a woman who says she is divorced or has children because she may not necessarily be searching for a husband or father for her kids.

The second major type is the woman who has not gotten married and has no children. These women are likely to be ambitious and financially and emotionally independent. They may feel they do not need to have a man in their life and are happier on their own. Given that it is still unusual for a woman in her mid-thirties to have never been married, it is highly likely she will be much more open-minded and secure than the norm. She also simply might not be looking for a serious relationship because she is so focused on her career. This means she is much less likely to be a gold-digger or expecting you to take care of her. She does not have as much baggage as a woman who has gone through the pain of a divorce, and she is much more likely to have her own place where you can enjoy each other's company without having to worry about babysitters or children that may prevent you from seeing her. Add the fact that she is entering her sexual prime and it gives you the perfect opportunity to meet a sexy, mature, financially stable, liberated individual who could be a terrific dating partner.

No matter what the situation is, my experience with this dating demographic is that they are generally much more pleasant to talk to and spend time with. Unlike younger girls who often are confused about their needs, older women are much more likely to know what they are looking for and unafraid to express it. Additionally, because so many men are entranced by youth and beauty, a more mature lady is likely to be more appreciative of a man's attention. As we all know, because of society's emphasis on a woman's youthful appearance, they are much less at ease with the aging process than men. When a younger man expresses interest in them, it makes them feel more attractive. They may be just looking for an energetic, exuberant guy to add some flavor to their lives. If you can uncover the fountain of youth for an older woman, she may show her gratitude in ways you can never imagine.

That is not to say that dating older women is not without its disadvantages. Their "experience" can often come with plenty of baggage that you do not want to deal with. She may be jaded or harbor anger toward men because of her separation from her spouse. Additionally, her kids may consume her life to the point where she never has time to get together. Another potential problem arises when she is looking for a father to her kids, which is a role I do not recommend you fill unless it is a really special situation. Those women who have not been married nor have kids may be stressed out that their biological clock is ticking. An older woman also may be really uncomfortable with the aging process and upset that her looks and charm are not as effective as when they were younger. She may also feel awkward being seen with a younger man. This may make her moody and unappealing to spend time with.

Despite these potential problems, I still highly encourage you to explore dating older women. You still need to apply the same principles you do with a younger girl, and that is to know what you are looking for and communicate that honestly to her. Additionally, use your common sense as the relationship progresses if it goes beyond casual dating. If you plan on settling down with her, make sure you are comfortable with the fact that she will age faster than you. Do not get attached to her out of the sheer novelty of the situation. Make sure that the basic components of a good relationship and "real love" exist so you can sustain your connection even if the physical attraction lessens. Otherwise, you may not only be hurting yourself down the line, but it will have a devastating effect on her as well.

I also strongly suggest that you do not get too serious about a single mother because this situation brings all types of responsibilities and hassles that you may not be ready for. First of all, there may be a biological father in the picture, and that can complicate your relationship with her. You also may have to accept the role of father figure for the child and all of the financial and emotional pressures that go with that. Not only that, you may face confrontation from the kids if they are confused about their loyalties between you and the actual father. Now, I am not saying that you absolutely never get involved with single mothers, but be aware about the complications that come with the commitment. There is nothing more harmful than hurting a woman who is trying to raise kids on her own because it affects her and the children. Use your common sense and evaluate the situation before settling down.

Overall, being open about age differences in your dating life is a wonderful thing because you never want to shut the doors to quality people enhancing your life. Mature women are not only generally better in bed, but much better conversation and company. Their experience often carries wisdom, and you may find that being with them can teach you all types of lessons. I realize that despite social progress, there is still a stigma to older women dating younger men. Just as with the double standard in sexuality between genders, you must be more open-minded and nonjudgmental if you are looking to erase this taboo. If you are a man who is looking to minimize drama and maximize enjoyment in his dating life, then sometimes older is better.

CHAPTER 42
What a Wonderful World
☆ ☆ ☆

"I myself subscribe more to the European philosphy of life, my pri-orities leaning towards wine, women and...well, that's about it."—Alfie (Alfie)

From the Taj Mahal to the Eiffel Tower to Iguazu Falls, my travels have taken me to some of the most breathtaking places in the world. Witnessing these wonders is an awe-inspiring experience, but they are not the only sensational spectacles you see when you circle the globe. When people look at my pictures on my various profiles, the two things that stand out are the phenomenal landmarks and the gorgeous girls. Perhaps the most fun part of traveling for me is being able to combine these two passions by meeting lovely ladies from all over the planet.

I have already encouraged you many times to make the effort to go overseas as much as possible. The benefits you will receive from the experience are immeasurable. You will become a much more cultured person who is comfortable with a wide variety of people and ways of life. Additionally, you will gain a broader perspective of the world and become more open-minded and intelligent. These are traits that strengthen your confidence, which, as we know, is the key to making all of your dreams come true. Speaking of dreams, when you are an American guy meeting girls overseas, you may feel that you have entered a fantasy world. You will discover a whole new outlook on dating that may influence whether you decide to settle down or continue to explore the glories of the women of the world. If you are a single man reading this who is interested in eventually getting married, I implore you not to get attached in a permanent relationship before traveling and meeting girls from different cultures.

It is true that you can still see the world with a romantic partner and that has charms of its own, but once you have settled down, you do not have the same freedom. I explained earlier how traveling solo can help you grow as an individual, and I promised to discuss the benefits of meeting foreign women. When you are with a wife or girlfriend, you will likely not have the options to experience the diversity of beauties you encounter in different countries. Think of a ship trying to set sail with an anchor. It is not going to get very far out onto the sea. When you have the responsibility of a relationship weighing you down, you do not have the ability to freely explore what is out there.

The problem with American society is that it confuses gender roles and creates a cultural climate that is not conducive to sexuality or long-term relationships. I have talked at length about the various double standards that end up making both men and women frustrated with the opposite sex. Men consistently encounter hypocritical women who not only expect to be treated as equals, but often want to be put on a pedestal at the same time when it comes to their own financial and emotional security. Many Western women are preoccupied with "fairness" and trying to prove themselves to make a point, thus appearing bitter and contemptuous toward men. Then there are the women who appear guarded about their sexuality, but who have no problem using it as a reward in order to get what they want. This constant power play is one of the reasons failure rates in marriages are at such an alarming level. Chances are good that you will come across one of these types in your dating life.

In no way am I saying that all American women are like this because there are plenty of quality girls out there who are not jaded or prudish. I also place a large blame on men for creating an environment that is hypocritical and stifling for women. That being said, as an open-minded, nonjudgmental guy looking to casually date a variety of women, it is often wearisome. It is baffling to me that I have probably dated more than five hundred women, but have met maybe less than a dozen I was impressed enough with to continue seeing. The confrontational attitude that so many possess can become extremely annoying, even as somebody that is not looking for anything serious.

When you go overseas, however, you may find your experiences much more pleasant. I can easily say that the sexiest, most well-rounded women I have met were abroad. There are cultures out there where the women are not raised with so many confusing messages, and they are much more likely to satisfy your needs. This book is not meant to be anti-feminist doctrine, but as a guy, why would you not want to meet women from places where they highly value taking care of a man? I haven't put extensive research into studying the gender roles and dating habits of every country in the world, but I can share my observations from my own experiences with foreign women and how they were vastly superior to what I deal with domestically.

First of all, one of the factors on your side when you travel is the appeal of being an American guy overseas. After all, this is one advantage that you do not have when you are at home. Unfortunately, as of this writing, this stock has vastly dropped in recent years because the global perception of the United States is much more negative now than in the past. There is still, however, a certain aura that comes with saying that you are from America. In many ways, the entire world still depends on our economy, and the country still sets the tone for the rest of the earth. Our movies bring imagery of the USA to every corner of the globe, and our celebrities are icons everywhere. This creates a certain glamour and prestige with the heritage. When I tell people I live in Hollywood, jaws drop because of the fantasy associated with the city. The fact that you are from the land of opportunities can give you a mythical quality when you are in a distant location, especially when you are in places that don't abound with such chances.

Additionally, since people from the States do not travel overseas as much as other cultures, you will be viewed as much more cultivated than the typical American. You should use that as a tool in luring the foreign women. Obviously, do not feed into the stereotype of the arrogant nationalist who feels the whole world revolves around his country. Instead, showcase that you want to understand a multitude of cultures, and that you find the women of the locality striking. When you present yourself as a cosmopolitan man attempting to expand his world knowledge, it will pique their interest. There is always something exotically appealing about a visitor from a different land so that should also work in your favor.

When you meet women, you should still utilize many of the skills and strategies I have described in this book, but you may find that you will not encounter as much of a power struggle. If you visit Europe, for example, the continent as a whole has a much more open attitude toward sexuality than Americans do, so women are not as guarded about sharing this pleasure with you. It is apparent just from walking on the streets. Women dress sexier, and couples are far more outwardly affectionate and playful. Even if you hate public displays of affection, this liberated environment makes it a haven for satisfying your fantasies. I believe this social acceptance makes European women more secure with themselves than their American counterparts.

This self-esteem means they are less likely to be argumentative or on a quest to prove their equality. When I talk to girls overseas, they seem much nicer and happier than the girls I meet at home. Additionally, since the continent has so much more history and Europeans travel much more often, the women are more worldly and open-minded. They are not constantly cautious of men's intentions. If I go to a bar and attempt to engage in conversation, a European woman is much less likely to have a bitchy reaction or pretend like she is not interested for the sake of pretense. This security makes them more comfortable with their sexuality and far more fun to be around. I have been to more than twenty-five countries in Europe alone. When meeting the women over there, I have enjoyed some illuminating conversations as well as some of my wildest escapades. Do not just take what I am saying at face value, but go out there and discover it for yourself.

Europe may be a good starting point to meet women on your travels, but you certainly should not limit your scope of exploration. In fact, the hottest times I have had with women were in more exotic regions such as Thailand, Costa Rica, and Brazil. These countries are hedonistic havens bursting with sexy sirens eager to satisfy your every desire. Think about what men have to go through in America to fulfill their needs and then imagine the tables turned where the women are so free-wheeling and ready to please that you will find yourself having the power to turn them down. Some of these places have it ingrained in their culture that the women cater to man's needs. You are most likely to receive this type of knightly treatment in Asia and South and Central America. The women there may not even speak English, but you may find that they are so receptive to satisfying your wishes that you communicate better with them than those with whom you do not have a language barrier. Believe me when I tell you that when you have experienced such heavenly pleasure, you will never come back to the American dating circuit the same. All of the trials and tribulations will seem like a bunch of meaningless nonsense.

One of the most alluring characteristics of women in many of the foreign countries you will visit is that they have a certain sex appeal most American women lack. Overall, the United States is not a very sexy culture. Most of the people do not bother to take good care of themselves and end up in terrible physical condition. They also generally do not dress in a very stylish or attractive manner. In contrast, when you go to many countries overseas, the sense of fashion and attention to their figure is stunning. When I went to Costa Rica, for example, it was on rare occasions that I saw a woman who was not slim and sexily attired. This also goes for places such as Sweden, Norway, and other parts of the world. Additionally, their friendly, open personalities enhance their sexiness

Now that you are hopefully getting more enthusiastic about vacationing overseas, I am sure you have the same question in your head that every guy seems to ask me. People always ask my opinion on which countries have the most beautiful women. I have included a list of my top ten countries for beautiful women at the end of the book, but let me get into some detail here. The concept of beauty is a subjective one based on personal tastes so I cannot answer that for you, but I can tell you which region I whole-heartedly feel contains the most stunning creatures on earth. Women of Eastern Europe are generally considered the most beautiful women on the planet for good reason. A relatively high percentage of the world's models come from that area, and the gene pool over there appears to be one that selectively breeds magnificent-looking ladies. Just to give you an illustration, even their women's tennis players are incredibly hot. Compare Anna Kournikova and Maria Sharapova with their peers, and you will see the evidence.

When I talk about Eastern Europe, I am referring to places such as the Czech Republic, Estonia, Slovakia, Poland, Russia, and Hungary. When you walk the streets of these countries, it often feels as if you have stumbled onto a runway fashion show. When I was strolling through a mall in Bratislava, Slovakia, I nearly broke my neck as I twisted and turned my head in amazement at the quantity of luscious ladies. Clubbing in Tallinn, Estonia was also an eye exercise in attempting to capture the astonishing attractiveness of the female constituents. I normally never give compliments, but I was so awe-struck that I was going up to random girls and simply asking them what type of magic potion they have in the water there that generates such spectacular specimens.

Slavic women, as they are often known, have striking features like high cheekbones, babyish faces, and often long blonde hair and ocean-blue or deep-green eyes. They also usually have really lovely accents that can make you enchanted just by hearing their voice. Not only that, they usually have very nurturing attitudes and hospitable personalities that make them terrific for long-term relationships. Most of all, they have a seductive sex appeal that can captivate your attention and fulfill every fantasy in your imagination. The last girl I was serious about was from the Czech Republic, and she had all of these attributes.

While I have emphasized the superior traits that these ladies generally possess, that is not to say you should stray away from your fellow American girls in your travels. On the contrary, you may find that the same girl who may reject you at your local bar will be more than willing to give you a chance when she is on vacation. Because she is in a retreat mentality, she is more relaxed and has her guard down more than at home. She will not only likely be much nicer, but she will also be in a mood to get wilder. This goes back to my theory of women needing security but craving excitement.

When they are away from their comfort zone, American girls generally have a much more adventurous attitude towards life and may do more of the things they hesitate to do in their everyday life. There is a reason why you see women get wild on spring break and at places like Mardi Gras in New Orleans. They see it as an escape from the drab reality of their everyday life, and they behave in a manner that allows them to unlock their doors and freely live out their fantasies. You should see this open door as an opportunity to share in their escapism and live out your own desires with them.

As you can gather from my journeys, traveling the globe can be an incredible way to meet the women of your dreams. If you have limited yourself to the girls in your locality, you have closed the door to a world of opportunities. When you open that gateway and explore the international dating scene, you will come to the conclusion that it is indeed a wonderful world.

CHAPTER 43
My Experience on the Tyra Banks Show
☆ ☆ ☆

"You got me goin'
You're oh-so charmin'
But I can't do it
You womanizer"
       —Britney Spears

As you've probably realized by now, I have had some incredible life experiences. One of the events that I get the most questions about is my appearance on *The Tyra Banks Show* episode focused on "Womanizers." Many of you may have seen me on the show or heard about me for the first time when I was on it. Although I was disappointed by the way I was portrayed on the program, as well as some of the lines of questioning, it was a seminal experience in my life as it was my first national television interview. If you have not seen the episode yet, I suggest you watch it before reading on. You can likely find it available somewhere online if you type in my name on Google. Since I receive so many questions about it, I thought I should share my version of the event.

First of all, I want to share a bit of the history that led to my appearance on the program because I feel there is a life lesson to be learned from it. Let me turn the clock back to when I was an innocent freshman entering college. I was moving into a dorm, ready to meet my new roommate. Although I did not click right away with him, I wanted to spice up our room with some eye candy. The very first poster I hung up on the wall was a breathtaking Tyra Banks poster.

Strangely, when my roommate came back in the room and saw it, he was upset and said it was offensive to women. Having never heard of a guy being turned off by seeing a beautiful woman in a bikini, I was surprised. Eventually, I discovered that he was more likely to be attracted to me than Tyra! I have no problems with gay people at all, but I will admit that it was a bit of an uncomfortable situation to come into my first year away from home. So it was really the poster of my fantasy girl of the moment that led me to realize that I may have been the fantasy of the guy I was living with.

Even back then, I was very open-minded and confident with myself. At the same time, I was inexperienced with girls and not ready to explore the dating scene with full abandon. Although I was not living the wild hedonistic life at a party school, I had the mental strength to spend college doing other activities that I loved doing. In that sense, I was living by the ideals of the Showstopper Lifestyle even before I coined the term.

Let us fast-forward to 2008. After college, I had experiences with countless women and have taken pictures with hundreds of beautiful ones. I was online searching through job postings for random jobs. One of the postings was looking for real-life "womanizers." Now, I do not really like that term, but I was curious so I sent in a link to my award-winning MySpace page. Since the page shows me with gorgeous girls and in front of landmarks all over the world, I felt it would show that not only do I get sexy women, but that I am also an intelligent, well-cultured, well-traveled man living life to the fullest.

The producers loved the MySpace page and wanted to hear my story. They were stunned by the photos with the wide variety of beauties, but they were even more intrigued by the fact that I was extremely well-spoken when discussing my skills with the ladies. As most people do, they had the misconception that guys who hooked up with numerous ladies were dim-witted sleazeballs who hate women and have no moral convictions. I tried to explain to them that the reason I get so many girls is because I love women but realize that my lifestyle does not allow me the emotional attachment of a committed relationship. The fact that I am extremely well-educated and cultured was shocking to them. This dichotomy made me a fascinating subject for their program, which was to be on the secrets of the life of "womanizers," inspired by the Britney Spears song.

The producers became captivated by my story and offered to fly me to New York to be a special guest on their program. Although I had my reservations because I knew the nature of talk shows and that the topic of the show could lead to some criticism, I decided to accept the invitation because I felt it would be a glorious opportunity to dispel the myth that "womanizers" only behaved the way they do because of some traumatic experience, or because they are hateful misogynists. My goal was to showcase that some guys just have a different set of priorities in life besides being in a committed relationship, and that as long as you are safe and honest with women about your intentions, then there is nothing wrong with that. I had never seen *The Tyra Banks Show* before, so perhaps I was a bit naïve in thinking that the ideals I believe in would be accepted by the audience.

The original plan for the program was to have my last "girlfriend" on the show to discuss how our relationship ended and to give a better portrait of the softer, more emotional side behind the "womanizer" image. I felt that this would have made for an excellent examination of my lifestyle because it was my relationship with her that made me realize that I was not interested in commitment. I regret the hurt I caused her, and I do not want to cause that type of pain again to anyone. Unfortunately, she was not able to appear on the program.

They asked for another option, so my second proposal was to have my best girl friend come on the show. As I mentioned before, when you are single and dating a plethora of women, it is vital to have at least one or two close female friends for balance and perspective. My friend understands that the reason I am with so many girls without commitment is because I am a nice guy who is having fun and not ready for it. Additionally, the fact that I have never slept with her or even attempted to is proof that I can have a serious emotional attachment to a girl without anything sexual. I knew she would humanize my story even more than anything I could say about myself. When they decided not to put her on the program, I became a bit leery about how I would be portrayed, but I felt my personality was strong enough that I could speak up for my own beliefs.

Instead of having an old girlfriend or best friend appear on the program with me, they decided to film me in a local bar in Hollywood interacting with various women to showcase my skills with the ladies. Unfortunately, I had a job in Las Vegas the upcoming weekend, so the only free time I had for filming was on a Thursday evening around six to ten o'clock, hardly the hottest time to find women in a bar. As I have made clear, the bar setting is a terrible place to meet women. I had some reservations about filming the scene, but I decided to make it a fun experience by exhibiting my charm and confidence.

Most of you have probably seen the episode, so you witnessed that there were a few successes and even more mishaps. That is pretty representative of what takes place in a bar, even for guys highly skilled at getting women. Keep in mind that it was a very staged setting because everybody knew there was a camera present and it was being taped for a television show. It is impossible to tell if the girls reacted the way they did to me because they were being filmed.

I did my best to have fun with the special and demonstrate how to approach girls without hesitation or fear of rejection. I would have no desire to hook up with many of the women I interacted with, but mainly talked to them to keep things interesting. The main things I want you guys to take out of that segment is that when you are in a bar, your main goal is to have a good time and not to be afraid of how women will react to you. Although the sequence may have come across as cheesy and unflattering on television, it was an absolute joy to participate in, and the camera crew and producers of the segment were terrific people and tremendously helpful.

The program was to be filmed the Monday after Halloween weekend, and since I spent that weekend in Las Vegas, you can imagine the type of mental state I was in when I arrived in New York. After sleeping about five or six hours total in the last four nights, I was essentially a walking zombie who was barely able to string together a comprehensible sentence, much less speak eloquently on a national television show. The producers pumped my body with coffee to bring me back to life from my catatonic state. Although I was in danger of appearing as a caffeinated catastrophe, I was able to compose myself enough to prepare my interview with the producers.

While I am on that topic, I must say that the producers of *The Tyra Banks Show* are absolutely first-rate professionals. I decided to do the show based on my wonderful interactions with them, and meeting them was the highlight of my experience. If you are reading this, I want to thank you guys for the opportunity and for being so kind and supportive throughout the process.

Unfortunately, despite the preparation, they could not possibly get me ready for the reaction of the studio audience that awaited me. Although I appeared second during the actual airing of the program, I was originally scheduled to open the show. The producers convinced Tyra that I would be the main ratings draw on the show and told her, "Shawn is your money." I love that line! Speaking of money, you guys would have paid to see the look on my face as I sat on her couch alone with a crowd of hostile ladies singing "I'm Every Woman." The main lesson here is this. Just as you want to research a company before you interview with them, you definitely would be advised to actually watch a television show before being interviewed on it! When the taping began with a woman in the audience calling me "a disgusting pig," I knew I was in for a long hour.

To give you an idea of how I felt when I saw the audience's unreceptive reaction to my views, just imagine somebody realizing that he voluntarily walked into his own hanging. Well, maybe I am exaggerating a bit, but I quickly realized that no matter how well-spoken or logical my points were, the live viewers were not interested in hearing them. Again, it was extremely naïve and egotistical of me to assume that I would be able to immediately win over the crowd.

People had warned me in advance that it was largely a program geared toward women, so the mere topic of "womanizers" would be frowned upon. The best advice that I received prior to my appearance was from Nina Hartley. Yes, that woman is nothing short of extraordinary! She told me that Tyra would be a tough host and the majority of the audience would be harsh. She also stressed that there are many people out there who have similar goals and beliefs to my own but are too afraid to live the lifestyle they want. As the cliché goes, if I could inspire one person, it would all be worthwhile.

Because it is available for viewing online, I will not discuss too many details of the content of the program. To summarize, most of the interview consisted of me getting chastised by Tyra and her audience as well as some "relationship expert." I was accused of being "a male slut," a former high school nerd, a commitment-phobe, a gay man overcompensating, and a sleazeball. I stood my ground as best I could given the unfriendly reception I received and stuck to the principles I have explained throughout this book. My aim was to get across to the world that just because you hook up with many women, it does not mean there is something wrong with you or that you are disrespectful toward them.

I felt the views I was expressing were rational. Not everybody desires to be in a committed relationship. It is better to be honest about what you are doing as opposed to lying to women and then cheating on them. You can be educated and close to your family, and still have desires and beliefs that do not fit the confines of a traditional relationship. I wanted to come across as a charming, confident, educated guy who just happens to date lots of women and is enjoying every moment of it. If you look at the expression on the faces of the girls in the crowd, you would think that I was barging into these girls' houses and forcing them into it or something. As Nina said, "Sex isn't something men do to you. It isn't something men get out of you. Sex is something you dive into with gusto and like it every bit as much as he does." If these appalled girls in the audience had bothered to stop and think about what I was saying, they would have realized that there are many women who have the same desires I do.

Many people have told me that the reason people were so shocked by my views was that I was obviously extremely educated and I did not fit the stereotype they expected. It is easy to dismiss some sleazeball or therapy case, but it is harder to accept somebody who is smart and stable and unapologetic about the lifestyle he is living.

I was extremely upset that the two other guys who were on the show got the last word. They were both really cool guys, but they presented the clichéd stereotypes that most people associate with "womanizers," and my goal for being on the show was to dispel those myths. One of the men explained that he dates so many women because of a bad childhood experience with his mother. The other was a hilarious guy, but he came across as a sexist pig. I wanted to get the message across that getting lots of girls is not always a psychiatric condition based on hurt or hatred toward women. Additionally, it is not just about sex, but it can be a manifestation of excitement toward life in general. Unfortunately, Tyra and the audience had other preconceived notions, and most were too close-minded to accept my ideals.

Since many want to know what Tyra Banks is like in person, I cannot make a judgment either way on that. Our personalities did clash during the filming and we started taking some subtle jabs at each other but it was nothing personal. I was originally supposed to talk more, but I was phased out of the filming as it became obvious that I found some of her questions ridiculous and I started giving sarcastic responses. When the program aired, I was moved from the opening to the middle of the show. That is an executive decision, and I totally understand that.

Those of us who appeared on the program did not get to meet Tyra backstage, so my entire interaction with her was in front of the camera. Many people told me that she was really rude and self-centered, and it may have come across that way on the program. I also realize, however, that when she is on television she has to put on a show that caters to her audience, so I cannot use her behavior on the program as a profile on her personality. Although I would have been happy if she had approached the topic more respectfully and had listened to me with an open mind, I know her main job is to draw ratings. Despite the fact that I was extremely unhappy with the interview after the taping, I am now more content realizing I did the best I could in a hostile environment.

As Nina told me prior to my interview, my objective was to reach the people out there unsure if they desired a traditional life, and who needed guidance or inspiration that they could be perfectly happy without being in a relationship. A few days after the filming, I received an email from one of the few guys that were in the audience and reading it made me feel that the whole experience was worthwhile. He said, "Hey Shawn, I saw you on *The Tyra Banks Show* and was disappointed by the reaction of the crowd. They did not understand your way of life, which is the one I want to live. You are my role model. Keep up the good work! Don't let the audience's reaction get to you. I support you!"

In the weeks following the actual airing of the show on television, I was recognized by many people as "the womanizer" or "that playboy kid" from *The Tyra Banks Show*. Some just laughed at the surprise of seeing me in person after watching me on the program, but many also expressed their support and complimented me on standing up for my beliefs. I have received hundreds of emails from all over the country. Some were condemnations of my lifestyle, and others were indecent proposals from all types of women. The main tone of the emails, however, was one of overwhelming support for having the courage to live the lifestyle I want to.

Despite my initial dissatisfaction with the program, I realized that I should use the experience as motivation to explain my philosophies on life to all of those out there who are open-minded enough to listen to them. My main awakening from being in front of that crowd was that most people still have a very close-minded attitude toward life and are afraid of witnessing something outside of the social norm. *The Tyra Banks Show* gave me an enormous platform to express my beliefs, but at the end of the day, I did not have a significant work to give me more substance beyond the words that came out of my mouth. This book has been a project of mine for years, but I had put it off because I was too busy traveling and actually maximizing life experiences instead of writing about it. Having my lifestyle criticized on national television made me refocus on my writing, so that the next time I would appear on an interview, I would have a work of substance that backs up my beliefs. So I must give some thanks to Tyra for the completion of this book.

Now I look back and think about when I was that young teenager beginning college with a Tyra Banks poster on my wall. I was not a nerd or shy at the time, but I was definitely filled with the same fears and insecurities about women that inhibit most men from approaching them. I could never have imagined that years later I would be invited for an interview on national television with Tyra Banks herself so I could discuss how I live my dream life and attract so many women. It just goes to show that it does not matter who you are or where you are at in your life, you never know what the future holds. If you approach each day positively and each situation with confidence, then all of your dreams can come true, and the world may be there to listen to you share them.

☆ SECTION 3 ☆
A Lifestyle of Big Decisions and Smart Choices

CHAPTER 44
Real Love
☆ ☆ ☆

"If you believe in love at first sight, you never stop looking."—Closer

One of the most confusing concepts that exists in the world involves the most popular of all four-letter words…and that is love. Although it is the consensus that love makes the world go round, most people just do not seem to capture the true definition of the term. In fact, too many people are obsessed with the idea of being in love that they forget what the meaning of loving a person is all about. To me, the only actual form of love that lasts is the kind you share with your family and friends. Even a romance is nothing more than a friendship on fire, as they like to say.

Despite what romance novels and movies tell you about "love at first sight," a real bond takes years of developing trust, respect, mutual understanding, communication, and friendship. Those are the five keys to a successful relationship, whether it is with your significant other, friends or family. Love is not just a product of some type of magical burst of wind that overcomes the hearts of two people and instantly connects their souls. You may be attracted to somebody when you meet them or have some type of feeling in your gut that they may be special, but discovering that unique emotion between two people requires a long journey.

That is why the closest people to your heart should be the ones with whom you have taken the time to develop the five components I mentioned above. Keep in mind that they are all interrelated and combine together to construct a connection between two people. Trust is absolutely paramount because if you cannot believe what the other person says and have faith in their actions, then you will not be able to take them seriously or depend on them. Additionally, this conviction allows you to express your innermost thoughts to that person. Without express honesty between two parties, a strong closeness is impossible. Obviously, if you are in a romantic partnership minus trust, you will be in a constant state of stress over the other's behavior, and that lack of belief in their words and actions will take a toll on both of you. You cannot love somebody without being able to trust them.

Mutual respect is also a vital factor in any form of healthy relationship. You must accept the other person for who they are, admire them for their strengths, and not judge them by their weaknesses. I am not just saying that you need to forgive all of their flaws, but you must respect them as an individual. If you do not have this admiration for each other, then the very foundation of reciprocal acceptance is shattered and whatever "love" you may share with that person may be fleeting.

With respect for the core of what the other person is about comes understanding. You must take the time to comprehend why the one you care about is the way they are, and appreciate them for what they bring to your life. If you cannot empathize with their emotions, then it may eventually create a divide between you. Common appreciation for the traits that make the other unique enhances the caring that makes love possible.

Even if trust, respect, and understanding exist between two individuals, if you are not able to convey those essential feelings to one another, then closeness may never develop. That is why strong communication is crucial to any form of healthy relationship. Take the time to express your emotions to the other person, whether they are supportive or not. If you hold back what you are feeling, then not only will trust break down, but this repression may destroy the understanding you have for each other. Millions of people who love each other lose that special bond because they are unable or unwilling to be open with their sentiments. Life is too short not to reveal those emotions, and it may cause you to lose somebody you really care about.

When you form a strong trust, respect, and understanding between each other and are able to communicate this, a friendship should naturally develop. Obviously, it is also necessary that the two of you must share some common passions and enjoy exploring them together. If you are to really be close with somebody, this enjoyment must be combined with the other factors to culminate in the deep connection between individuals.

As we have seen, the collective emotional traits that define true love are not just those that describe a romantic companionship, but any type of relationship that is important to you. Most human beings are lucky to find a few of these people with whom they can share this mutual caring. When you find them, make sure you appreciate how special that bond is and do anything you can to maintain it. If you feel that you developed these feelings with someone you are romantically interested in, only then can you really say that you are in love.

CHAPTER 45
Perfect Partner
☆ ☆ ☆

"A loving relationship is one in which the loved one is free to be himself—to laugh with me, but never at me; to cry with me, but never because of me; to love life, to love himself, to love being loved. Such a relationship is based upon freedom and can never grow in a jealous heart."—Leo Buscaglia

The various topics this book has covered may make you believe that it is mainly a guide for the single man. While some of the issues I have discussed may be geared toward those who are unattached, most of the principles apply for everybody. In fact, the ideals of peace of mind, confidence, independence and developing into a well-rounded human being are paramount in being part of a successful relationship. After all, if you are not secure with yourself, you cannot make your significant other happy, and your bond will suffer. Once you have achieved this self-assurance and security, and you feel you are ready for a commitment, here are some steps to make sure you find the perfect partner.

First of all, before you get into a serious relationship, make certain that you have maximized your life as a single man so you are not overcome by temptations and regrets. Make sure you have dated a variety of women before choosing the one you want to be with. Those experiences will make you more comfortable with women and will give you a better idea of the type you'll eventually want to settle down with—if you decide to do so. It may also lead you to the conclusion that you prefer to be single and casually date. If you do not explore the dating circuit, then you may rush into a long-term commitment with the first girl you become involved with and then regret it later. You may also settle for somebody you are not compatible with and face heartache in the future. If you are not at ease with being single, then you likely will not be content in a relationship. As you date various women, begin to understand the traits that capture your attention and enhance your companionship. Define the standards of what things are important to you when seeking an ideal mate, and make sure any woman you consider getting serious about lives up to your own wants and needs.

Not only should you date numerous women, I feel you should also take steps to develop into a stronger individual person before tying yourself to a relationship. I have stressed the benefits of education many times. It is very important that you should finish your studies before getting attached. Additionally, I suggest getting your career on the pathway to success. Of course, amassing cultural experiences such as world travel and volunteer work also aid immeasurably in making you a well-rounded person. When you are educated, financially stable, and cultured, you not only develop into a more mature, powerful individual, but you also become more prepared for the responsibilities that come with a relationship.

Perhaps most of all, make sure that you have maintained strong ties to a solid group of family and friends who can support you and guide you through your trials and tribulations. These connections do not have the instability, fickleness, and limited timeframe that most romantic partnerships are often plagued with. Having truly close, quality people in your life also assures you that you are less likely to get into a serious relationship because you are bored or lonely. These are the people who will be there for you through the ups and downs of your romance, and they will stand by you even if it falters.

When you meet someone you see as a potential long-term partner, make sure you date them for awhile before you make a commitment. You want to build a base upon which your relationship can blossom. Do not let a sudden chemical attraction mislead you into the illusion that you are suddenly "in love." In actuality, this foundation takes a long time to create if you want a fruitful long-lasting connection. Remember that real "love" takes years of developing trust, respect, mutual understanding, communication, and friendship.

When you can form that genuine bond with somebody that you do not necessarily need in your life, but someone you truly want in your life, then you may want to take things to the next level. Do not forget that a perfect partner is not someone who completes a void of emptiness or loneliness, but one who complements the inner joy that you already hold in your heart. Too many guys forget that a girlfriend is really a close friend who shares the same interests, wants and needs as you and to whom you happen to be attracted. When that initial chemistry disappears, there is often nothing left. If you take the time to develop the elements of a loving relationship, then you will have found a friend who may be with you for life, even if the romance fades.

If you are lucky enough to have discovered this special person and have taken the time to formulate a genuine connection with them, then you have the makings of a flourishing relationship. Because you have made the decision to commit, you want to make the most of this companionship. Make the efforts to consistently do activities together that you both enjoy. Combine your unique personalities with your mutual interests and share as many joyous moments as you can.

As time goes by, make sure you keep things fresh and exciting by exploring new adventures together. There are too many people who get into relationships and just start going through the motions. In the process, they not only lose that spark that made them love the other person, they also lose track of themselves. Do not lose track of what made you happy and confident when you were single. At the same time, do not start taking the other person for granted and remain with them merely to have somebody in your life. There should be an undeniable electricity in the air when you share time with her. When you lose that passion, not only will the sex lose its allure, the very premise of why you are in a relationship will be on shaky ground.

Remember the principle of living each moment as if it is your first. This principle can also be applied to a relationship situation. You need to see each day you are with someone you love as a blessing and make continuous efforts to get to know your partner all over again. You should schedule vacations, attend family outings, search for cool events, and do everything you can to sustain that chemistry and the thrill that bonded you together.

Another important step is to weave your relationship into your circle of friends as seamlessly as possible. Too many people make the inexcusable mistake of forgetting or alienating the people they care about when they have a girlfriend or wife. Just because you have a significant other, does not make the rest of the people who love you insignificant. Ideally, if you have truly found somebody that you connect with, they will naturally fit in with your loved ones. Make sure you not only introduce your companion to your friends and try to enjoy time with them as a couple, but also ensure that you spend time with your buddies. The bottom line is that you do not want to separate your dating life from the rest of your personal life if you want to maintain both a successful relationship and close friendships.

Just as vital is to make certain that your significant other has her own circle of friends. Too often, a woman does not have a solid set of platonic companions and becomes reliant on a relationship. This is not only detrimental for her but for you as well. You do not want to become the sole focus of another person's life because it places an excess responsibility on you to spend all your time and energy on making her happy. On the other hand, when she has her own friends, her whole life will not revolve around you. Each of you will have your own social groups and will not become completely dependent on each other.

The biggest mistake people make when they get involved in serious commitments is that they often lose track of who they are as an individual. If your whole life revolves around another person and you can no longer enjoy yourself on your own, then there is a major problem. Although a relationship requires making a strong connection, you also want to retain a sense of autonomy. If you do not, you will not only become overly dependent on your partner, you are also setting yourself up for disaster if the bond breaks. That is why it is of utmost importance to spend significant time on your own and with your other loved ones doing various activities. Remember that you were perfectly satisfied alone but chose to be with someone to enhance your life. Do not allow yourself to lose the inner strength you had coming into the relationship. An ideal relationship allows you each to attain your freedom. This not only means that you are able to continue to enjoy things on your own, but also that you should be free to be who you are.

By that token, you should not feel compelled to change just to fit into your mate's ideals of who you should be. Making adjustments that make you and your relationship stronger can be a tremendous growth process. Ideally, you will both grow stronger as a couple and as individuals. Unfortunately, too many people go on an endless quest to fulfill the image of what they feel the other wants to see. In the process, they lose touch of who they are and the connection is no longer genuine. At the same time, you should not force the other person to conform to your own portrait of who you think they should be. There is a reason you cared for her enough in the first place to get into a relationship. You should respect her unique individuality as well. Remember the old saying by Andre Gide that "it is better to be hated for what you are than to be loved for something that you are not."

Finally, perhaps the most important part of a relationship is to know when to call it quits and move on. There are various indicators that things are not going smoothly. When you find that spending time with your companion is more of a burden than a blessing then you have a good idea that it is time to break up. If your conversations are getting increasingly dramatic and you are forced to answer unwanted questions, then there is a sign that jealousy or insecurity may be creeping up. If routine discussions are turning into arguments, then sustaining the connection may be more trouble than it is worth. Do not forget those necessary elements of respect, trust, understanding, communication and friendship. When any of those key factors begin to dissipate, then it is time to consider ending the relationship.

Just as dangerous as things going sour is when your partnership becomes one of convenience instead of passion. If you start getting lazy and losing track of your priorities, then you need to either regain that zest for life or reevaluate your situation. Make sure you are keeping focus on your career goals, staying in shape, and maintaining your sense of adventure. If a relationship turns into an obligation that drains the adrenaline and the exhilaration out of your existence, then you need to call it quits.

I completely understand that ending a relationship is a potentially frightening decision and it can cause heartbreak, but you need to gather the strength to do so. That is why I stressed the importance of becoming a confident, free-thinking individual before getting into a serious commitment. When you have that strong sense of self, it is easier to come to terms with a relationship ending. Many people stay in bad relationships just because they have become accustomed to having the other person in their life. This is unhealthy for both partners and can take a real toll on your individuality and your self-esteem. Summon your inner power and take the initiative to tell your partner respectfully that it is time to move on.

I realize many couples believe that all of the time they invested in the relationship would go to waste if it were to end. In actuality, you are not only wasting more time struggling to maintain a bad relationship, you are also tainting the good times you shared. Just because you are breaking up does not mean that all of the time you put in was squandered. As long as you maintain the mindset that you will cherish all of the good times you had together, then those memories will be with you forever. If the friendship is strong even when the romance fades, then she should be close to you for life as well. That is the ultimate example of the perfect partner.

CHAPTER 46
The Greatest Show on Earth
☆ ☆ ☆

"The music at a wedding procession always reminds me of the music of soldiers going into battle."—Heinrich Heine

When Barnum and Bailey presented their world-famous circus extravaganza, they promoted it as "the Greatest Show on Earth." Over the years since then, I believe that the true "greatest show" has become a display nearly everybody has or will become a performer in. It is the institution of marriage as well as the ritual of the wedding. Let us start by analyzing some important issues that many people do not even take into consideration. If two people truly love each other and want to spend their lives together, why do they need to go through the formality of a wedding and be married? If their caring for each other is truly some type of eternal bond, why do they need to label themselves as husband and wife? Shouldn't the emotions and the friendship that they share be enough without having to be attached to a legal document? Do you really need to justify your relationship to your family, friends, deity, the government, and the outside world? I am not a religious or a political person and I am not presuming to have the answer to these issues, but I am telling you to ask yourselves these questions before deciding whether you want to take such a gigantic step.

Remember, I grew up as a product of a stable marriage and my parents were together for thirty-five years before my father passed away, so I understand the benefits of the symbolic union between a couple and how it helps raise children in a secure environment. Increasingly, however, the institution of marriage has become as much a complication as it is a connection. Let us take a look at some statistics that have been backed up in multiple studies, including my own research. More than fifty percent of marriages in the United States, at the time of this writing, end up in divorce. Of those that last, around forty percent of couples classify themselves as truly content in their relationship. So when you combine the numbers, you find that less than twenty percent of marriages are likely to have the "happy ending" that two partners promise each other when they exchange vows. Is that really the "holy matrimony" people profess marriage creates?

I know this sounds a bit cold and unromantic, but you cannot dispute statistics, and the result of these numbers does not equate to a warm, fuzzy fairy tale with two people living happily ever after. While marriage is generally an emotional decision and is usually entered into with the best of intentions of both parties, you must not allow your emotions to cloud your judgment. Don't complicate common sense!

It has largely been my belief that a major reason people get married is they feel that they need the paper and the ritual to justify to others as well as themselves that their relationship is real. After all, besides some legally binding documentation, how does it really improve your relationship? If you really love each other, you should not feel the need to prove to the world that the compassion is heartfelt. When two people are really meant to be together, it is the closeness in their hearts and the companionship they share that will keep them so. If this "love" wears off and the company is no longer so pleasant, the paper that says you are married will not magically rekindle the passions you once shared. Unfortunately, conventional thinking has still not allowed most people to view a long-term relationship as something other than a union that leads to a wedding.

Speaking of weddings, there is nothing that personally turns me off more to the idea of marriage than the unnecessarily complicated, contrived spectacle that weddings often become. This is coming from somebody who enjoys going to weddings and loves the reunions of friends and family that take place there. I simply feel that a gathering of that nature could be just as possible and enjoyable without the cheesy speeches, the overpriced presentation, the stressful preparation, and the necessity of two people vowing to live the rest of their lives together. I mean, can't we just have a get-together at Chuck E Cheese or something? Seriously speaking, think about the cost and the planning that go into a wedding. The expenses often total up to astronomical amounts of money for a celebration that lasts a few hours, all for an institution that is far more likely to fail than succeed. Again, this may sound cold, but these are the facts and they need to be considered before planning a formal ceremony.

Even taking into consideration the altruistic motives of bringing friends and family together for the "most important" moment of your lives, think about how much of this planning is done more to impress others than to celebrate the occasion. If the couple really loves one another and the people in attendance are so close to them, they do not need all of the fancy presentation and the pageantry to commemorate the event.

Now let me make this clear. If you can afford to spend the money on the festivities, and you truly enjoy planning the wedding, and are doing so because you genuinely love the whole process as well as the grand party, then by all means, have the wedding of your dreams. If you, however, are doing it just because you feel that the only way to celebrate a romance between two people is to put on an expensive exhibition to show the world you care about each other, then you should reconsider it. I interviewed thousands of subjects, and my surveys showed that less than fifty percent of people who got married actually enjoyed their own wedding. The majority said that it was much more stressful and costly than it was worth, which is not surprising given the fact that for the most of them, the marriage ended. Now, I know the wedding and marriage itself are about more than the two parties who are professing their love, but if you are going through the time, effort, and the expense of such an event, shouldn't you at least take pleasure in the experience?

Step back and think about how much you can do with the money you spend on a wedding. You can travel all over the world. You can place the down payment on the home of your dreams. You can use that money to put in a college fund if you plan on having children. In fact, if you have even more lofty ideals, you can use much of that money to help people who really need it.

Remember, this book is not meant to be an instruction manual on how to live your lives. My primary purpose is to make you question the institutions that too many people take at face value and accept as the only way of living. Our world is based on emotion, and without the love and caring of your fellow human beings, it would be a miserable place to live. There is no place where it is etched in writing, however, that the only way to express this affection is to go through a symbolic ritual that substantiates your feelings. The fact that the majority of the people in the world still have it ingrained in their minds that they need to go through a wedding and be married to prove they have someone special in their lives, despite the fact it so often ends in failure, is why I call marriage the greatest show on earth. I hope you do not discover too late that it is often far less entertaining, and considerably more crazy, than any circus you can ever imagine.

CHAPTER 47
Before Getting Married
☆ ☆ ☆

"Women marry men hoping they will change. Men marry women hoping they will not...so each is inevitably disappointed."—Albert Einstein

By now, you realize that I am not so much against marriage itself but the false ideas that too many people have ingrained in their minds that being married is the only signifier of a lifelong commitment or the only path to fulfillment. That being said, because the previous chapter analogized a wedding to a circus, I wanted to make sure that you are absolutely ready before deciding to participate in such a festival. Many of you are either deciding whether or not to get married now or whether you will do so in the future. Before arriving at such an enormous decision, there are many issues you need to consider that may have permanent consequences for your life.

I am going to assume that you are getting married to have a solitary emotional, physical and spiritual partner for the rest of your life, although those components can be exclusive of each other and still enhance your relationship. For now, I am assuming that you are thinking about taking the vows of a "traditional" marriage, where both parties agree to be monogamous. I am hoping that when you arrive at this decision, you already have the type of "real love" I have described, as well as the necessary components of a good relationship that I explained earlier.

First of all, let us look at the logistical issues of being married. You have to keep in mind that you are deciding to have one sole partner whom you share just about everything with for the rest of your days on earth, from your name to your finances to any type of economic or health issues either of you face. You will become essentially attached to another person you will need to include in any major decision that you encounter.

Do not forget that men, and even women, are sexual creatures, and only you know about your nature in that regard. So keep in mind, and tell your body, that you are also forsaking any other physical partner for the rest of your life, unless you plan on lying or cheating on the one you profess to care about. It is amazing how much deception takes place in a married relationship in the pursuit of one's erotic yearnings. Instead of waiting until after you are married to realize that perhaps it is unnatural to exclusively be with one sexual companion the remainder of your days, just make it easy on yourself and your partner, and do not make that commitment.

Also remember that the person you find so attractive at the time you get engaged may not be so appealing to you years later. I am not saying this to be superficial or that looks are everything. I am plainly stating the obvious fact that we all age and our appearance evolves over time. Marriage is, in theory, supposed to be a lifelong commitment, not a temporary way to keep someone attached to you until something better comes along. If you are not comfortable with the thought of your mate looking older or less beautiful, and you feel you will want somebody younger when her charms or looks wear off, then the thought of marriage should not even cross your mind. If you have fantasies or ideas of various sexual partners that you are either interested in sleeping with or will do so if given the opportunity, then remain single and explore those options.

In my studies, I ran into countless people, and in my personal life, I have seen numerous friends who enjoy the idea of having an emotional and physical companion who will consistently be there, but simultaneously want to sleep with other people. I simply cannot understand why you would choose to be in a relationship with "the one" you "love" while being dishonest to them about your sex life. In my opinion, there is nothing wrong with enjoying your physical pleasures with multiple partners, as long as you are safe and are not deceiving somebody you care about. All too often, when people cheat and have extramarital affairs, they forget that they had made the decision to tie themselves to one person. If you are not willing to do so, the decision is easy. Do not be in a "committed" relationship or get married!

Even more important to consider than the sexual element is the emotional one. When you are married, or even in a relationship, your individual problems become matters both of you have to deal with. There is nothing wrong with that, as people should support one another in tough times. Unfortunately, this often includes dealing with issues that are trivial to one party but of great consequence to the other. Before getting engaged, make sure you each have the strength to bear the burdens of the other. If you can do so, it is a beautiful thing, but too many people find that their own worries are difficult enough and taking on somebody else's is overwhelming.

You and your partner deserve each other's consideration through your trials and tribulations when taking such a major step. Realize that habits of the other that you deem merely tolerable while you are dating may become downright annoying or unacceptable when you are married. If your potential spouse has the tendency to get on your nerves or has certain characteristics you do not like, those traits can become magnified when you see that person everyday. If there is something about their personality that bothers you, do not assume that it is just going to magically change over time. It is not your responsibility to try to transform them. One of the biggest mistakes people make in life is getting into a relationship thinking they are going to change the other person.

Let us say, for example, that your girlfriend does not like your friends or the idea of you spending too much time with them, but sharing that time is extremely vital to you. You must weigh whether being in a permanent relationship with her is more important than spending extensive time with your buddies. If she changes her mind about them, then great, but do not assume she will. You have to accept the person for who they are and be prepared to spend nearly every single day of the rest of your life with this person, accepting the good and the bad.

Think about all of these things prior to getting married. Do not forget that there is no specific timeline that a relationship needs to run on, and you have the power to wait until you answer these key questions before getting engaged, if at all. The problem with marriage and why it ends in heartbreak so often is that people often do not consider the effects it will have on their lives in the long term. Obviously, when you first decide to offer the ring, everything appears to be all rosy and beautiful. At the time, you genuinely intend to remain together as a happy, loving couple, but how will it change in the days ahead?

In many ways, you have to be psychic before making the decision, because you need to see well into the future, and not just be overcome by the emotions that exist in the present. They say love is blind and the sentiments associated with it often cloud your rational thinking process. You need to look decades into the future and think if this is the person you want to grow old with and share your life with. Additionally, you have to take the risk that the emotion you feel at the moment about that person is the type of love you will have for them your entire existence. Not only that, you do not know how your companion's feelings will change over time. Ideally, that love will grow, but realistically, that intense caring you enter into a marriage with does not last, and unfortunately, often changes to intense dislike.

Of course, it is impossible to see what the future holds, and you cannot predict how your feelings may change in the future. That is why people need to get into a marriage realizing it is not just about "being in love," but it is equally about the duty and responsibility that accompanies your promises to each other. My parents barely knew each other when they got married so it definitely was not a case of a passionate couple deciding to tie the knot. It was an arranged marriage, but the love grew over time, as the friendship, respect, trust and communication developed. Although the relationship was not born out of a romance, it lasted because of a sense of duty and loyalty to each other and the responsibility of raising a child.

I am not advocating an arranged marriage, but I am making the point that a lasting relationship is not merely about the initial emotions that a man and woman experience as they get married. It should be a combination of that love with a close friendship between partners, respect for each other, trust, good communication, and knowing the duty and responsibility that come with the symbolic union.

Then there is the matter of children. The primary reason people get married is to raise a family. If you want to have kids, you need to be certain that the person you are thinking of marrying possesses the qualities of a solid parent. They must be nurturing, responsible, emotionally stable, and exhibit the ability to be a good role model for a young one. The decision to get married is not just about the couple but about their potential offspring as well. If you make an irresponsible decision about the one you choose to marry, nobody will suffer more than your children.

Even if you have all of those things with your potential spouse, also keep in mind what you may be losing the day you choose to spend the rest of your life with somebody, and that is your individuality and your freedom. When you are married, it is difficult to be your own person because everything you do has an effect on the couple, as I mentioned before. When people think about you, they also think about your spouse. With rare exceptions, you are spending almost every single night with that person. It is extremely difficult to sustain your unique identity when your entire existence is intertwined with another.

This loss of individuality generally results in your freedom being compromised. You may not be able to spend as much time doing the things you love. You may not have as many opportunities to see your friends. If you have desires to travel or live on your own, or take some type of employment risk, then it is much easier to do that when you are single. If you want the power to have your entire life in your hands, and have the autonomy to do what you want when you want, then it is not in your best interest to get married.

Taking all of this into consideration, if you still decide that you want to get married, make sure you are doing it for the right reasons. It is essential that you have the elements of a good relationship: respect, trust, communication and friendship. Also, make sure that you are with a person who does not keep you from doing the things you love, but makes them more enjoyable. Make sure they allow you to balance time with the other people you care about so your entire life does not revolve around one person. When you can find a partner you enjoy sharing your time with but who will still allow you to keep your individuality, then you are very lucky. The rule for a successful couple is that the whole must be greater than the sum of its parts. Your mate should complement your existence, not complicate it.

Even if you are with somebody who has all the qualities of the perfect partner, you must remember that you always have the option of being in a relationship with them without getting married. It may not be mainstream or socially acceptable as of yet, but it is your life, and if you two are happy with each other, do you really need the ceremony and the paper to substantiate it for yourselves and to others? Many people get married just to "validate" their relationship or to feel secure that the other person will stay with them. Some feel some type of power knowing that they have a wife or husband attached to their identity. Unfortunately, when things go bad, you may feel utterly powerless. As long as you enjoy each other's company in the present, do not feel pressured into making promises you may not be able to keep that will affect your future. If that person is "the right one" for you, they should stay with you regardless of whether you make a vow to remain with them or not.

If the relationship ends, it is for other reasons than the fact that you did not have a paper to legalize the union. It is your life, and you should not have to measure your relationship by societal norms. Remember, the norm these days is to be in a marriage that will not last and will end in further difficulties for yourselves and your children. Be strong enough in yourself and confident enough in the bond with your partner to make the most of the time you share together, and above all, be responsible and intelligent in deciding whether or not to get married.

CHAPTER 48
Bachelor Party: The Last Meal
☆ ☆ ☆

"The bachelor party is like the last meal before the electric chair."—Unknown

One of the most bizarre rituals in the world is the bachelor party. Because I am such an open-minded person who is often the life of the party, everybody assumes that I would be an advocate of throwing the ultimate bash for such an occasion. On the contrary, the idea of this "last night of freedom" and why it is such a phenomenon in our culture has always puzzled me. If you have such a desire to have a night of drinking and debauchery and male bonding, then why are you getting married? I have likened the concept of the bachelor party to the last meal before the electric chair.

Men look at this occasion as some type of final wild rite of passage before settling down into a life of monogamy and stability. Of course, given the statistics, we know how often that lasts. Even disregarding the likelihood of divorce, what is this fascination with being straddled by naked women and drinking yourself into oblivion just prior to promising the one you "love" eternal loyalty? Now, please do not get me wrong. I see nothing wrong with the beauty of the nude female form or the enjoyment of an alcoholic beverage, but if they really desire this type of decadence, I cannot understand why men would not rather just remain single.

In actuality, I believe that the type of rowdy behavior which takes place at a bachelor party is what many grooms want to engage in more often, but are afraid to when they are single. Because the occasion gives them a convenient excuse to behave in this manner, they take advantage of it to full capacity before settling into something more socially acceptable. I am not condemning the often outrageous activities that take place at such an event, but I am criticizing the decision to do it as a precursor to a wedding. If you really want to party and enjoy erotic ecstasy, then I recommend you just remain single, and summon the courage to do these things. It should not arise out of the repressed desire to live out your fantasies before the fun and the freedom ends. It sounds harsh, but it really appears that is the attitude many grooms have when participating in the custom. That is why I liken it to the last meal before the electric chair, where the one who is sentenced gets to choose all of the things they want to eat before they die.

The type of escapist pleasures that so many men only experience at a bachelor party is the sort of thing I enjoy all of the time, except it is as a single man without restrictions who is not vowing his life to another woman. I believe that if you live out the fantasies you envision at your bachelor party before you get engaged, then you will not have the yearning to experience them right before you get married. In fact, if you have the guts to live out these desires, you may enjoy it so much that you may not want to tie the knot in the first place.

If marriage really is such a sacred institution where both parties pledge their everlasting love and support to each other, both emotionally and physically, then the bachelor party is a complete contradiction of those principles. If you are idealistic enough to believe that a man and a woman can be eternally happy in marital bliss, then you should not need to celebrate your "last night of freedom" as if it is some type of justification for all of your excesses. You should use it as an occasion to celebrate your upcoming nuptial with the friends you care about.

If I were about to get married, then my bachelor party would consist of gathering together my closest friends and going out to eat before hanging out and watching movies or sports. Even better, it might be going on a mini-vacation to a cool place where we can share stories while enjoying a cultural experience. That way it would be about quality time with my buddies, not just a hormonal haven of unleashed testosterone.

Again, I do not find anything morally wrong with the actual events that generally take place at these festivities, but I question the motives of those future husbands who crave them. Here is my advice. If you are a guy about to get married, and the thought of a raucous rendezvous with your guy friends and some naked women is extremely enticing, then seriously consider why you are getting married. The conclusion you may come up with after you ponder that question is that you want to remain single and sustain the power and the freedom to do what you want without hurting a significant other. If you want to engage in this debauchery simply because you were too scared to do so when you were unattached, then the bachelor party really is the last meal before the electric chair, because in all likelihood your marriage will be doomed.

CHAPTER 49
Protect Yourself From Disaster
☆ ☆ ☆

"Prenuptial agreement: Paper a lawyer prepares to protect the party of the first part from the party of the second part should they discover the party's over."—Rheta Grimsley Johnson

As we have learned in the previous chapters, the statistics of marriage failure rates are pretty frightening. Let us assume that you disregard these damning statistics and choose to get engaged. Before you get married, there is one extremely important document I would advise everybody to sign and that is the prenuptial agreement.

Let us revisit those statistics in case you forgot. More than fifty percent of marriages end in divorce, and studies show that fewer than forty percent of those that last are actually satisfying, so you can conclude that the actual success rate of marriage is below twenty percent. It may not be a romantic way of looking at things, but let us analogize marriage to a business deal, which in many ways it is. If you are entering a business agreement that has a less than one in five chance in succeeding, and you have the opportunity to protect yourself from potential complications and losses, why would you not take it? Business tycoon Donald Trump writes a chapter on the importance of this document in his book *How to Get Rich*.

The primary reasons people do not get prenuptial agreements is that they are under the delusion that their marriage will defy statistical evidence and last forever. Please do not let your emotions get in the way of your good judgment. Don't complicate common sense. After studying community property in law school, I have learned about the grave financial consequences that a divorce can have on a person. I do not want to go into a detailed explanation here because I did not write this book to give legal advice, and the laws differ depending on jurisdiction. You should study your local community property laws before getting married or seek the advice of an attorney who specializes on such matters. It is true that it is the last thing on your mind when your judgment is clouded by sentiments of everlasting love and commitment, but reality indicates that such emotion may be fleeting. In case there is a separation, you should be prepared to protect yourself and your assets.

Of course, another reason that couples do not get prenuptial agreements is that one of the parties, generally the man, is afraid to approach their spouse with the suggestion. I find this apprehension simply preposterous because if your partner truly loves you, then they must understand that you need to minimize complications in the future in case problems arise. I am not even saying that signing the document will eliminate all of your monetary worries in the event of a divorce, but it does lessen the burden you will bear if you are the primary earner in the marriage.

If you are a man and your wife refuses to sign a prenuptial agreement, it is generally because of one of two reasons. The first one is that her belief in the relationship is so strong that she does not even want to consider the possibility of future difficulties, much less divorce. In this case, while her intentions are noble, she is quite simply letting her emotions get in the way of her reasoning. Additionally, you do not know where her intentions will lie in the event of a separation, so why take the risk? Unfortunately, the other major motive why a wife refuses to sign a prenup is that she wants to be in an advantageous position in the event of a divorce. I am not even saying that in a condescending manner because it is her every right to look out for her own best interests.

I am not giving you this advice to steer you away from marriage, nor do I want you to get the idea that all women are evil and looking to take advantage of you. I am merely telling you that you should also look out for your own well-being and guard your assets the best way you can. Go into the marriage with high hopes of a lovely future, but comprehend the idea that the worst is always possible. I would approach her with the mindset that signing the document is a non-negotiable matter and that it is beneficial for both parties because it lessens tricky obstacles in the event of a divorce. Marriage is largely an emotional decision, but it has legally binding consequences, and you want to be in a favorable position in the eyes of the law. If she still declines to sign the agreement, you must analyze her motivations and decide whether or not this marriage is a step you want to take. Bottom line is that it is best to protect yourselves from the potential frustration and future financial complications and get a prenuptial agreement.

CHAPTER 50
Swinging Is Not Just for the Playground
☆ ☆ ☆

"Si Non Oscillas, Noli Tintinnare"—Inscription in front of the Playboy Mansion, Chicago

When Hugh Hefner opened up the Chicago Playboy Mansion, inscribed on the door were the Latin words *"Si Non Oscillas, Noli Tintinnare."* Translated to English that means, "If you don't swing, don't ring." While the thought of cavorting with a bunch of beautiful Playmates would fulfill just about every man's fantasy, that is not typically the visual associated with swinging. Of course, there are those who are so shut out to the idea of swinging that the only thing they think of when they hear the word is children swaying back and forth in a playground.

Unfortunately, when people do imagine the swingers' community, most just picture a bunch of naked, overweight senior citizens carousing with each other. Not that there is anything wrong with that image per se, because there is no law that says you have to be a certain age or weight to enjoy sex, but it is an enormous misconception. Others have the misbelief that these parties exist as part of some cult-like subculture of sexual deviants taking out all of their yearnings in a secretive setting. Just think of the movie *Eyes Wide Shut* for those of you who have seen it.

While those types of parties may exist, it is not the norm in the lifestyle. The truth is that swingers consist of all types of regular people who just happen to be really open-minded. If you decide to explore the lifestyle, you may find that you can meet someone who would love to cater to any fantasy in your imagination.

Let me speak from my personal experience. I have been in just about every social setting imaginable, but nowhere have I seen nicer and more open-minded people than the swingers community. I have attended countless parties across the country and even hosted weekly lifestyle events for about a year. Not only has my experience allowed me to fulfill some of my most titillating fantasies, but more importantly, it has introduced me to amazing friends who will last a lifetime. Since you are already open-minded enough to be reading this book, I highly recommend that you attend a party when you get a chance. I know what many of you are thinking. You are afraid of what you will see, or you are scared you might end up with somebody that you may not be attracted to. Most of all, you are apprehensive about stepping that far out of your comfort zone into an atmosphere that seems so foreign and surreal.

Let me clear up your concerns. These parties are not all hormonal orgies where random people are grabbing legs, breasts and thighs like it is KFC. On the contrary, people are highly respectful, and the setting is very comfortable because the attendees are so open-minded and nonjudgmental. When you are literally willing to put everything out there, there is not much to hide, nor is there much room to be dramatic or critical. Nobody is forced into anything, and there is always an understanding that nothing will happen unless all parties are willing. If you are a woman reading this or a guy who would like to attend a party with one but are afraid about how she will be treated, I can reassure you that a lady will be given much more respect at a swingers party than at a regular bar or club. You should not be afraid, as it is generally a very pleasant setting and the men realize that "no" means "no."

If you are new to the lifestyle, you are not alone. In fact, there are newcomers at just about every party who are there just to watch or soak things in. If the thought of watching people have sex makes you feel awkward, there are always mingling areas where people are talking, drinking and snacking on food. In fact, if you attend a party for the first time, it is advisable that you hang out in this common area awhile before you even think of hooking up. I assure you that you will meet the friendliest people you will ever see, and as you spend more time there, the idea of participating in the festivities becomes much more enticing.

Now I know that many of you are interested in attending these parties and have always fantasized about it but either lacked the courage to go there or do not know how to find one. As far as your trepidation goes, my main advice is to simply get over it and realize that life is too short to be afraid to do the things you desire. Having both attended and thrown parties myself, I can assure you that you are missing out on a broadening experience. If you simply do not know where to find such events, I advise you to preview some swinger websites. Two of the best are Swing Lifestyle and Lifestyle Lounge. You can register for free and view the events sections to find out about the local parties. You may be surprised by what you will discover, that the swingers' community is not nearly as big of a minority as you would imagine, and there are gatherings going on everywhere. Not only that, when you see the pictures on the profiles of the attendees, you will realize that there are many attractive people who attend these parties, and you can meet somebody that suits your preference.

I realize that most of you reading this book are likely either single males or men in a relationship looking to explore your options. You may have heard the rumor that it is necessary to have a partner to get into a party. Generally, the rule is that you need to show up with another female to attend, but there are plenty of parties that do allow single males. As I mentioned above, research the details of your local parties and you are likely to eventually find one that allows single men. Even if you cannot, I urge you to set up a profile on these sites and try to find a single girl or a couple that likes to play with single men. There are plenty more out there than you would imagine, and often parties allow admission of single men if they are occupied by a couple or another single woman. If you want to make this fantasy come true, I can assure you that if you are persistent and honest with women about your curiosity regarding these parties, you will find somebody who is interested enough to join you.

What you will discover when you are a single guy at the party is that you can find women who are open about their sexuality as opposed to having their guard up all the time and acting like they are doing you a favor if they decide to sleep with you. Let's face it. Men are, by nature, sexual beings. Inexplicably, most guys try to fulfill their needs by going to places where they have little to no chance of getting what they are looking for. At these parties, you are likely to find many women who have similar sexual attitudes to your own, and they are in an environment where it is socially acceptable to act on these desires.

Remember what Nina Hartley said about a woman's sexuality: "Sex isn't something men do to you. It isn't something men get out of you. Sex is something you dive into with gusto and like it every bit as much as he does." Here is a setting where women admit fully that they enjoy erotic pleasure just as much if not more than men do. If you are comfortable enough, you will find that there are many couples where the female partner likes to have fun with other men and, if you are willing, you can fulfill her fantasies.

That is the beauty of the swingers setting. There is no illusion about why people are there. People will not pretend that sex is something taboo or that it has to be practiced exclusively between couples. These parties celebrate sexuality instead of repressing it, and as long as you practice safely, it can be a very healthy way to live out your fantasies with like-minded individuals.

Now let us contrast this to the bar setting. If you are a guy at a bar looking to go home with a girl, you are most likely to leave with nothing but frustration and disappointment. Most girls will tell you they are just there to "dance" or "hang out with friends." Even those who are looking to hook up will likely be guarded by their protective friends or not admit to their true desires due to social restrictions. Once you become comfortable with the swinger scene, you will find it is almost impossible to go back to the frustration and illogical nonsense of traditional nightlife.

A swingers party is a much friendlier and more open environment where many women are there specifically to fulfill their sexual wants and needs. Even if you do not end up sleeping with a girl at a party, you are highly unlikely to encounter the rejection and uppity attitude that most women have at a bar. As I said before, going to a bar to have sex with a girl is almost like going to Burger King to get a lobster dinner. Once you become involved with the swingers community, you will inevitably meet women whose mindsets are in tune with your own and you will fulfill the longings that eluded you in more common venues. Additionally, if you go back to the nightclubs after enjoying the lifestyle parties, you will return with the added confidence of experiencing something most are too closed-minded to explore. You will not be as worried about sleeping with a girl because you know there is a far better venue where you can fulfill those desires if you so choose.

So let us assume that you are a single guy who has summoned up the courage to attend a party and has found an event that accepts single men. Once you are there and become comfortable with the idea of having a sexual encounter, you may wonder how to approach a woman or a couple at one of these parties. Having been to many parties as a single guy, I can outline the best way for you to maximize your time there. First of all, although the venue is completely different and the people have a different mindset, the basic attitude with which you should arrive is the same as the bar scene. Come in looking to have a good time and meet cool people, and do not worry if you hook up or not. If you come in with a positive attitude and without expectations, then you will surely enjoy yourself and will be more likely to find what you are looking for. Here are some steps to maximizing your experience.

☆ Step 1: Survey the scene and watch for people who show interest in you.

Of course, nothing will happen if you do not make it happen, so here is the best way to fit into the swinger environment as a single guy. There may be single girls there, but let us be realistic and assume that almost all of the women there are with a male companion. First of all, survey the scene by walking around with a drink in hand and reading people's facial and body language. Often, you will notice the female partner checking you out, or the couple motioning you over with their hands or their eyes. If that happens, go talk to them without hesitation. When they express interest, the power is usually within your hands whether you want to play with them or not.

☆ Step 2: Befriend the men at the parties.

If you are not good at reading those signals or do not notice them, my main advice is to befriend any guy who seems approachable at the party, especially those there with a woman. Most of the men there are very cordial with everybody because the atmosphere is festive and they know they will likely fulfill some type of fantasy that night. Unfortunately, there are often single men at the party who are uncomfortable in the atmosphere or are just looking for a cheap thrill or voyeuristic pleasure. Those guys will likely find the experience disappointing, and others may find them too creepy to be with.

When couples see that you are cool and friendly, not just some sexually frustrated guy looking for an easy release, they will be more comfortable with you. That comfort could result in you playing with the guy's female companion, but even if it does not, it is good to blend into the environment and appear as a genuinely likable person who is there because you are open-minded, not just because you are lonely and desperate. Once the gentlemen at the party are at ease with your presence, you will feel much more secure with yourself and with the situation. It is true that most couples there are looking to play only with other couples, but when people see a cool guy having a good time getting along with everybody, you instantly become more attractive to those looking to enjoy the company of a single male. When that happens, you may find that the choice is yours as to what extent you are willing to explore your desires.

You may wonder why I am advising you to become friendly with the men at the party first even though the women are usually there for the same reason. The women are generally equally as responsive at these gatherings, but if you just start chatting up every female half of a couple, it may come off as disrespectful and aggressive. As I mentioned earlier, there are sometimes single guys at these events who will give you a bad name, as they come across as awkward or perverted. That is why it is best to establish that you are a smooth guy who enjoys life and is comfortable in any setting, even if you do not get laid. Conversely, this easy-going attitude will result in you getting more action.

☆ Step 3: Ease into conversation with small talk about "the lifestyle."

When you do strike up a conversation with a couple, ease into it by making some small talk. Ask them how long they have been in "the lifestyle," as the swinger community often calls it. After you get an idea of how the conversation is going and gage their interest level, slowly transition into asking them what type of fantasies they enjoy. If they find you attractive and enjoy your company, you may soon discover that their fantasies include you. If they are not interested in playing with you, do not get angry or frustrated; instead, remain friendly with them and slowly move on to somebody else. The key is to be outgoing and engaging, and eventually your desires will come true.

☆ Step 4: If you discover a single woman at the party, make sure you talk to her.

So far, I have explained how to handle yourself when you are a single male approaching couples. You may also find single women at these parties but they are few and far between. Just realize that when you find them, they are an absolute goldmine because they are usually hot-blooded passionate women who love sex and are eager to satisfy your wildest erotic dreams. Talk to them in the same smooth manner as you would a couple, and soon you two may form your own couple for the night and have the time of your life. By the way, if you are a single woman reading this who attends these parties or wants to, we men appreciate you, and you should be cherished.

Many of you may be in a relationship, but that does not mean that these parties should be off limits. Let me make this clear first. If you are completely happy in your relationship and the thought of being at a party where others would be engaged in sexual activity is disconcerting, then I am not recommending that you attend a party just for the sake of it. There is no point unnecessarily complicating a relationship where things are already going well.

If you are happily with a significant other, but are looking to explore some new sexual experiences, then perhaps you should consider looking into the swinger scene. I will admit that all of my experience in the lifestyle has been as a single guy attending parties either alone or with a casual partner, or as a party host. I have not been involved in the swinger scene as part of a committed relationship so I cannot speak from personal knowledge what it is like to do so. I have, however, encountered countless couples with whom I have discussed their lifestyle at these parties. Additionally, I have interviewed plenty of couples who have been involved in the lifestyle to varying degrees. My studies and interactions have revealed that it is rare to find those who have a negative attitude toward their swinging experience. Some of the couples attended a party or two mainly out of curiosity, but did not participate in any sexual activity. Although they did not play, most of them had very positive things to say about the experience and enjoyed the general atmosphere and the friendly nature of the people there.

For those who have explored erotic adventures with other couples, the majority of people in my research were thrilled with the experience and spoke about how it brought a whole new dimension to their relationship. Not only did it allow them to fulfill their fantasies in an honest and open manner, it also enhanced the pleasure they felt with each other in the privacy of their own bedrooms. The common theme was that they were emotionally monogamous but sexually polygamous. Most people are still too close-minded to be at ease with that dichotomy, but there are those who can love a partner but also be secure enough to understand that their sexual desires sometimes include others. Instead of cheating or lying about it the way so many people do, the swingers community is a way of giving into those temptations without giving up the person you really care about. Being a happily single guy, I am not going to tell a happy couple what to do, but if you and your partner are looking to broaden your sexual horizons while maintaining your relationship, then a swingers party may be an avenue to do so.

As you can see, most of the preconceived notions people have of the swingers' community are false. These are not just unattractive people exploring their perversions or a strange subculture of masked deviants having cold and callous sex. On the contrary, it is the most friendly and open atmosphere you can ever encounter, and I highly recommend that you check out a party and find out for yourself. You will discover that swinging is not something just for the child's playground, but an environment where adults can play out their biggest fantasies.

CHAPTER 51
Kids...the Greatest Gift?
☆ ☆ ☆

"Having children makes you no more a parent than having a piano makes you a pianist."—Michael Levine

The biggest decision that anybody can possibly make in their life is whether to have children. If you are truly prepared for all of the responsibilities and challenges that come with raising a child, then it can be the greatest blessing in your life. Unfortunately, there are too many people who have kids before they are ready. Although I do not have kids myself, I wanted to share some things everybody needs to consider before making that most crucial decision.

☆ **Rule 1: Make sure you find a partner who will be a good parent.**

First of all, make sure you have found that "perfect partner" that you are absolutely sure is compatible with you for a long-term relationship. If all of the elements of true love and a strong relationship are not there, then you should not take this major step. Even if you share closeness and chemistry with your romantic partner, that does not necessarily mean she has strong maternal instincts. Some women make terrific girlfriends or wives but may not be able to handle the responsibilities that are associated with child rearing. Before even thinking about kids, make sure that the woman you are with has the parental characteristics to be an ideal mother to your prospective child.

⭐ Rule 2: *Analyze your own qualities as a potential parent.*

Of course, just as important, you also need to come to terms with your own qualities as a potential father. Are you living a lifestyle that is conducive to being a role model for an infant? Are you ready to take on the financial and emotional responsibilities that are necessary for the well-being of a young one? Are you prepared to put all of your own needs aside for the sake of bringing someone into this world?

All of those things are important, but that last question in particular needs to be pondered extensively. What many fail to consider when having offspring is that all of their own interests are supplanted by those of the children they are volunteering to bring into the world. Be prepared to refocus your entire life so it revolves around your child. This may mean making enormous sacrifices and delaying or giving up goals that are much more realistic before becoming a parent. It is true that there are many things you can do even with kids, but why rush it? You need to be absolutely certain that you have lived out your dreams as a single man and as a free couple before experiencing the joys of parenthood.

⭐ Rule 3: *Wait until you are mature before having children.*

I have always felt that people should wait until they are a little older until they have children. Obviously, I have already stressed the importance of waiting before deciding to get into a long-term relationship, and the same applies to having kids. If you have someone in your life you really love, enjoy your relationship freely for awhile. This will even benefit your children. After all, what we teach our kids is largely from learning from our own life experiences. Most people in their twenties have yet to enjoy the diversity of events in their lives that they can teach to their young ones. When you are more mature and savvy about the world, then you will have a much larger body of knowledge to share. Additionally, by spending a few years together first, you will understand how strong your relationship is and whether you can handle the permanent connection of having a child.

If you are ready to make this decision, then also make sure it is for the right reasons. Let me run through a list of terrible reasons to have children, all of which I have encountered both in life and in my studies.

☆ Rule 4: Do not decide to have a child to make you more responsible.

Do not decide to have a child because it will *make* you happy or more responsible. It is true that you may become happier and that you are forced to take on added responsibilities, but that is an awful premise upon which to make the decision. If you are living carelessly or are depressed, then that will have a negative effect on the person you bring into this world. You should already be happy and responsible so you can use those qualities to benefit your child.

☆ Rule 5: Do not have a child simply to fill a void in your life.

Do not have a child simply to fill some type of void in your life, or just to know that somebody will love you unconditionally. There is nothing more disturbing than when I hear somebody say they are having kids so they have someone who cares about them. If you do not have any true friends and family in your life already, having a child is not the answer to your problems. A child needs somebody who is strong and stable, both mentally and financially, not just someone needy for affection. If you go into this crucial decision with such a negative mindset, you may find that even your own flesh and blood will not give you the love you seek.

☆ Rule 6: Do not have a child in attempt to fix a shaky relationship.

I have already emphasized the importance of having a solid partner with whom you share a strong relationship. One unconscionable mistake many couples make is to have a child merely to bring them closer together. This is fine if you already have a healthy bond, but if you feel that you will not last as a couple, having a kid is not the answer to your problems. In fact, it may drive you further apart. Fix your relationship first, or end it and move on. Countless studies show the advantages of being raised in a stable two-parent home so I am not going to go into detail there. If your relationship is rocky, then you are bringing someone into an unstable environment and you will all suffer as a result.

☆ *Rule 7: Do not have a child to fulfill a social expectation.*

Above all, do not decide to have children merely because it is the social expectation that it is our purpose in life to do so. In fact, there are many people in the world who are not fit to be parents. There are also those who would be terrific at raising a child but are much better off not having kids. Just as you are not a failure if you do not get married, you can be a perfectly content person without a child. An even bigger failing is being stuck with a responsibility you see as a burden. Do not give in to the pressures of society or your loved ones. This is your life, and you should not be living it out according to other people's wants and needs. There are plenty of other glorious contributions you can make to this planet other than having kids. Live your life according to your own standards and make the decision that you feel happiest with.

While I am on this topic, when I tell people that I have no desire to have kids, they ask me what type of legacy I want to leave. In fact, too many people are consumed by what they will leave behind when they leave this earth instead of concentrating on how to maximize the enjoyment of their time here on it. We do not know what lies ahead when our days are done, so just concentrate on making the most of every day you are here. For many people, a child enhances their joy, but for others, the enormous responsibility inhibits it. My answer for people is that I am not concerned as much with my legacy as I am with making the most of my life. After all, what better legacy can you leave than departing this planet with others admiring you for maximizing every moment on it?

☆ *Rule 8: Do not have a child just to have someone to take care of you when you are older.*

Additionally, do not just have kids so you have somebody to take care of you when you are old. I get asked this question often as well. Do not be swayed to have a child when you are hesitant to do so merely because you want a future caretaker. Is it really worth changing the entire course of your life for the possibility that there will be someone to take care of you at the end of it? I am not saying this should not factor in your decision, but just do not make it the sole basis for deciding to have children. There are other options for support when you reach an advanced age than to have a child you do not really want.

Personally speaking, I have never had the desire to have children. I have always placed an extremely high value on my own freedom and living each moment without worrying about a permanent responsibility. I realize that my lifestyle flourishes as a single guy with little serious attachments and that having a child would be catastrophic to my own wants and needs. That may sound selfish, but I feel it is much more self-serving and dangerous to have children you are not ready for. I am completely aware that I would not be a good father with the mentality I have now. I live very spontaneously and adventurously and could not provide the stability and support a child needs.

That is not to say I do not like children. In fact, since I am in many ways a big kid myself, I enjoy the company of children for limited sessions. A few years ago, I discovered a perfect program that allowed me to share this enjoyment with a child who needed it. I highly recommend the Big Brothers and Big Sisters of America for all of you who love kids but are not sure if you are ready to have your own. The volunteer program pairs a young child in need of an older role model in their life with a compatible adult. It is up to you to arrange monthly meetings with the kid, but the company also organizes various events to bring you closer together. It was one of the most fulfilling experiences of my life.

My Little Brother was an incredibly cute, well-mannered eight-year-old boy whose father left him when he was a baby. Although his mother was a really nice, responsible person, she wanted a strong, educated adult male friend to share company with. He was a really amazing kid, and I shared many joyous moments with him. Unfortunately, after I finished school, we had to conclude our relationship with the organization because I wanted to travel the world and would be unable to see him as much as I wanted to. Nonetheless, we have each made a friend for life. If you love children, especially if you are not ready for the permanent responsibility of your own, I strongly suggest looking up your local chapter of the program. In fact, if you did not know, just by purchasing this book, you have aided the foundation because I am donating five percent of the profits to Big Brothers and Big Sisters of America.

In the future, when I am more financially stable, I want to do further volunteer work to help the needy kids of the world. Traveling to so many countries has allowed me to witness some of the darker sides of this planet, particularly the impoverished living conditions so many people suffer. Because

I do not want kids of my own, I feel that I will be able to dedicate time and resources to help many people. This would be a legacy I would be proud of.

I hope you do not get the wrong message that I am suggesting you shouldn't have children just because I do not want them. On the contrary, I am merely stressing that you should not decide to do so until you are completely prepared to take on the enormous responsibilities that come with raising a child. If you are prepared to set your own needs aside for the good of a child, and you are in a financially and emotionally stable relationship, then bringing someone into this world is the greatest gift that you can give. If you are not ready, you may find that a kid is the gift that keeps on taking, and both you and your children will suffer as a result.

CHAPTER 52
Ups and Downs of the Lifestyle
☆ ☆ ☆

"A man's errors are his portals of discovery."—James Joyce

When I am asked to describe the Showstopper Lifestyle in one phrase, I tell people I am making all my fantasies come true. In a world where so many people are apathetic about their existence, I have been fortunate to spend nearly every moment delighted to be in an unbelievably exciting, surreal paradise surrounded by gorgeous women, breathtaking settings, and incredible people. This paradise is a result of my knowing what makes me happy and making my lucid dream a reality. It is a rarity when I am spending time not doing what I love. That is not to say that the Lifestyle is without its downfalls. In fact, when you live your life according to a set of values and goals that stray from mainstream society, it is sometimes difficult to fit in. I wanted to share some of the dark side of utopia so you can get a more complete picture of the Lifestyle and can avoid some of the mistakes I have made.

The average person has the desire to get married, have children and raise a "traditional" family. Now there is absolutely nothing wrong with wanting the conventions of a typical household. As I said, I was raised in a "normal" home and the benefits of that stability have allowed me to become a strong, self-assured person who has been able to thrive doing what I want. Thankfully, most people have been tremendously supportive of me standing up against these norms and living how I want to live. Despite this, I sometimes have internal struggles that make me feel like an outsider.

When my friends talk about their families, jobs, dating life, and personal problems, I often have a hard time understanding their situations. Being a person who does not want a regular job, steady girlfriend, or a traditional family of my own, the confines of those institutions bear no relevance to my own wants and needs. I am open-minded and have encountered a diversity of experiences, and that is why I have been able to intermingle with people from all walks of life. However, since I have taken the road less traveled, it has sometimes made me unsympathetic to the wants and needs of others. As a result, I find that while I am able to get along with everybody, I often cannot really relate to anybody. This has even caused barriers with some of my best friends and sadly, I have drifted apart from some of them.

My unfettered belief in my way of life has allowed me to live out many of my fantasies, but it has also left me frequently detached from reality. Unfortunately, this detachment has often manifested itself in an air of arrogance. Oftentimes, when I discuss my life, I have an aura of superiority that makes others feel as if I am communicating to them in a condescending manner. Truth be told, there have been times where I was disrespectful and unreceptive to the idea that a person could be content in a monogamous relationship or a steady job, but I have grown to recognize that many people are perfectly pleased by those conventions. Many thrive in stability and for those who do so, having a serious relationship allows them to maximize life experiences. I have learned over the years that the very core of being open-minded is to appreciate all ways of life as long as people are not harming others and are happy with themselves. Just make sure that in your learning process you do not alienate those who love you.

If you follow the principles I have outlined in this book, you should become an independent, self-assured, well-rounded person. When you spend each day exhilarated to be alive, others may not be able to relate to your enthusiasm. I have often had people try to write off my natural excitement as phony or overcompensation for being unhappy. That cannot be further from the truth because I genuinely am in high spirits and merely want to express this passion.

You must come to terms with the fact that many people are not so fortunate to enjoy this self-belief, and even those who do may not share the same goals you pursue. It is a fact that many people are so consumed with the confines of conventional thinking that they cannot accept or understand somebody completely satisfied outside of that realm.

Earlier, I mentioned the story about working out with former Mr. Universe Tony Atlas. He provided an excellent analogy that explains why so many are insecure and pass judgment on the lives of others. He was telling me how many celebrities face persecution from those who do not even know them. Atlas also made sure to point out, "You notice that people do not make fun of people in hospitals or wheelchairs?" He stated that it is because most individuals already feel superior to them. They really want to bring down those who they feel are above them in some way. When you display belief in your abilities and security with yourself as a person, many envious people might want to knock you down. If you truly believe in yourself, this criticism should not affect you.

At the same time, you should never let your confidence manifest itself in arrogance and feel that you are better than other people. When you do not rely on others for happiness, people often may perceive that you are selfish. If you are not self-centered, and you share your joy with others instead of merely basking in the glory of your existential excitement, then you can help erase that perception.

Perhaps the most challenging thing I have encountered in my lifestyle has been finding women who I can form a close connection with. That may sound ironic because I have had such a large number of women in my life. Of those I have met, however, only a select few have truly understood my thinking process. I have been extremely successful at consistently having various ladies floating in and out of my life, but most cannot handle the idea of a guy being so independently happy. As I explained, although women yearn for adventure, most eventually want something more secure, which I am unable to provide.

Additionally, the fact that I have had such little emotional investment in many of the women I have dated has occasionally resulted in my being callous or uncaring toward them. Over the years, there have also been many beautiful, sweet girls who have really liked me whom I have had to push away because I knew that I could not make the commitments they wanted. Part of it was because I did not want to get too attached myself, and the other reason was that I did not want them to become too close to me and be disappointed. Truth be told, I do appreciate the caring, companionship and intimacy that a romantic relationship can bring, but my lack of desire for drama or commitment makes this type of connection nearly impossible. The most devastating part about that is I have lost some precious women who were terrific friends because of my unwillingness and inability to share serious emotional intimacy. I have learned from my mistakes the hard way and have vowed to truly be grateful for the women I love and who care for me.

Casual dating can be an excellent experience, particularly if you are not ready to be part of a committed relationship. It is much better to enjoy short-term pleasure with women you may not be too close to than to cause long-term pain to someone whom you do care for. Not everything has to have long-term ramifications to be meaningful as our lives are an accumulation of experiences that make each moment enjoyable. Just do not let the cumulative effects of those joyful happenings result in you becoming emotionally distant from real personal feelings. The true beauty of life is in the connections you make with quality people who enhance your life, and once you meet one, it is a gift that you should cherish.

My freewheeling mentality has allowed me to take chances and enjoy escapades that many are afraid to try. Unfortunately, sometimes it has resulted in reckless behavior that had harmful consequences on myself, and potentially could have hurt others. I have not done drugs or practiced unprotected sex, but have done stupid things that have caused me damage. The lesson here is simple common sense. Free your mind and enjoy life to the utmost, but there is a fine line between being carefree and being careless. If you cross that line, you may find the freedom you enjoy useless without your good health and peace of mind.

I sincerely hope that the principles of the Showstopper Lifestyle I have described in this book will help make you a more open-minded person who reaches out for their dreams. I feel that I was blessed with the inner strength to live according to my own standards, and the aptitude to recognize what does and does not work in our society. When you develop this power, you will not only learn from your own mistakes, but more importantly, you will learn from other people's errors and avoid making them. I want to illustrate some of my own mistakes in the hope that you will not fall into them yourself. If you appreciate the good experiences and grow from the bad ones, you will be in control of the Lifestyle and not let it control you.

Finally, I wanted to share the most emotional experience of my life. My friends often ask me how I was able to handle the loss of a parent without losing my sense of excitement and childlike wonder. When my father passed away from cancer a few years ago, I stood in tears at the hospital, realizing things would never be the same. It was the lowest moment in my life, but it also taught me the highest understanding of what is truly important. While his death brought immeasurable sadness, it also provided me with a lucid awareness. The helpless feeling that took over my body during those final days was the ultimate test of inner strength. Ever since that transcendent experience, I have not allowed myself to be stressed out by trivial matters. The lesson I learned is that unless something is truly out of your control, it is not worth worrying about.

So the next time you are overcome by frustration, ask yourself if the matter is really worth the aggravation. Often, you may find that the situation is in your hands and you have the power to make the best of it. As the old saying goes, don't sweat the small stuff. If you face everyday happenings with a positive attitude, then when you are confronted by life's true challenges you may discover that you have the strength to persevere. That is the ultimate test of your inner superhero that you will face during the ups and downs of the Showstopper Lifestyle.

CHAPTER 53
Meet Joey Showstopper
☆ ☆ ☆

"And in the end, it's not the years in your life that count. It's the life in your years."—Abraham Lincoln

Ladies and gentlemen, my name is Joe Average, and I am here to tell you about my life. I am a forty-year old American man. I am currently single with no children, and I recently left my job in a corporation to start my own business. I wake up every morning with the anticipation of what thrills my day will bring. I have been blessed with an incredible life, and I wanted to share some of my story.

I lived with my parents, and I went to school until I was 18. My parents cared for me so much growing up. They couldn't wait to see my wedding and the day I would make them grandparents. I have nothing against the idea of marriage, but I made it clear to them from a young age that it was my life, and if I were to settle down, it would be when I felt the time was right. They respected my decision and even enjoyed the fact that they would keep their "baby boy" longer. Both of my parents worked when I was a child and I spent much of my time alone, thinking of creative ways to entertain myself.

I was a big dreamer as a kid, and I would often sit alone and think about the spectacular adventures and gorgeous girls that I would enjoy when I grew up. I learned early on the importance of generating your own excitement as well as having individual strength. This realization that being alone does not necessarily mean being lonely has aided me as I've gotten older.

When I became a teenager, while most of my friends chased girls and got into a continuous series of month-long "relationships," I focused on playing sports, developing a wide variety of hobbies, being involved in student organizations, and getting good grades. I believe spending so much time alone as a boy made me relish being single while most boys were overcome by hormones. While I may not have had girlfriends, I became really close to my parents and formed connections with a tremendous set of friends that have been with me to this day. Additionally, while many in my school succumbed to the peer pressures of drinking and other temptations, I avoided those things because I was so busy and focused on my goals. I figured that I was too young to handle unnatural substances in my body and did not need them to have a good time.

As a result of my involvement in a variety of clubs and athletics, I became very popular in my school, both with the guys and the girls. My focus on my coursework and my body attracted many of my female classmates to me because they were turned on by the idea of an intelligent, well-built guy who was a challenge. I believe people also respected how I got along with everybody and did not feel the need to drink, smoke or chase girls to be cool. I was lucky enough to learn early that there is nothing cooler than being yourself and finding your own path.

By the time I was in my late teens, I was much more mature and confident than the majority of my peers. My high school years were an incredible all-around experience, and a stepping stone to even better days ahead in college. Because I was happy at home, close to my family, and not much of a partier, I decided to save our family some money and start my university years off living at home. My family was never fond of traveling, but I convinced them to spend some of the money that we saved on my room and board on some overseas family vacations. These trips not only made me closer to my parents, but they gave me an appreciation for the sheer scope of wonders that lay out there on this earth.

After my first two years of school, I moved away to live on campus. Although I was content living at home, I felt it would expand my horizons to assert my independence and move out. Living at school allowed me to meet a whole new circle of friends. I also began dating a lovely young blonde named Betty. She was a wonderful person whose companionship I cherished, and we shared an incredible chemistry. At the same time, I had other avenues I wanted to pursue so I told her that I was not ready for anything serious. She was upset but appreciated my honesty, and we decided to remain friends. In fact, soon she was even helping me pick up other girls at parties and bars! Betty would be my only significant relationship during my college years.

That is not to say that I was living a Casanova lifestyle full of wine and women. On the contrary, my main focus was on maximizing my educational opportunities. I took a diversity of courses, ranging from economics and accounting to film studies and public speech. These classes gave me a foundation of knowledge that has prepared me for various career paths. Additionally, I got involved in volunteer work, intramural sports, and numerous college clubs that catered to my interests. This, in turn, allowed me to meet friends who shared the same hobbies that I did, and we would get together weekly to enjoy these passions.

Many people, including some of my close friends, became overwhelmed by the freedom of being away from home and the access to free booze and babes. There is definitely nothing wrong with that, but I believe that developing a strong-willed, independent streak as a boy made me less obsessed with being free to do whatever I wanted as a young adult. I did enjoy an occasional beer with my friends and went to some parties, but I was just as happy chilling out and spending time with my buddies at home.

That is not to say we did not experience our wild adventures together. A group of us took a trip to Cancun for our spring break in my junior year, which was an amazing vacation that brought us closer together. After the success of that trip, we took a few other journeys together, including a two-week trek across Europe to reward ourselves after graduation. Not to be outdone, my parents took me on a month-long tour of East Asia with the cash they had saved up because of my scholarships. These retreats allowed me to strengthen ties with many of my loved ones, as well as to broaden my horizons as a person.

By the time I was in my early twenties, I was single, educated, and had traveled to nearly twenty countries, which made me an extremely cultured person. In addition, the vast amount of life experiences I had compiled made me a very self-assured, open-minded, well-rounded person. Being surrounded by a circle of loving friends and family also gave me immeasurable support and inner strength. Confidence is the key to making all of your dreams come true and combining that with my free-minded attitude, I was already well on my way to living the life I fantasized about when I was a child.

I decided to go to graduate school for a Masters in Business Administration, but first took a year off after my undergraduate studies. People advised me against the extended time off and their concerns made sense, but I followed my gut and have not regretted it. If I have learned one major thing in life, it is to do what you want to do, not what you have to do. For many people, taking a year off to find themselves often ends up with them losing track of their priorities. While I have enjoyed a free-wheeling, spontaneous lifestyle, I always have been focused on my goals. It is important to live for the moment, but also vital to prepare for the future.

Knowing that I would be commencing graduate school in a year, I wanted to exploit my freedom to the fullest extent. I spent my year doing community service and working some odd jobs that revolved around my passions, like writing movie reviews for the local paper. I used this money to take a few more trips to various destinations around the world. I also strengthened my work-out regime by adding some yoga and Pilates to my weightlifting routine. All of these activities combined to strengthen my mind and body. Most importantly, I spent this year developing a large-scale vision of which people, places and things were important to my life. When I formulated this picture, I realized that my goals differed from those of the mainstream, but it did not deter me from living each moment doing what I loved. I figured that as long as you are spending as much time as possible doing what makes you happy without harming others, then you are living your lucid dream. This outlook further escalated my self-assurance and I summoned my inner superhero, Joey Showstopper.

With this added power and freedom, I really fully entered the dating universe for the first time. Although many of my friends began to get into committed relationships, I knew I was not looking for anything serious. As Joey Showstopper, my confident attitude, intelligence, and open-mindedness made me successful with the ladies in the casual dating circuit. I lived a pretty spontaneous, fun-filled life and I began to realize that though women often need security, they also crave excitement. As a result, I met plenty of like-minded women who were looking for drama-free companionship. I enjoyed some short-term thrills with some of them, while others developed into long-term friendships that I share to this day.

By the time I completed graduate school and decided to enter the work-force, I had decided that I would not be just another employee with a boring personal life going through the motions of a job he hates. I had established the core values and traits that allowed me to live life to the fullest, even while taking on further responsibilities of employment. I continued to take vacations as often as I could with the money I was earning. As my friends began to get married and have kids, I increasingly came to terms with the fact that they would no longer be able to freely join me on these trips. Since my years of learning how to do things on my own had built up my self-reliance, I began traveling on my own. Amazingly, I learned that it was a blessing because it forced me to reach out and make new friends from all over the world as I stayed in travel hostels.

Thankfully, because I was so happy in my personal life, I took that joyous outlook into my job and really enjoyed my work. Not only was I highly educated, but people saw that I had a charismatic, outgoing personality. My boss found my enthusiasm refreshing, and we became friends as I started working my way up the corporate ladder. It is amazing what a positive attitude and genuine inner happiness can do for all aspects of your well-being. It helped that I was doing something I loved and had my own office and a gorgeous secretary.

I know what you are thinking. I do not mix business and pleasure, so that raven-haired goddess I work with is off limits. There are more than three billion women in the world, and there is no reason to complicate life at my workplace. Besides, my dating life was flourishing, and my years of experience meeting a variety of different women had given me immense confidence in this arena. There would be weeks when I would have dates with different women of varying ages and ethnicities. Keeping a free mind and being honest made me enormously successful with all demographics. I recognized that women were so accustomed to dating bland men who lacked a passion for life that they found my lifestyle alluring. They knew I was getting all kinds of girls, and I freely shared that fact with them, thus creating an aura of unattainability that fascinated them. This allowed me to fulfill many of my hedonistic fantasies, including some I never even knew I had. At the same time, the reason this type of drama-free dating was so much fun was that I was already content as a single man and did not need a serious romance in my life. I have been able to attract women because I am excited about life. I am not excited about life merely because I am attracting lots of women.

Ever since I turned thirty, people have been questioning me about when I am going to settle down and get married. Thankfully, my parents have never put any pressure on me so I am not filled with guilt that I am disappointing them. This is largely because I have retained close ties with them to this day and they see that I am extremely happy and successful. At the end of the day, that is truly what mothers and fathers want from their children. Some wonder if my adventurous lifestyle is getting old, but truth be told, it keeps getting better each day. As I grow older, I have maintained ties with that wide-eyed child who dreamed spectacular dreams as a youth. I formed the mentality to live every day as if it was my first. With this vision, I have sustained the ability to appreciate the beauty and the awe of each moment in life as if I am an excited, innocent child enjoying it for the first time.

What allows me to achieve my dreams is my realization and appreciation for the real things that are important in my life. I have already discussed the importance of being close to my family. Additionally, I have maintained ties to the friends I have met at various stages in my life. Many of them have the responsibilities of a spouse and children, but we still make efforts to get together. Just as they have accepted my free-wheeling lifestyle, I have to respect the choices they have made to raise a family. Thankfully, because I am constantly experiencing new adventures all over the world, new friendships are always blossoming and many of them have wants and needs more in tune with my own. This has given me a constant circle of people who not only provide me with emotional support but also provide me amazing companionship. They are part of the reason I am so comfortable being single. Remember, being alone does not mean being lonely.

As for my life now, it could not be better. I recently quit my job after fifteen years of learning and making friends in a terrific environment. It was an amicable split because even my company understood that it was time for me to branch out and form my own enterprise. I enjoyed my job but wanted to do something greater where I was in charge. It is important to always be happy but never be satisfied, and I felt it was time to take my career to the next level. Years of working hard and making sound financial decisions have allowed me to take the risk of starting my own business. Because I do not have a wife or kids depending on me, I can afford to make some bold decisions without worrying about my choices having a detrimental effect on people I am responsible for.

Despite my unattached status, you may be interested to know that for the past year I have been casually dating a beautiful woman named Marilyn who fits the description of everything I look for in a mate, both in looks and personality. She is an amazing person who accepts me for who I am and does not place judgment on my way of life. We were physically attracted to each other from the beginning and enjoyed an undeniable chemistry from our first date, but thankfully she is also not the type who is needy or clingy. We each enjoy our own lifestyles and set of friends, but have become increasingly close over time. What began as lust at first sight has blossomed into "real love" between two people who share mutual understanding, respect, trust, good communication and friendship. Now I am not one for labels, and thankfully neither is she, so I cannot tell you what the future holds for me and Marilyn. What I can assure you is that our relationship has made us both happier because we complement each other's strengths, not complicate them.

As for now, I still consider myself single and am unashamed to admit it. People might find it abnormal that I am forty years old and unmarried with no children and no steady job, but who is to say what is normal? I do not consider myself a failure just because I do not conform to what society expects. In fact, more than half of my friends who did get married are in relationships that are on rocky ground. Fortunately, I have made common-sense decisions that cater to the way of life I desire. Thanks to being surrounded by tremendous family and friends, and formulating the inner strength to live life according to my own standards, I have been blessed with perpetual bliss. I consider each day a gift, and I try to spend it maximizing life experiences. After all, our lives are not so much about having to find a permanent partner or job, but about the sum of a wide variety of joyous experiences that this beautiful world provides us. With confidence, an open mind, and an adventurous spirit, I have been able to date ultra-hot women, gain unlimited inner power, and enjoy the greatest feeling of all, ultimate freedom. I can proudly say that I am living the Showstopper Lifestyle.

APPENDIX
Reflections of a Showstopper
☆ ☆ ☆

SHOWSTOPPING WORDS TO LIVE BY

- Always be happy, but never be satisfied.

- Don't do what you have to do. Do what you want to do.

- I am not excited about life because I get women. I get women because I am excited about life.

- Most people are dreaming about living when they should be living out what they are dreaming.

- Some men see the beautiful woman on their arm ask why…I see the beautiful woman on each arm and ask why they deserve to be seen with me.

- Confidence is the key to making your dreams come true.

- Minimize worries and maximize life experiences.

- People don't realize how short life is and how big the world is.

- Women need security, but they crave excitement.

- Live every day as if it is your first.

- Create the aura of unattainability.

- Don't complicate common sense.

- A smart person learns from his mistakes, but a brilliant one learns from the mistakes of others and avoids making them.

- Live for the moment while preparing for the future.

- Settling down should not mean settling.

- Being alone does not mean being lonely.

- Do not become a prisoner of your own decisions.

- Anybody can live the Showstopper Lifestyle. All it takes is an open mind and an adventurous spirit

COUNTRIES WITH THE MOST SHOWSTOPPING BEAUTIES

- Sweden: Does this even need an explanation? Everybody knows the myth of the blonde bombshells and the Swedish Bikini Team. Swimming in this sea of golden haired goddesses is an absolute must for the Hugh Hefner in all of us.

- Brazil: Brazilian ladies are the absolute epitome of sensuality and sex appeal. The country has one of the world's most fascinating mixtures of cultures and ethnicities, and the results are some of the most exotically luscious specimens you will encounter.

- Norway: Although it does not get as much hype as nearby Sweden, Norwegian women are equally as lovely. Scandinavia is a haven for men looking to meet sweet, friendly, and gorgeous girls.

- Costa Rica: This is the crown jewel of Central America and an absolute paradise of spectacular sirens. Like Brazil, these women are exotic and sensual and know how to make a man happy.

- Czech Republic: Eastern European women are the most beautiful women in the world. A large percentage of the world's models are descendants of that region and when you walk the streets of Prague, you may feel like you are witnessing a fashion show.

- Poland: This is my personal favorite of the Eastern European countries. Not only are the women magnificent looking, they are also a pleasure to spend time with.

- Thailand: If Asian women are your fancy, Thailand is the ultimate vacation spot. No matter what your tastes are, if you go there, you will discover that these ladies can make all your fantasies come true. Just be sure that they are ladies first.

- Estonia: As I said, Slavic women are the sexiest in the world. In this small country resides a large population of phenomenally attractive females. A weekend night at a Tallinn dance club can be an eye-opening experience.

- Hungary: A few of my friends went to medical school in a small town in Hungary and they all came home with sweet and stunning wives. When you go there, you will discover that these women are a gift that you may want to take home as well.

- Slovakia: I spent a mere two days in Slovakia but I have never forgotten what I witnessed. I have never seen such a high proportion of breathtaking beauties in any other place I have visited. They do not need fashion magazines here because the atmosphere is like a photo spread come to life.

- Explore For Yourself!: I have been to over forty countries, but there are countless places I have not been. My tastes tend to sway towards women of Slavic and Scandinavian appearance, but yours may differ. This list can be a starting point for you, but you will find the real joy in traveling and meeting women will be discovering what you love on your own!

THINGS EVERY SHOWSTOPPER BRINGS TO A BAR/ CLUB

- Camera: You should never leave home without your camera. When you are living every moment to the fullest, each outing could bring memories you want to capture forever.

- Sunglasses: Some may find it cheesy, but when you have the attitude and the swagger to pull it off, then you will have a sexy, mysterious aura that will make women intrigued. Additionally, when you disguise your eyes, they will be much more likely to compliment how beautiful they are when you reveal them.

- Business Cards: I highly recommend designing an original card that showcases your strengths and one that will make a memorable impression on the people you give them to. This can be a terrific icebreaker.

- Pen: You can put in the phone numbers you get in your phone, but it does not hurt to bring a trusty pen whenever you leave home.

- Phone: This is not only a tool to store contact information, but you can also use it as an accessory when you are bored or want to create an image of popularity and power.

- Cologne: Women are attracted to men who smell appealing. Bring a bottle of cologne in your car and spray it on before you go into the bar for that fresh scent.

- Breath mints or gum: Nothing can be a bigger turn-off than having bad breath. Additionally, since women always seem to be looking for gum, you can offer a piece as an introductory tool.

- Picture of a Beautiful Girl In Your Wallet: This can be any picture of you with an attractive female. When you are in the middle of a conversation, you can come up with a story that will lead to showing this picture. Women are attracted to guys who get hot girls, and this image will be your social proof.

- A Beautiful Female Friend: Of course, the picture cannot substitute for the real thing. A gorgeous platonic female friend is your ultimate nightlife accessory.

- Condoms: Just like you should never leave your home without a camera, you should never go out without protection. You never know where the night may take you.

MOVIES EVERY SHOWSTOPPER SHOULD WATCH

- *It's a Wonderful Life*: The film has become so synonymous with Christmas that people forget it's a celebration of the people and values that are most important to us at any time of year. If you are not crying at the end, you may not have a heart.

- *A Place in the Sun*: Montgomery Clift was the personification of cool on screen. Notice the wide-eyed expression on Clift's face when he sees Elizabeth Taylor for the first time. When you look at your significant other with such a stare, you know you have something special.

- *Philadelphia Story*: In fact, you should watch any movie of Cary Grant's and witness the personification of sophisticated sex appeal.

- *The Wild One*: Marlon Brando provides a definitive portrayal of the anti-establishment rebel. Most Brando movies from the 1950s are a worthy watch.

- *From Here to Eternity*: This film contains one of the most brilliant illustrations of a man standing up for his own moral code. Watch any pre-1955 Clift film.

- *Rebel Without a Cause*: This is the movie that has defined coolness for the generations that have followed. Pay attention to James Dean's gestures, walk, and general laid-back demeanor, because the man earns every bit of his legend.

- *Top Gun*: Forget about the planes. You should examine the self-assurance and swagger of Tom Cruise and, even more so, Val Kilmer. Whatever you think of Cruise, his film characters are a study in confidence.

- *Office Space*: This hilarious parody of the workplace will make you rethink your steady job if you have one.

- *American Beauty*: This is an excellent film exposing the dark side of the American dream and the consequences of what happens when passion and excitement are replaced by routine and apathy.

- *Eyes Wide Shut*: Stanley Kubrick's final movie is an intelligent, thought-provoking examination of the male ego and human sexuality. Nicole Kidman's revelation of her secret fantasy is a virtuoso scene.

- *Vanilla Sky*: A poignant portrait of how we discover what truly makes us happy when it seems as if everything is taken away from us. Discover your own lucid dream.

- *Troy*: Not only is Brad Pitt's Achilles an icon of larger-than-life presence, watching him on screen will give you motivation to stay on a healthy exercise regime.

- *Alfie* (2004 version): This film embodies nearly every element of the free-wheeling lifestyle, both good and bad. It is a must-see for every man.

EXPERIENCES EVERY SHOWSTOPPER SHOULD ENJOY

- Mardi Gras in New Orleans, Louisiana (USA): Just imagine a sea of hot young women in sexy clothing completely uninhibited and ready to unleash their repressed fantasies all for a necklace of beads. Better yet, go there and experience it for yourself!

- Carnaval in Rio de Janeiro, Brazil: This is actually supposed to be a more spectacular celebration than Mardi Gras, though I suggest the latter. Nonetheless, it is a spectacle that every guy should enjoy, if nothing else, for the luscious Brazilian ladies.

- Clubbing in Ibiza, Spain: This Spanish island is reputed to be the biggest party place on earth, and it lives up the hype. Entering one of its large-scale dance clubs is an out-of-body experience that could result in sensory overload.

- Spring Break in Cancun, Mexico: Sure, it may be overloaded by tourists, but there is a reason people flock to the Pearl of the Mayan Riviera. Not only are there a bevy of young beauties leaving their inhibitions at home, there are also some of the most awe-inspiring nightspots in the world.

- AVN Awards in Las Vegas, Nevada (USA): Vegas is the biggest party city in the United States. Now add to that atmosphere all of the biggest adult video stars in the country celebrating their industry. All of the sexy sirens you fantasize about on your screens come to life in this surreal adult playground.

- Amsterdam, Holland: I do not think I need to go into details here, but this is a place where you can fulfill every hedonistic desire. Pick your poison, and be careful.

- Halloween Parade in West Hollywood, California (USA): There are a variety of sensational festivals all over the U.S. every Halloween, but the most amazing I have seen takes place on the streets of West Hollywood. Some partiers spend months designing their costumes and it shows. Los Angeles is the world's center of creativity, and this event is a showcase of that artistry.

- Party at the Playboy Mansion: Hugh Hefner lives the life millions of men desire and it is safe to say that every young boy grows up dreaming about visiting the hallowed halls of his home. Invitations are usually exclusive or expensive, but if you get an opportunity to go there, take it, because you get a chance to party in a historical landmark of male fantasies.

- These are some of the most unbelievable experiences I have enjoyed and recommend. The world holds many more showstopping adventures. Get out there and discover them for yourself!

ABOUT THE AUTHOR

Shawn Valentino is the founder of the Showstopper Lifestyle. Shawn is also an avid world traveler, model, relationship expert and self-help counselor. He has graduated from law school and has passed the bar exam in multiple states. Despite his many talents, he has stated that his main aim in life is to change the way the world thinks. Shawn's goals include dating gorgeous supermodels, visiting more than a hundred countries, helping people around the globe with charity work, and getting on *People* magazine's "Fifty Most Beautiful People" list. He has been interviewed on *The Tyra Banks Show* and plans on doing more television appearances on his Showstopper Lifestyle World Tour. Inspired by Hugh Hefner, Shawn feels more people should follow Hef's example by living every moment to the fullest on their own terms. He wrote *The Showstopper Lifestyle* to be a *Playboy Philosophy* for a new era. Shawn is the man of many nicknames. He is commonly known as "The Hollywood Showstopper," "The One Man Revolution," "The Lord of the Flings," "The Heartbreak Kid," "The Face That Kissed One Thousand Lips," "The Lady-Killer," "The Womanizer," "The Human Postcard," and "The Living Dream." He currently lives in Hollywood and is working on his next books, *Adventures of a Showstopper* and *Child of the Eighties: A Thrilling Journey.*

Contact Shawn:

Email: shawnvalentino@showstopperlifestyle.com
MySpace: www.myspace.com/hollywoodshowstopperhbk
Facebook: www.facebook.com/shawnvalentino
Twitter: www.twitter.com/shawnvalentino

SUBSCRIBE TO THE FREE SHOWSTOPPER LIFESTYLE NEWSLETTER AT
www.showstopperlifestyle.com

CPSIA information can be obtained at www.ICGtesting.com
Printed in the USA
LVOW040112271211

261017LV00002B/78/P